IMAGES
of America

BROADMOOR VILLAGE

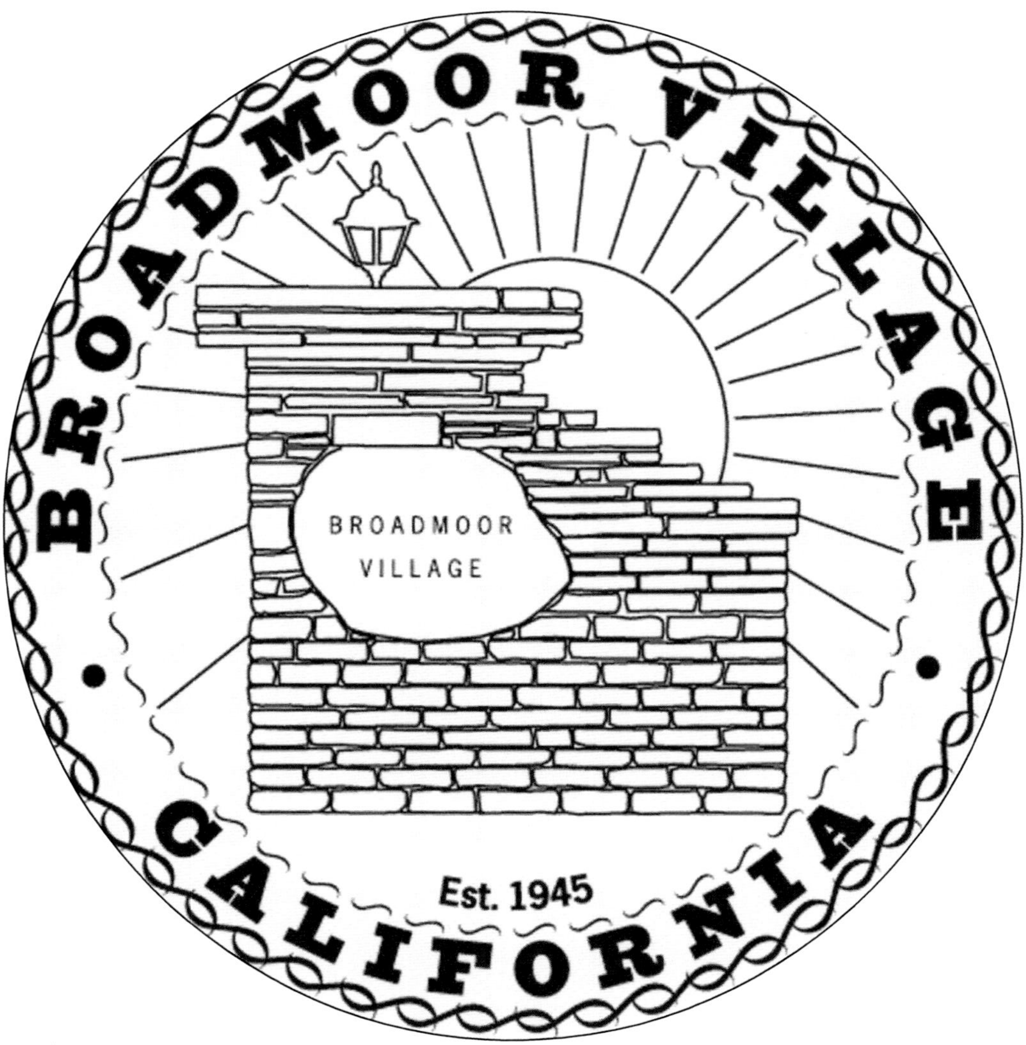

This is a gift to the community of Broadmoor Village. Broadmoor is simply an unincorporated community in San Mateo County. Because Broadmoor stayed unincorporated, it does not get the recognition like incorporated cities of San Mateo County. The hope of this author is that this seal, this book, and the contents in it will help give Broadmoor the identity it deserves.

On the Cover: Pictured around 1958 or 1959, from left to right are Michael Alberigi (nephew of David and Raymond Crapse), David Crapse, and "big brother" Raymond Crapse. Across the street is the home of Reverend Tweedy, who presided over the Broadmoor Presbyterian Church. (Photograph by Otis and Susan Crapse.)

IMAGES
of America

BROADMOOR VILLAGE

Dave Crimmen
Foreword by Quentin Kopp

ARCADIA
PUBLISHING

ISBN 978-0-7385-8092-0

Published by Arcadia Publishing
Charleston SC, Chicago IL, Portsmouth NH, San Francisco CA

Printed in the United States of America

Library of Congress Control Number: 2010921323

For all general information contact Arcadia Publishing at:
Telephone 843-853-2070
Fax 843-853-0044
E-mail sales@arcadiapublishing.com
For customer service and orders:
Toll-Free 1-888-313-2665

Visit us on the Internet at www.arcadiapublishing.com

This book is for all who have kept Broadmoor alive.

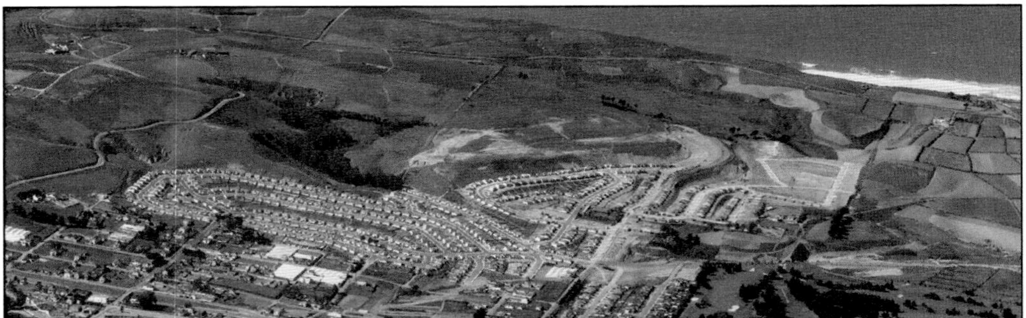

Broadmoor Village is pictured on February 23, 1948. North of Broadmoor and to the right is farmland; west of Broadmoor, at the top of this picture is farmland; to the south of Broadmoor, on the left side of this photograph is more farmland. Before Doelger, Westlake and Westmoor High School, there was Broadmoor Village. (Courtesy HJW Geospatial Inc. and Pacific Aerial Surveys.)

Contents

Foreword

My association with Broadmoor Village began in the 1960s as a young lawyer retained by some of the then 20,000 or so residents to furnish legal service to incorporate the area as a city; I reflect on the disappointment allayed with pleasure. The thwarting by Daly City and San Mateo County to Broadmoor Village's desires of city hood represents denial of a commonsensical democratic choice.

Pleasure occurred about 25 years later, as a state senator. I was able to preserve Broadmoor Village's shrunken identity by a law rendering further Daly City annexation unlawful without election approval by all Broadmoor Police Protection District voters, not just those to be annexed. Survival was sweet, as Dave Crimmen, native son, demonstrates in this unique recordation of history.

—Quentin Kopp
Retired San Mateo County Superior Court Judge

ACKNOWLEDGMENTS

I would like to start out by thanking three people who went beyond the call of duty to help with this book. First is Ray Mogel at the San Mateo County Department of Public Works, who helped me find old maps and pointed out what was Broadmoor and what is not, per county records. Second is Chief Greg Love of the Broadmoor Police Department, who supplied old pictures, old stories, and good coffee. Third is Edie Epps of the Visitacion Valley Historical Project, who made the phone call to John Poultney at Arcadia Publishing and got this whole project started.

I want to thank all who opened their doors and their lives and shared their love to help create this: Allan Wegscheider, Alvina Feno-Wegscheider, Ana Goldman, Andrew Volokitin, Arlene Smith, Arnez Amper, Betty Schultz, Bunny and Ken Gelespi, Carol Simms, Christine Holmlund, Chiyeko Harada, Christina Moretta, Curt Harada, Dana Smith, Darold Fredricks, Dave Holbrook, Dave Parenti, David Ruiz, Debra Crimmen, Deborah Osterberg, Edie Epps, Edward Graham, Elinor Charleston, Elio Fontana, Eloisa Avendano-Johnsen, Gary McLane, Gene Chasey, Gregory Love, Gus Vasquez, Jana Wirch-Wright, Janette Razor, Jeff Thomas, Jennifer Tagg, Jim Porter, Jim Dickson, John Poultney, John Schmale, John Travinsky, Joseph Avendano, Joseph Curran, Judith Christensen, Kathleen Manning, Kim Clifford-Salvador, Kirsten Arnold, Lauri Carlson, Leif Carlson, Leo Gomez, Linda Boscono, Marian Mann, Marie Brizuela, Marilyn Olcese, Mark Fontana, Mark Sanguinetti, Mark Weinberger, Martha Poyatos, Mary Lou Moss, Michael Crilly, Michael Rocchetta, Michael and Shirley Suanevik, Michael Wilson, Michele Courtney, Mitch Bull, Mrs. Noonan, Opal Fuller, Otis Crapse, Patricia Hatfield, Pat Stark, Pete Gascoyne, Phyllis Alberigi, Ralph and Cathy Hutchins, Ralph Warren, Ray and Loraine Gerribaldi, Ray Mogel, Raymond Crapse, Renny Wright, Richard Rocchetta, Rob Keil, Robert Barnhill, Roland Wright, Sharon Caren-Crimmen, Sue Medina-Larson, Susan Crapse, Susan Kennedy, Sylvia Payne, Terrie Powers, Tim Wilson, Vicki Kissinger, and Virginia Garcia.

All images in this book, except where individually cited, are from the archives of the author.

INTRODUCTION

Broadmoor Village is a community, not an incorporated city or town, located in Northern San Mateo County. There are basically four different entities that have to be taken into consideration when discussing Broadmoor Village. First—Broadmoor, second—Daly City, third—the town of Colma, and last—"Unincorporated Colma."

California got its statehood in 1850, and most of what is now San Mateo County was, at that time, San Francisco County. Citizens on the peninsula decided to break away from San Francisco due to what they perceived as corruption with the city and county governments. Thus, in 1856, San Mateo County became a reality.

What is currently the "Top of the Hill" in Daly City at the San Francisco/San Mateo County line all the way south to the cemeteries was originally the community of Colma. In 1911, the northern portion of this community decided to incorporate, and it became Daly City. The citizens in the southern part of this community decided to incorporate as well and, in 1923, became Lawndale. Lawndale changed its name to Colma; and this is where the confusion begins, as we now have two Colmas: the incorporated town and the unincorporated area. "Unincorporated Colma" is the land in between Daly City and the town of Colma that neither wanted to claim and/or annex at that time.

Local business owners, farmers, and citizens have used the phrase "Unincorporated Colma" for over 70 years to differentiate the strip of land between the town of Colma and Daly City. It is, however, a verbiage that is not recognized by the County of San Mateo, the City of Daly City, or the Township of Colma. These organizations prefer the term "Unincorporated San Mateo County" This is done for legal, as well as political, reasons. Much of this stems from the fact that unincorporated districts in any county come under the jurisdiction, and budget, of the county and not neighboring incorporated cities.

A good metaphor for "Unincorporated Colma" might be that of the illegitimate child, as initially neither Daly City or the Town of Colma wanted to claim these lands. But a more accurate analogy would be the phrase "forgotten or abandoned parent," as, historically speaking, the towns of Colma and Daly City were created from the lands of the original community. This author has decided to use the term "Unincorporated Colma" to honor the original community and its citizens. The phrase is also to eradicate confusion because there are many parcels of land and communities in San Mateo County that are unincorporated. This phrase used in this book refers to a specific one.

Lands that were Unincorporated Colma, west of Junipero Serra Boulevard, were purchased by the Stoneson Development Company to build a subdivision. That subdivision is Broadmoor Village; thus, Broadmoor is part of Unincorporated Colma. Because the subdivision was in this area, citizens used the phrases Broadmoor or Colma for their mail; due to the closeness of Daly City, however, this phrase was also used. This fact adds to the confusion as to where Broadmoor Village really is. Over the years, Daly City grew and came to encircle Broadmoor; thus, many believe that Broadmoor is simply a district or neighborhood of Daly City. More citizens further still are not even aware that there is a Broadmoor and just think that all of the lands are simply Daly City.

Today the small but proud community works to maintain its individual status. The citizens have fought long and hard over 65 years and have accomplished this goal.

One

Where It's At

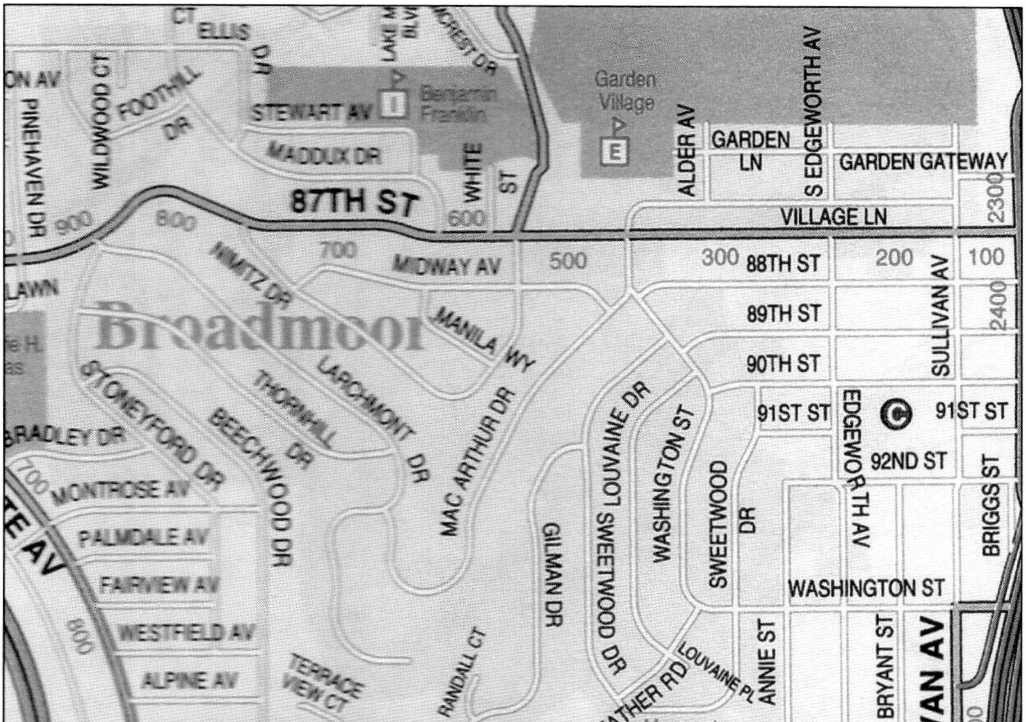

The first place to start looking to answer the question, "Where is Broadmoor?" One only needs to look at current maps. Above is a 2010 G. M. Johnson city map. It clearly shows the name Broadmoor, and the community is highlighted in a lightly shaded area, different from the shades used to show Daly City.

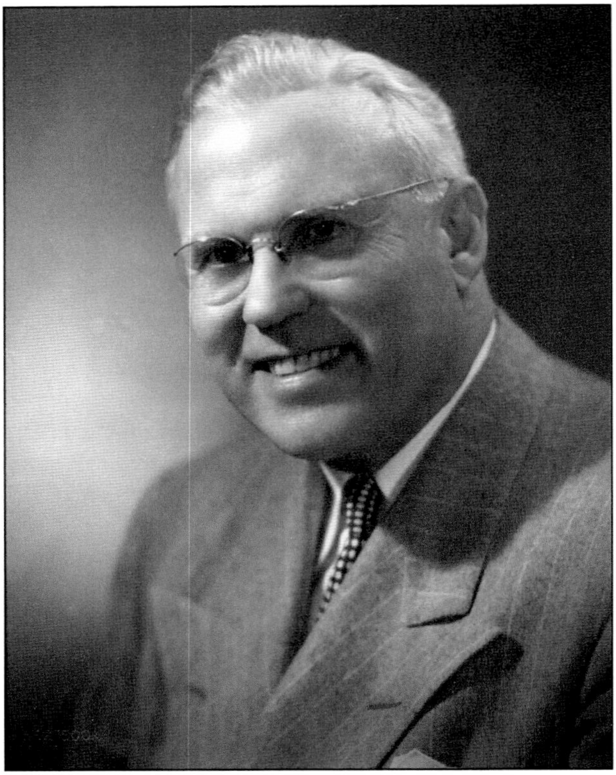

Ellis Stoneson is the eldest of the two brothers who created the Stoneson Development Company and built Broadmoor Village. He was born on July 15, 1893, in Victoria, British Columbia. Ellis was a veteran of World War I and a registered Republican. His occupation is listed as "Home Builder and general Contractor."(Courtesy San Francisco Public Library and the *San Francisco News-Call Bulletin.*)

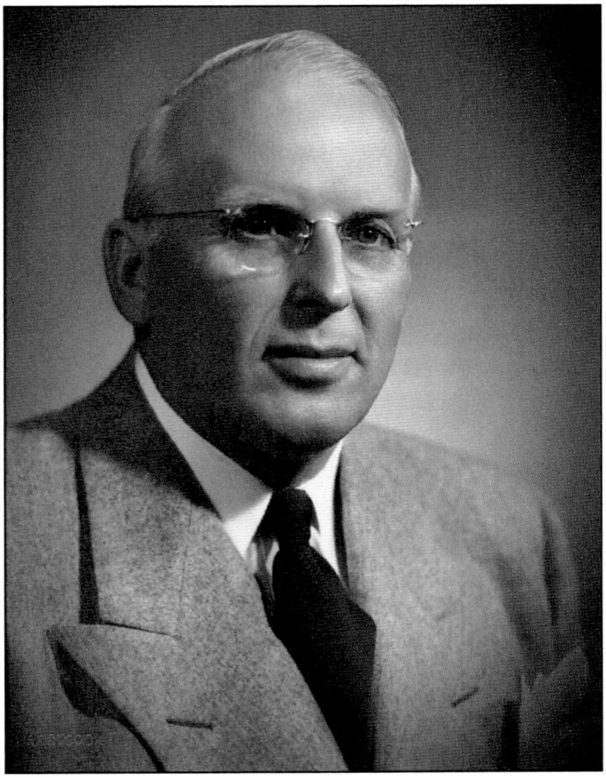

Henry Stoneson was born on May 17, 1895, also in Victoria, British Columbia. Henry was also a Free Mason. Both brothers directed six family-owned corporations including the Stoneson Development Company. It was through this company that the brothers built Broadmoor Village, Lakeside Village, and Stonestown, among other developments. (Courtesy San Francisco Public Library and the *San Francisco News-Call Bulletin.*)

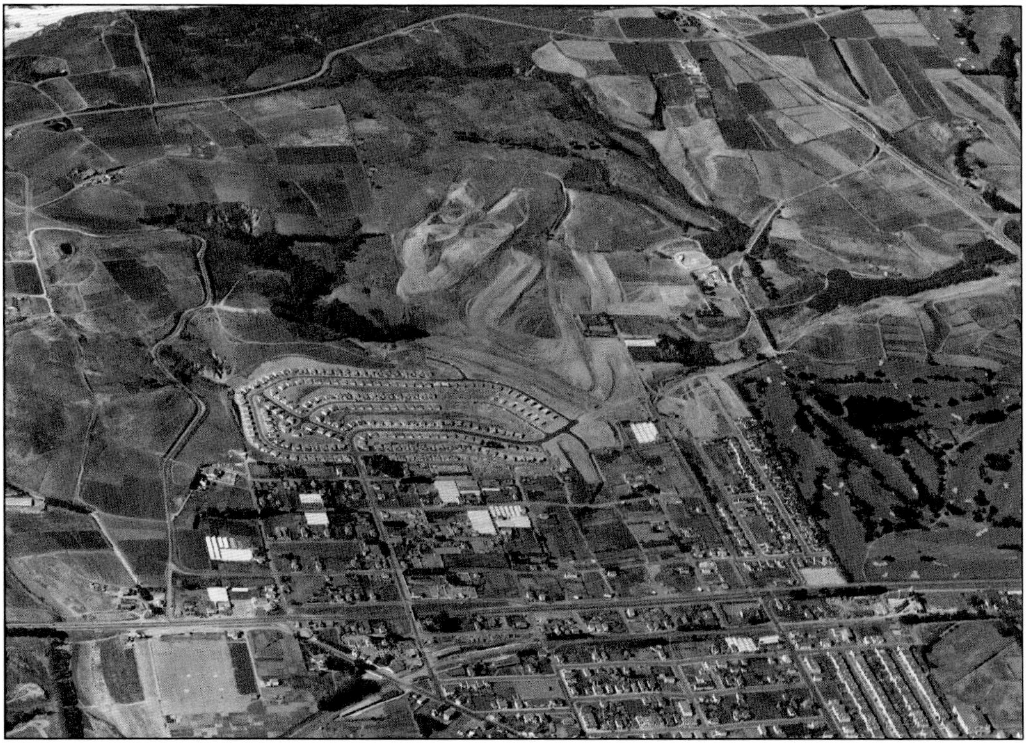

This aerial photograph was taken on November 2, 1946. In the middle of the photograph is the genesis of what was to become Broadmoor Village. To the right (north) is farmland that will become Westlake Shopping Center. The top of the photograph (west) is farmland that will be developed by Henry Doelger. On the left (south) will be Westmoor High School. (Courtesy HJW Geospatial Inc. and Pacific Aerial Surveys. Oakland, California.)

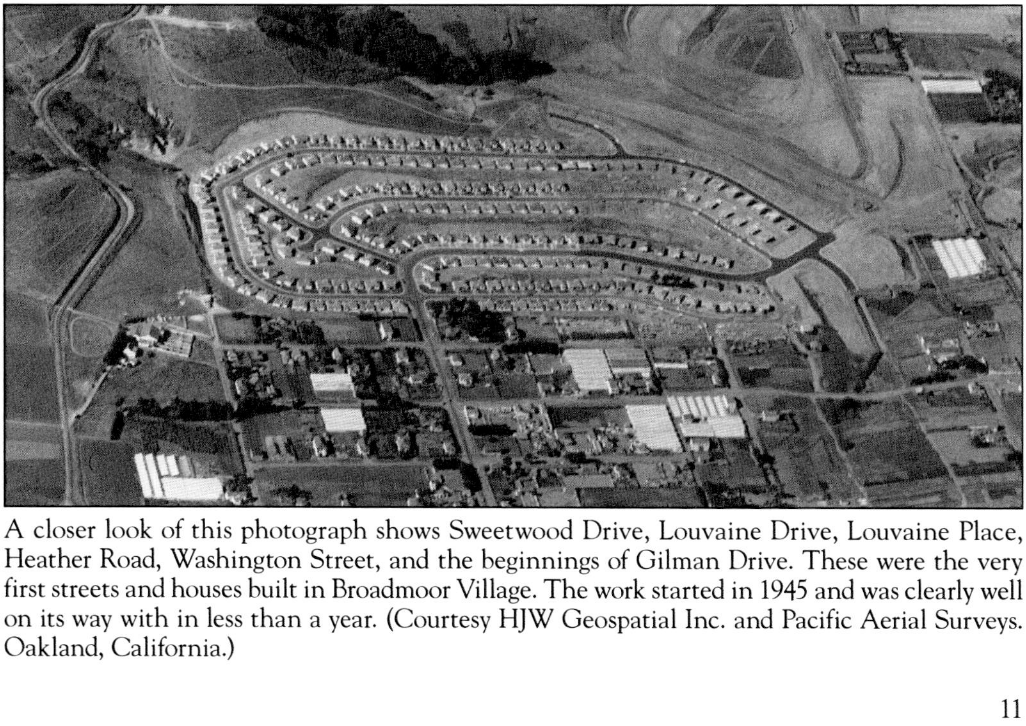

A closer look of this photograph shows Sweetwood Drive, Louvaine Drive, Louvaine Place, Heather Road, Washington Street, and the beginnings of Gilman Drive. These were the very first streets and houses built in Broadmoor Village. The work started in 1945 and was clearly well on its way with in less than a year. (Courtesy HJW Geospatial Inc. and Pacific Aerial Surveys. Oakland, California.)

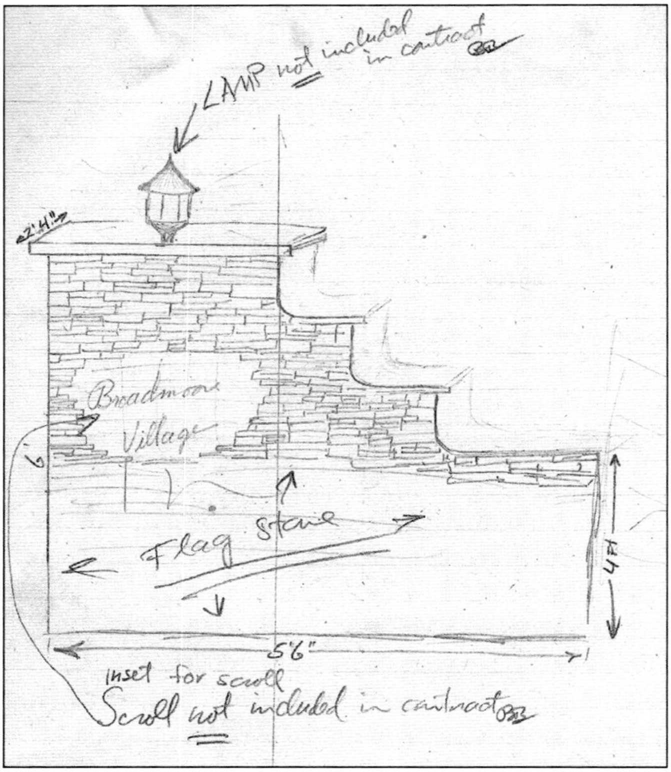

This is an artist's original drawing of the "Broadmoor Portals." The Broadmoor Property Owners Association built the portals in 1951 to mark the entrances to Broadmoor Village. Two were placed at the corner of Eighty-seventh Street and Washington Street. Another two portals were placed at the other end of Washington Street just east of Sweetwood Drive. (Courtesy Mary Lou Moss, Broadmoor Property Owners Association.)

This photograph shows the portal on the south side of the Washington Street at Sweetwood Drive as it appears in 2010. The portals marked the two main ways to get in or out of Broadmoor Village. The light fixtures at the top of the portals were removed due to vandalism.

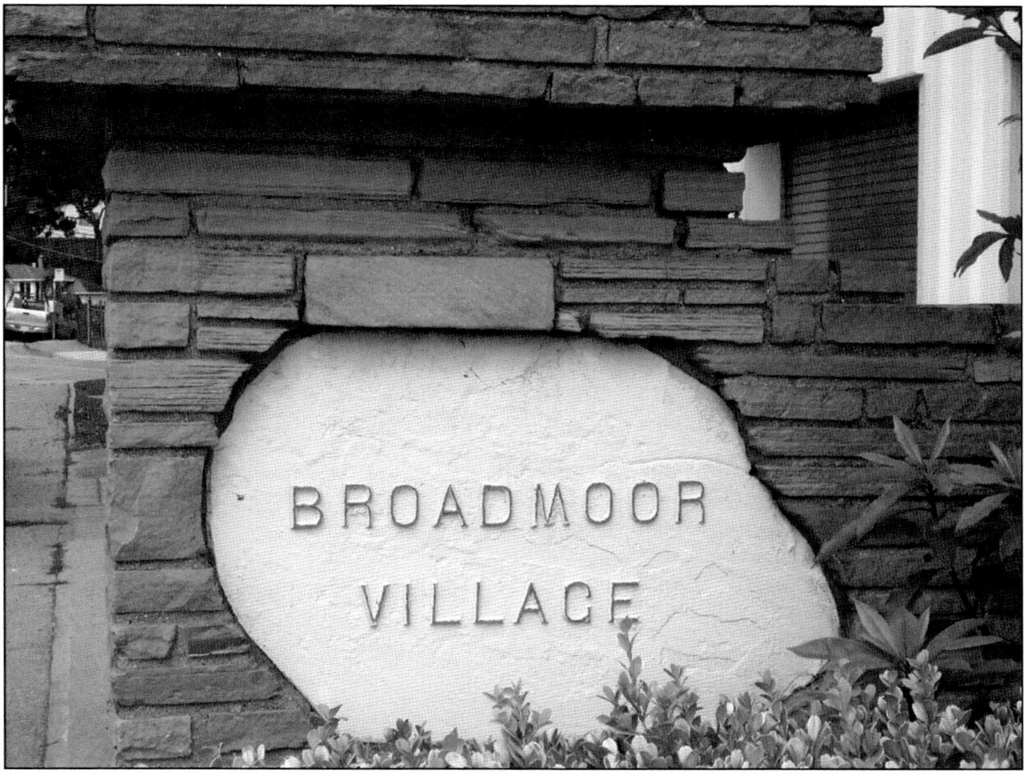

Here is the portal on the north side of Washington Street at Sweetwood Drive in slightly better condition. Pictured is the portal from the Daly City side looking west into Broadmoor Village as if one is entering the community. The stonework is amazing. One can only wonder what this cost the Broadmoor Property Owners Association when they had these built.

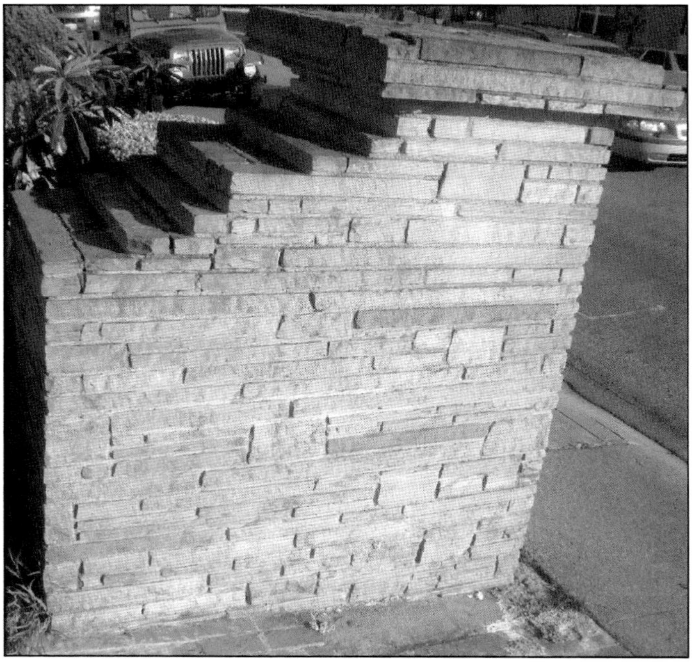

Here again is the north portal from the back on the Broadmoor side, facing east to the Daly City side. The two portals located on Eighty-seventh Street at Washington Street were removed by San Mateo County in November 1971. The portals on Washington Street are still a very good way to know if one is in Broadmoor or Daly City.

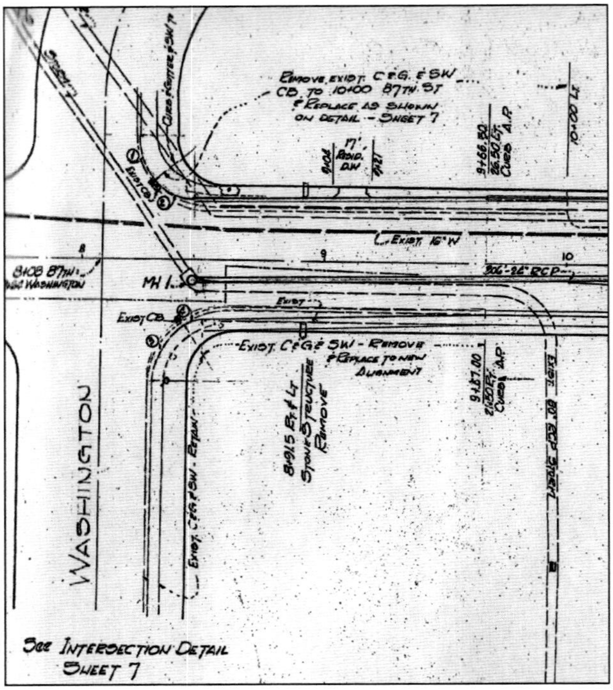

Here is a partial view of the map containing the plans for the removal of the Broadmoor Village Portals on the corner of Eighty-seventh and Washington Streets. Looking at the photograph sideways, one sees "Stoneson Structure Remove." These portals were actually paid for by the Broadmoor Property Owners Association and not built by Stoneson Company, who constructed the subdivision. (Courtesy San Mateo County Public Works Department.)

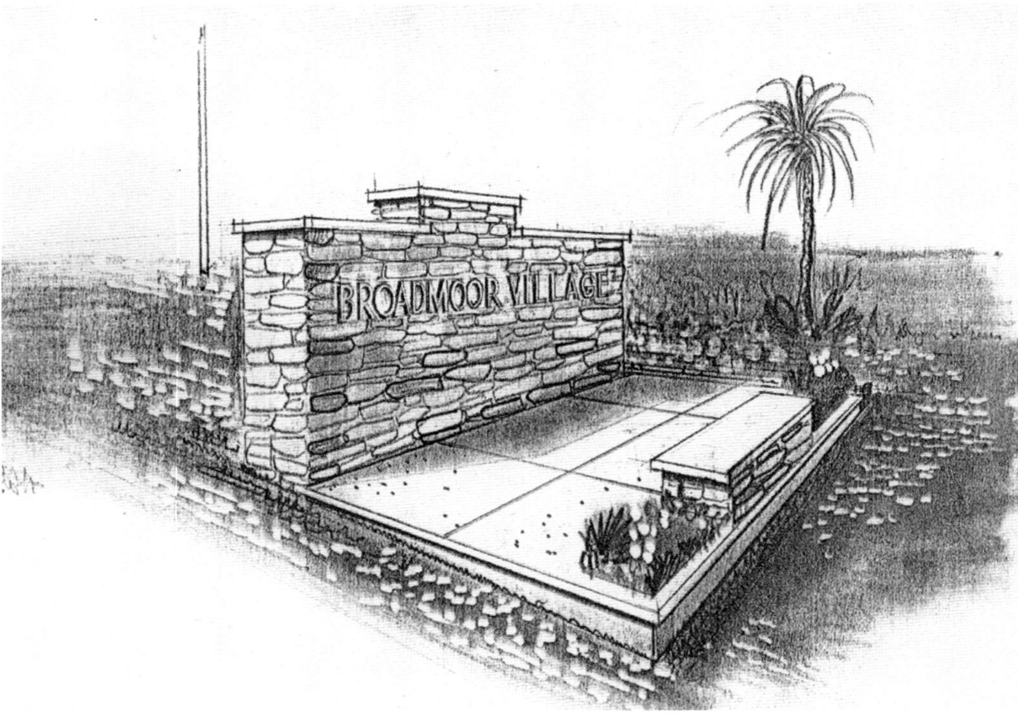

From 1967 until 1971, both the Broadmoor Community Center and the two portals just to the east of Washington Street on Eighty-seventh Street greeted homeowners and visitors as they entered Broadmoor Village. In November 1971, San Mateo County took down the two portals to widen the sidewalks. Above is a line drawing of the propose replacement. (Courtesy Mary Lou Moss, Broadmoor Property Owners Association.)

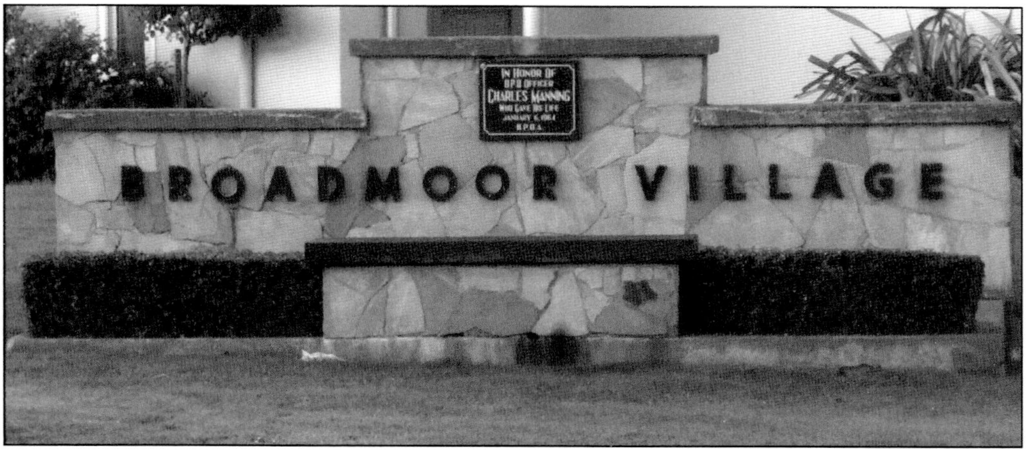

The property owners association wrote a letter to the county engineer proposing that a monument be built on the lawn of the community center. It was agreed and became a replacement for the two original portals. This is the monument as it looks in 2010. This was not part of the original plans when the community center was built in 1967.

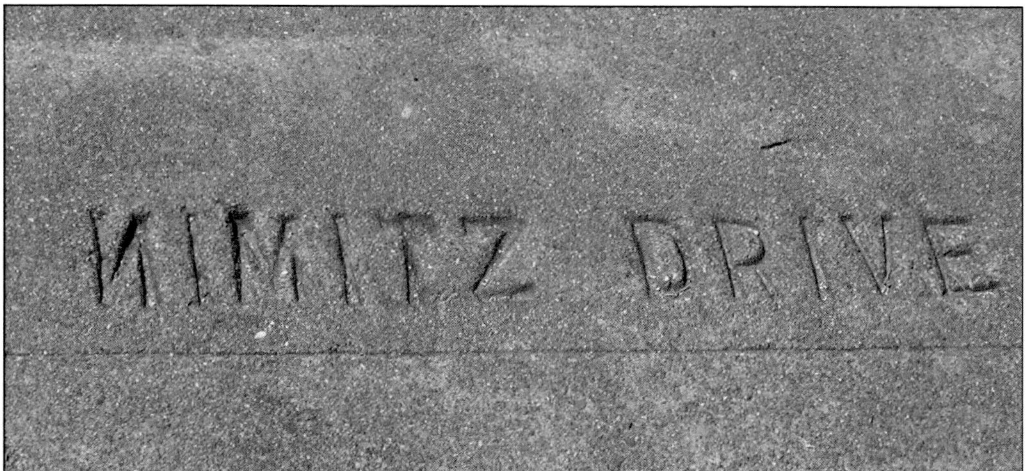

Another little secret in Broadmoor Village is that the names of the streets are stamped into the cement at the intersections where the green street signs are. This stamped street marker was done on a day when, perhaps, the Stoneson worker did not have his morning coffee. The letter "N" for Nimitz Drive is backward.

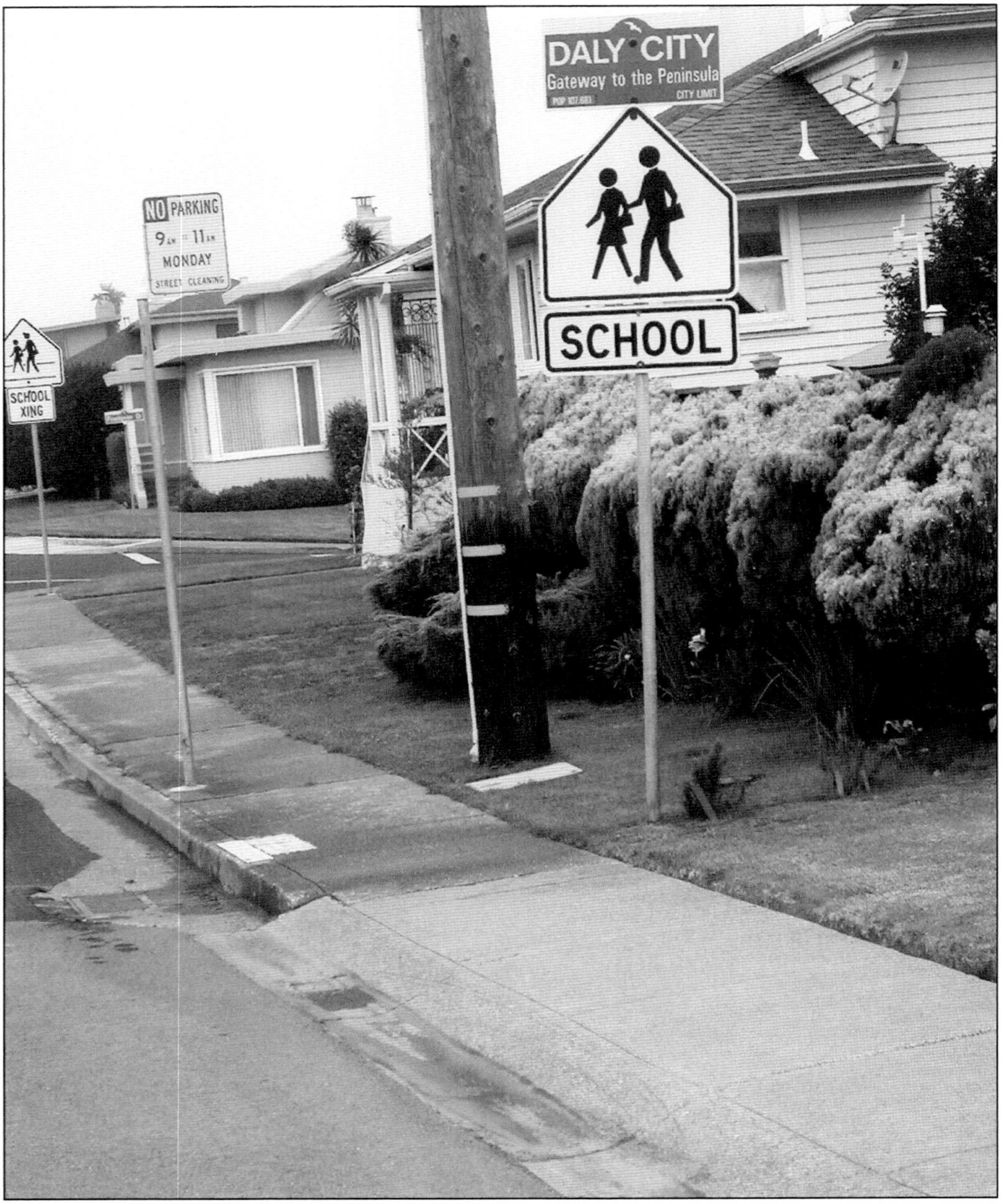

Pictured here is the western end of Eighty-seventh Street as one leaves "Stonesonville" (i.e. Broadmoor Village) and enters "Doelgertown" (i.e. Daly City). At this time, the sidewalks were not rolled up at sundown. In this day, the sidewalks simply ended. Eighty-seventh Street just stopped at this point. Doelger then started building Westlake or Westlake Shopping Center, to the north of Broadmoor Village. Later came these houses to the west of Broadmoor on Southgate Avenue, Mayfair Avenue, and beyond. To the south of Broadmoor Village would come more "Little Boxes Made Of Ticky-Tacky" along with Westmoor High School. In the meantime, there were sand dunes, deer, gophers, and the like. Note that the sidewalk on the Broadmoor side has a round curb that changes to a square shape once it crosses into Daly City. The only explanation is that Broadmoor comes under county building codes, while the city of Daly City has its own set of codes.

Here is more evidence of a county sidewalk, the round, Broadmoor side, becoming a city sidewalk, and the square, Daly City side. This one is found on Bradley Drive. The chain-link fence marks the play yard for Marjorie Tobias Elementary School, formerly Vista Mar, just a few feet over the line into Daly City.

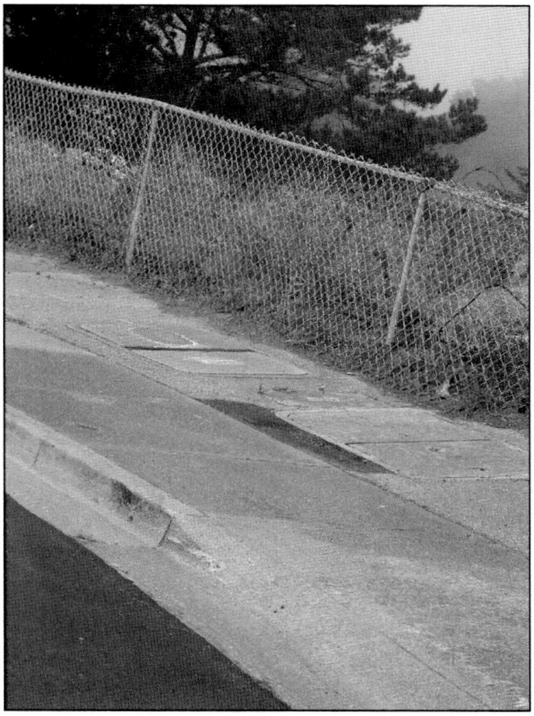

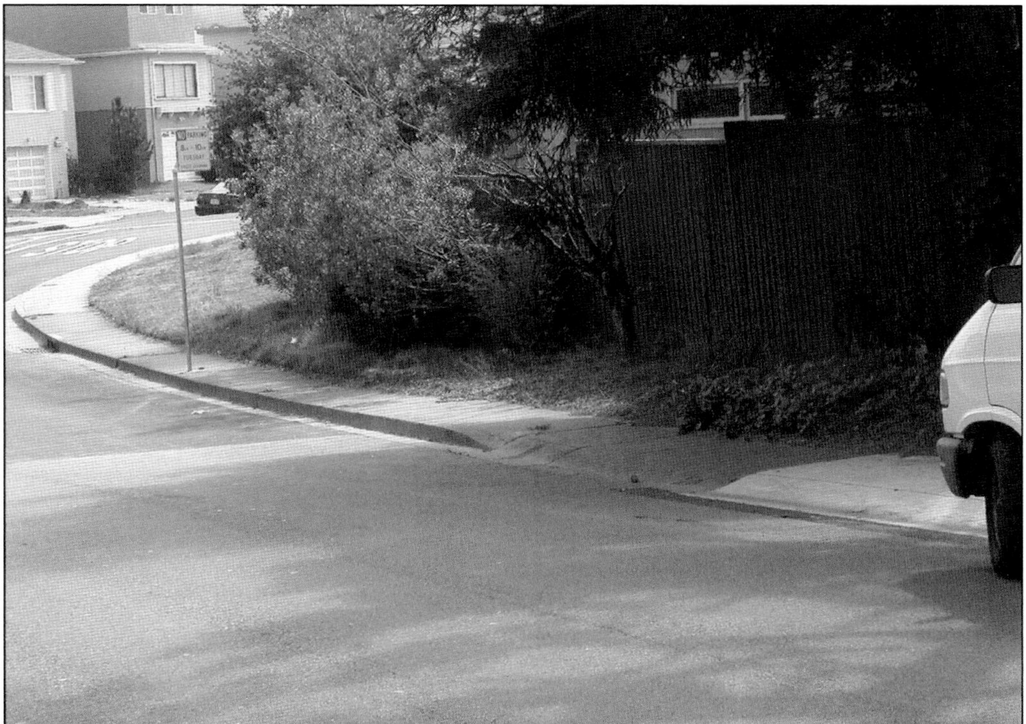

Here is Stoneyford Drive, round on the Broadmoor side and square on the Daly City counterpart as it intersects with Montrose Avenue in Daly City. This is a common walk for kids in Broadmoor Village who attended Westmoor High School but are not old enough to have a driver's license.

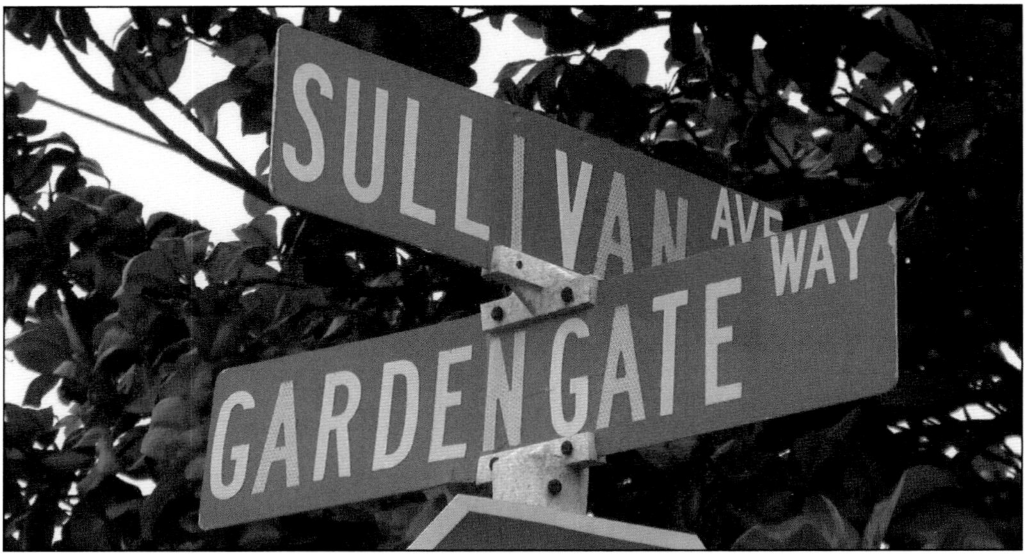

Round curbs, stamped names on sidewalks, and portals aside, the most definitive, accurate way to figure out if one is in Broadmoor, or, for that matter, most of unincorporated San Mateo County, is to look at the street signs. Here in Broadmoor Village, the street signs are green with white letters.

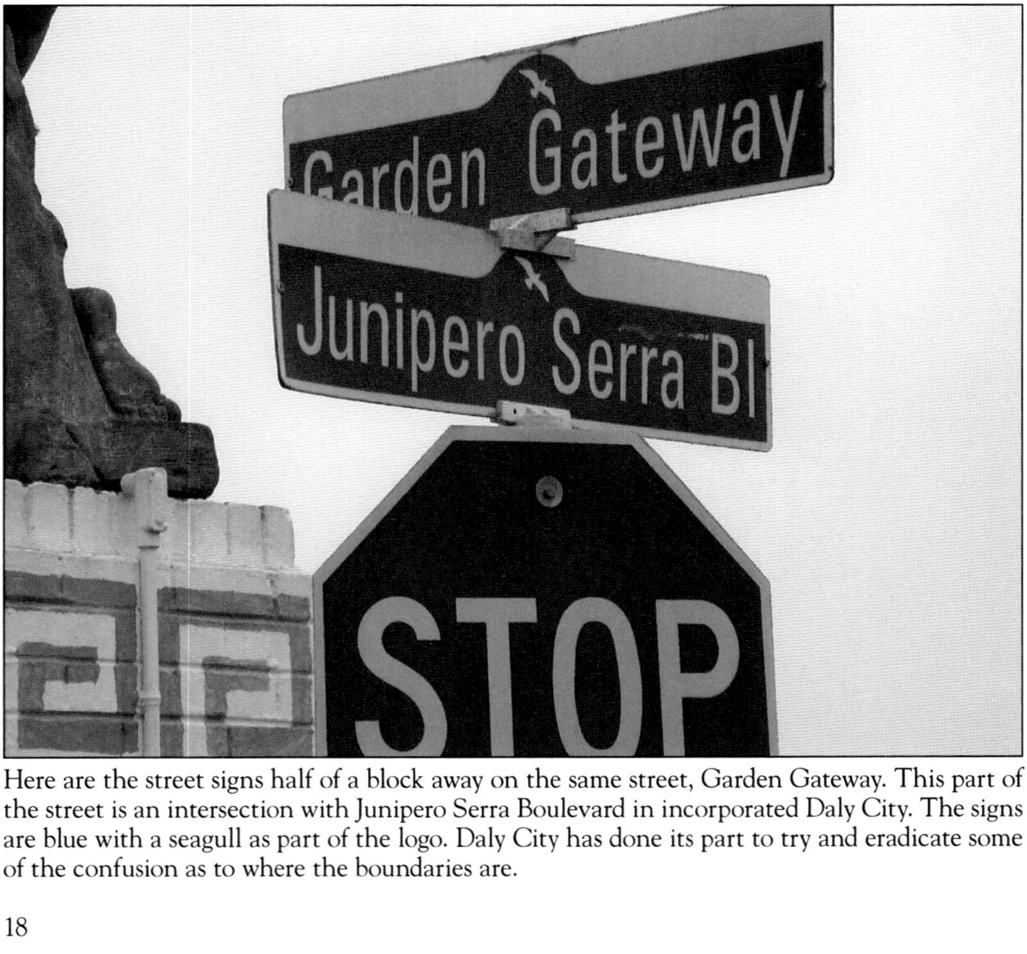

Here are the street signs half of a block away on the same street, Garden Gateway. This part of the street is an intersection with Junipero Serra Boulevard in incorporated Daly City. The signs are blue with a seagull as part of the logo. Daly City has done its part to try and eradicate some of the confusion as to where the boundaries are.

Two

The Veterans and Their Kids

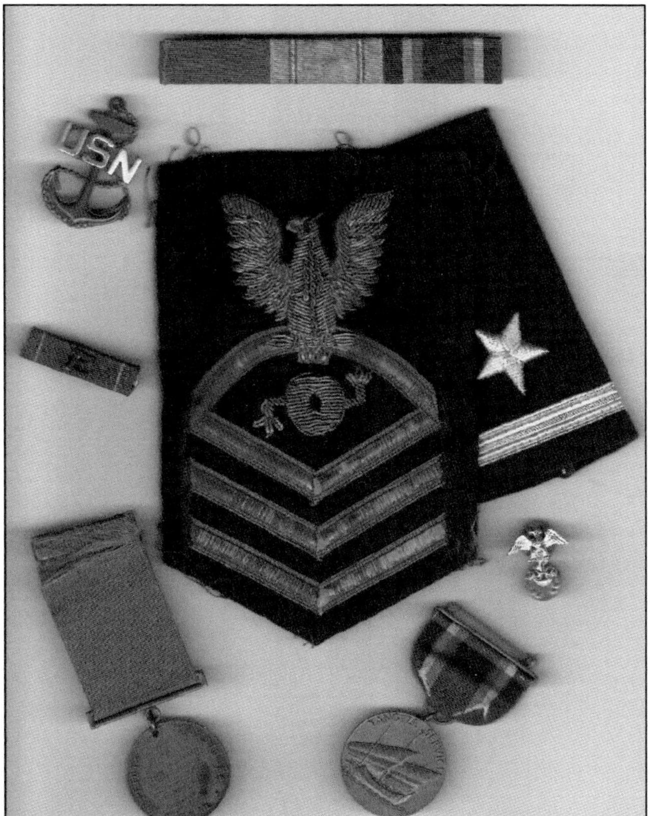

Many of the citizens of Broadmoor Village and surrounding communities were veterans of World War II or the Korean War. One such veteran was Chief Water Tender Otis Crapse. Above are some of Chief Crapse's military memorabilia. Also are a few things from his eldest son, Raymond, who went on to graduate from the U.S. Navy Officer's Candidate School.

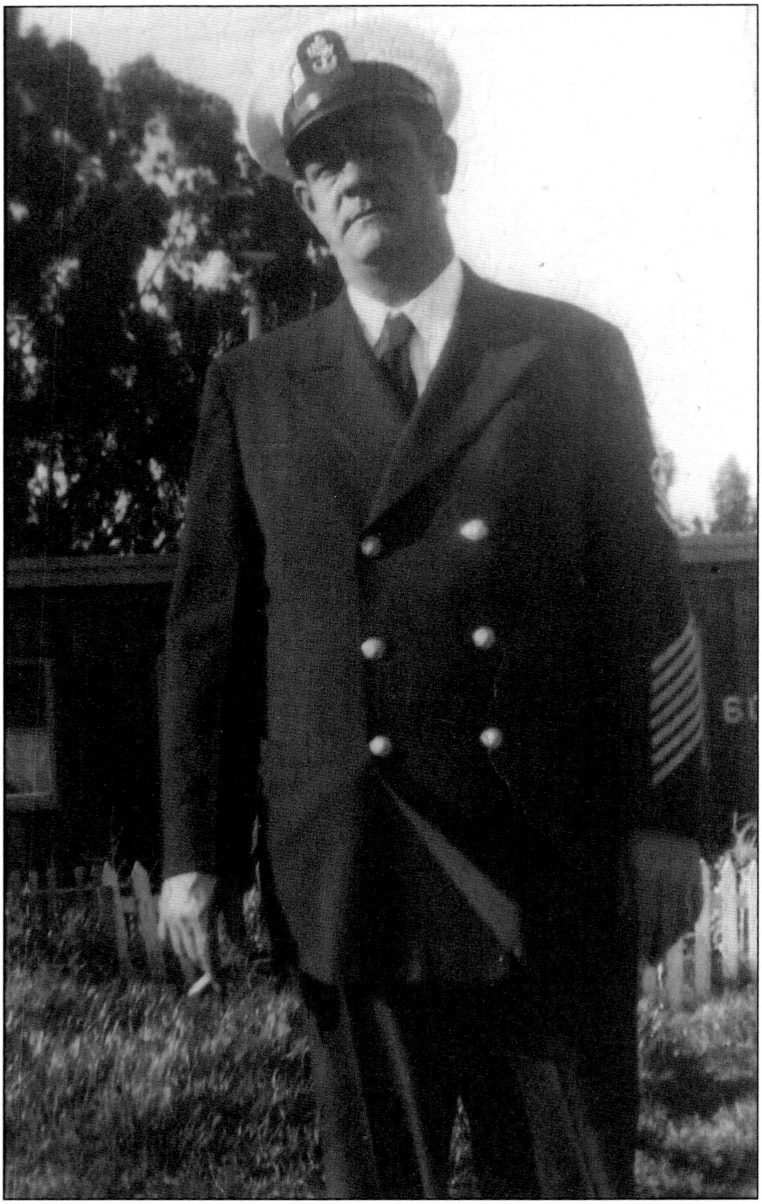

Chief Petty Officer Otis A. Crapse, like many of the folks who moved into Broadmoor in the 1940s and 1950s, was a veteran. Chief Crapse spent 30 years in the U.S. Navy and served honorably before he and his family purchased their house at 1131 Nimitz Drive in 1954. Having previously lived on Mariposa Street in San Francisco, Chief Crapse was working for Southern Pacific Railroad in the late 1940s when he was called back to active duty for Korea. He was permanently retired after his hitch and resumed his work at Southern Pacific. He and his family wanted to find a home that was closer to his work, and the homes in Broadmoor were preferred over Westlake because the lots were slightly bigger and there was more space between the houses for a little added privacy. The previous page shows Chief Crapse's ribbons, his Good Conduct Medal—awarded in March 1928, the American Defense ribbon—awarded December 1941, and lastly the Yangtze Service ribbon—April 1939. Shown along with Chief Crapse's memorabilia are momentos from Ensign Crapse, his son.

Chief Crapse's wife, Susan, and his two eldest daughters, Arlene (right) and Phyllis (left), are pictured here. As young adults, the girls will be trailblazers for women's rights, achieving jobs as draftsmen for the phone company. With the G.I. loan and monies earned by Arlene and Phyllis for the down payment, the family purchased their home in Broadmoor, moving in during summer 1954.

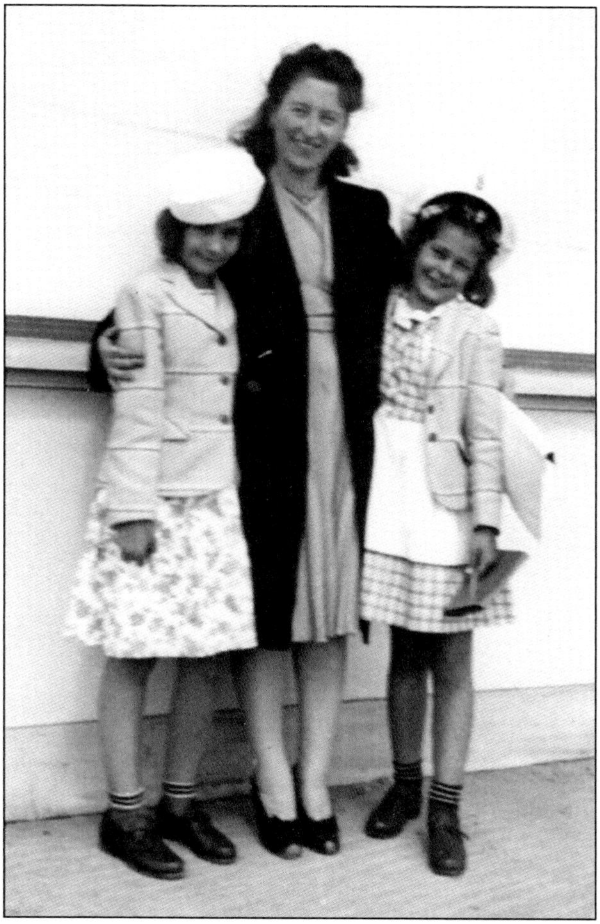

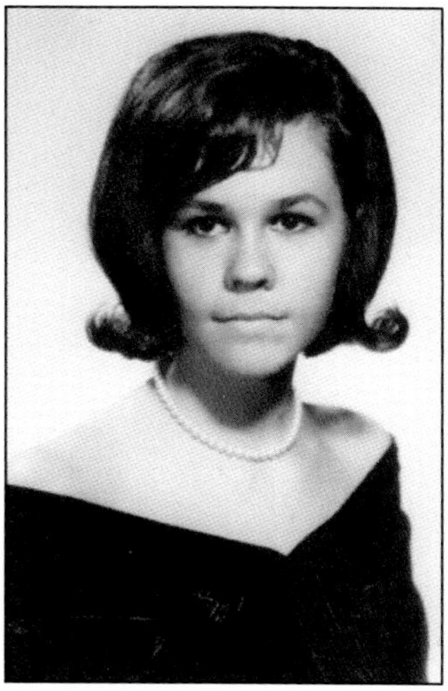

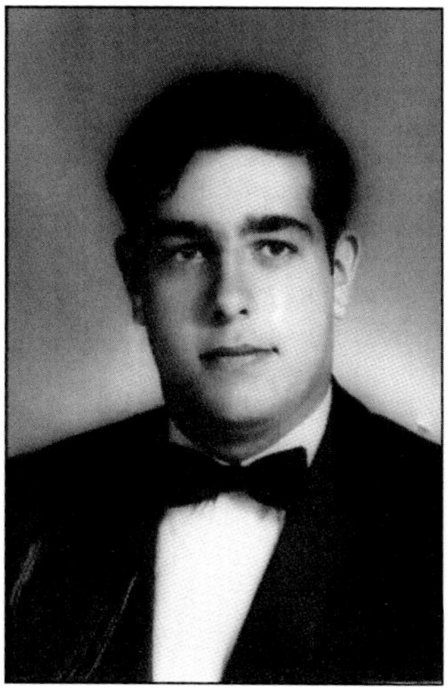

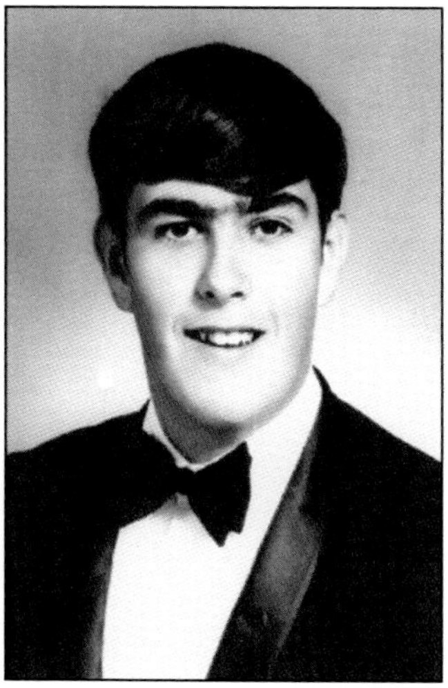

This is the remainder of the Crapse clan, in chronological order (left to right), Virginia, Raymond, and David. All were graduates of Broadmoor's two schools, Garden Village Elementary and Ben Franklin Junior High. The younger three siblings were also graduates of Westmoor High School (Daly City) classes of 1964, 1972, and 1973, respectively.

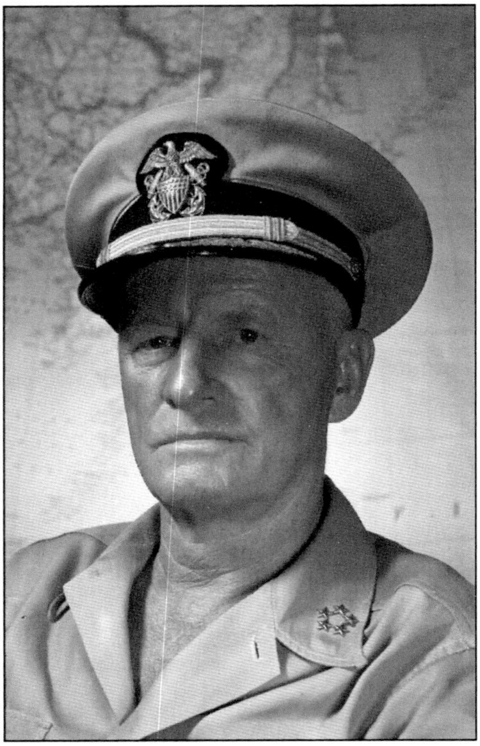

Some of the streets in Broadmoor were named after World War II–related heroes and campaigns like Macarthur Drive, Midway Avenue, and Manila Way. The street the Crapse family bought their house on was named after Fleet Admiral Nimitz. Ironically, Chief Crapse served under Admiral Nimitz in World War II and Korea. (Courtesy Naval Historical Foundation.)

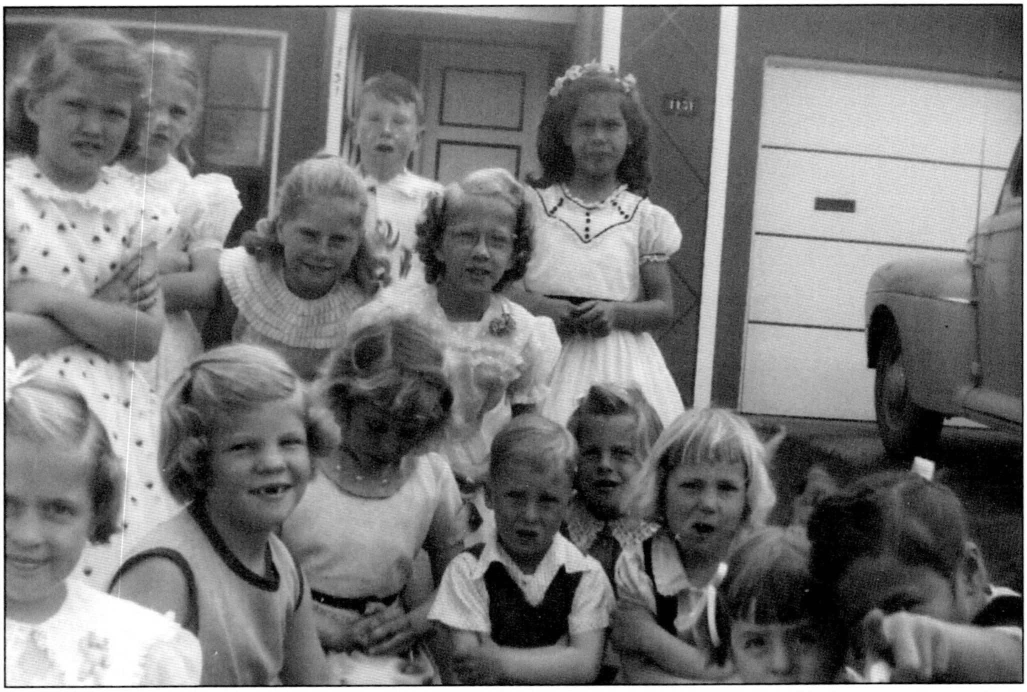

The Crapse family took up residence at 1131 Nimitz Drive in summer 1954; here is the eighth birthday party for Miss Virginia Crapse, months after the family moved in. The house has three bedrooms and one bathroom. One can only marvel at the time management that had to be used for a family of seven with one bathroom.

It is rush hour here in the backyard of the Crapse house. Behind Raymond and his chauffer is the type of fence regularly found at a Stoneson built house. This photograph, taken in the late 1950s, shows the small pine trees that were given to the owners to help ward off the landslides that had occurred during previous winter rains.

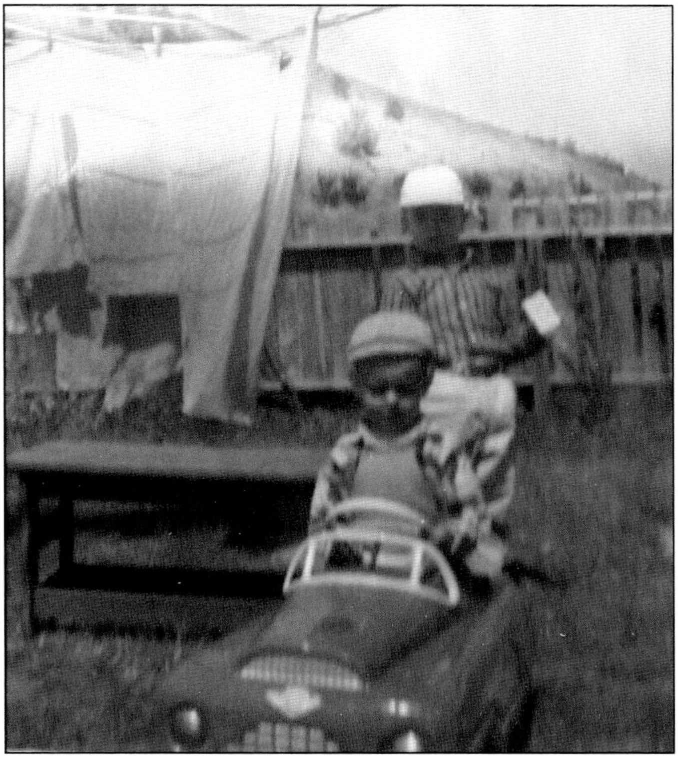

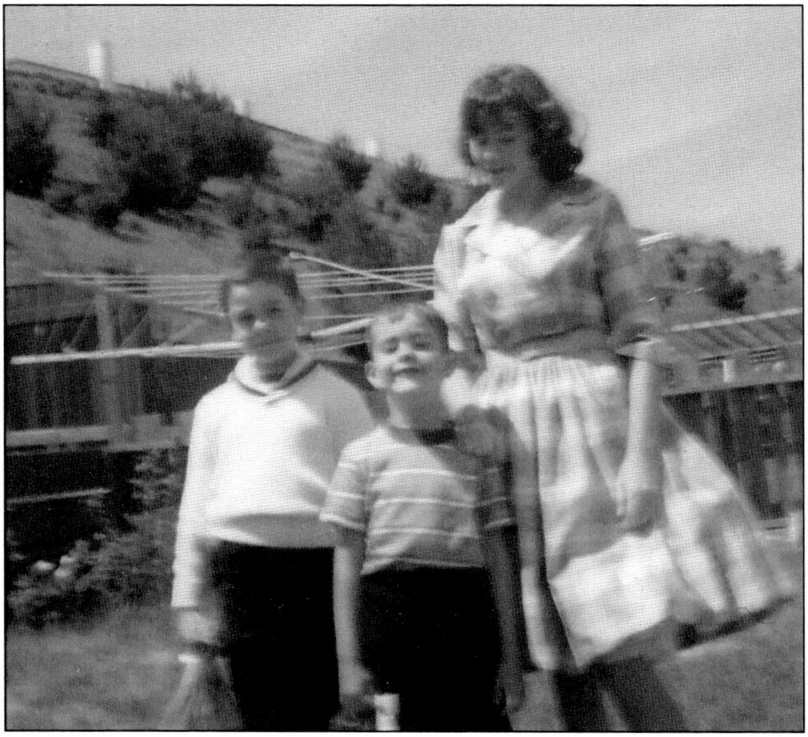

This photograph, taken in June 1960, shows big sister Virginia (Ginny) helping mom keep the boys in line. To their backs, at the top of the hill is Larchmont Drive. The pine trees have grown a little, and the neighbors have put in a patio.

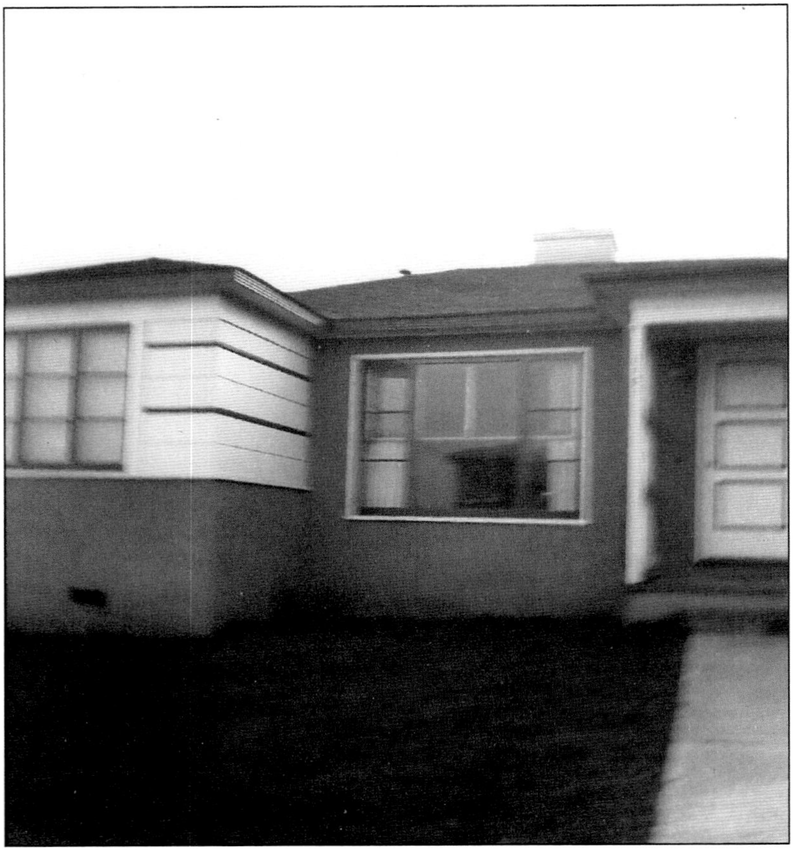

The Crapse residence at 1131 Nimitz Drive as it appeared in 1954 when the family purchased it. They were the second family to live here and remained there until the mid-1980s. By October 1955, Chief Crapse's eldest daughters were adults working for the phone company. Virginia, the third eldest, was at Garden Village School, Raymond was a toddler, and the youngest, David, was an infant.

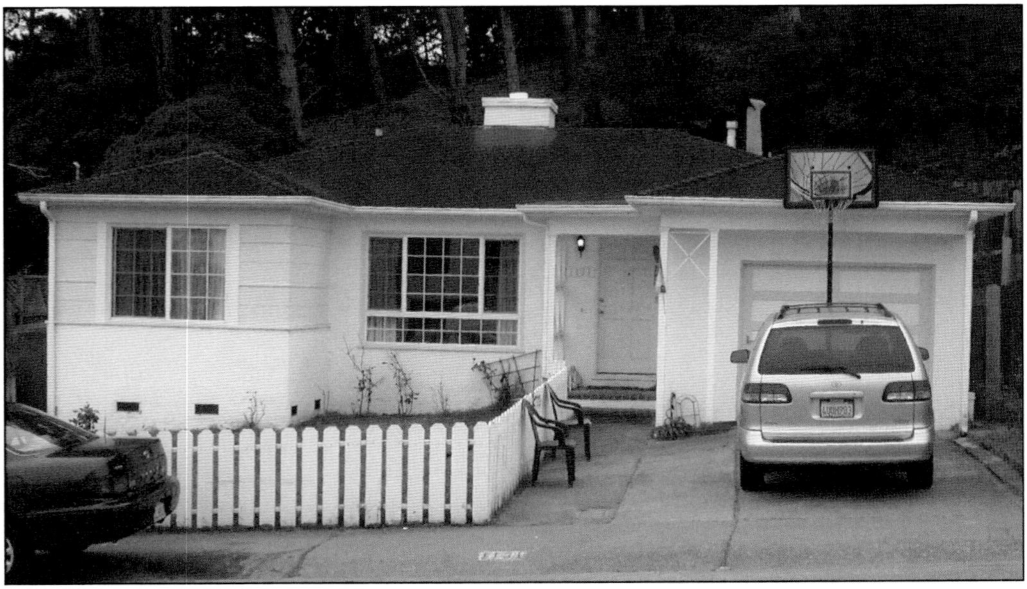

The same Stoneson built house is pictured in 2010. The house has new owners, new paint, new windows, and a new fence in the front yard. The house to this day retains its original charm in a quiet neighborhood. The trees in the back have grown into a virtual forest.

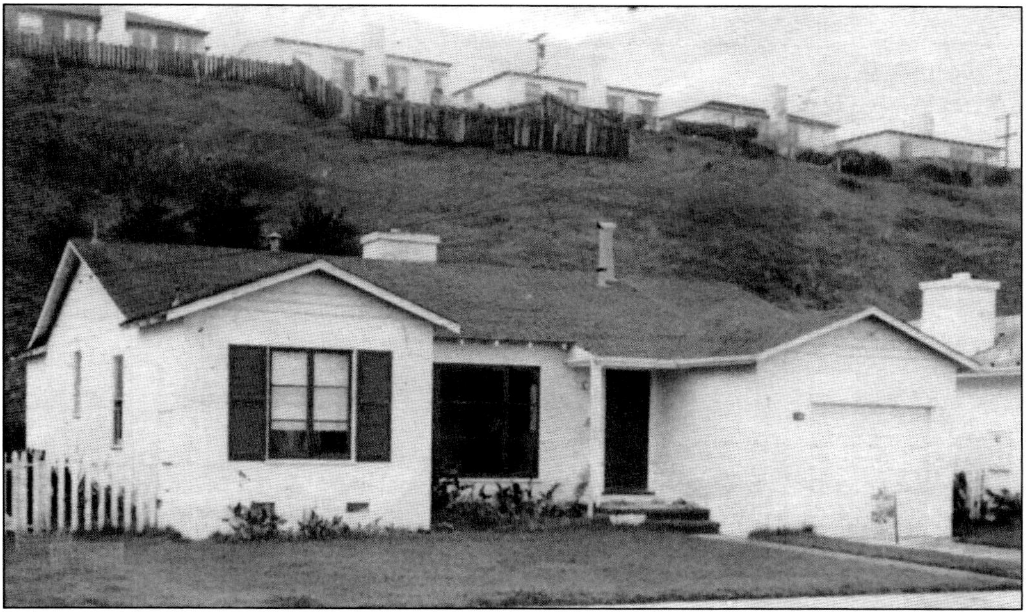

Just up the hill from the Crapse family was the home of Calvin and Chiyeko Harada at 1155 Nimitz Drive. Here is the original Stoneson house as it looked in 1956. This is a postcard from a local realtor listing the house. Behind the Harada house, one can see the houses on Larchmont Drive. (Courtesy Mrs. Chiyeko Harada.)

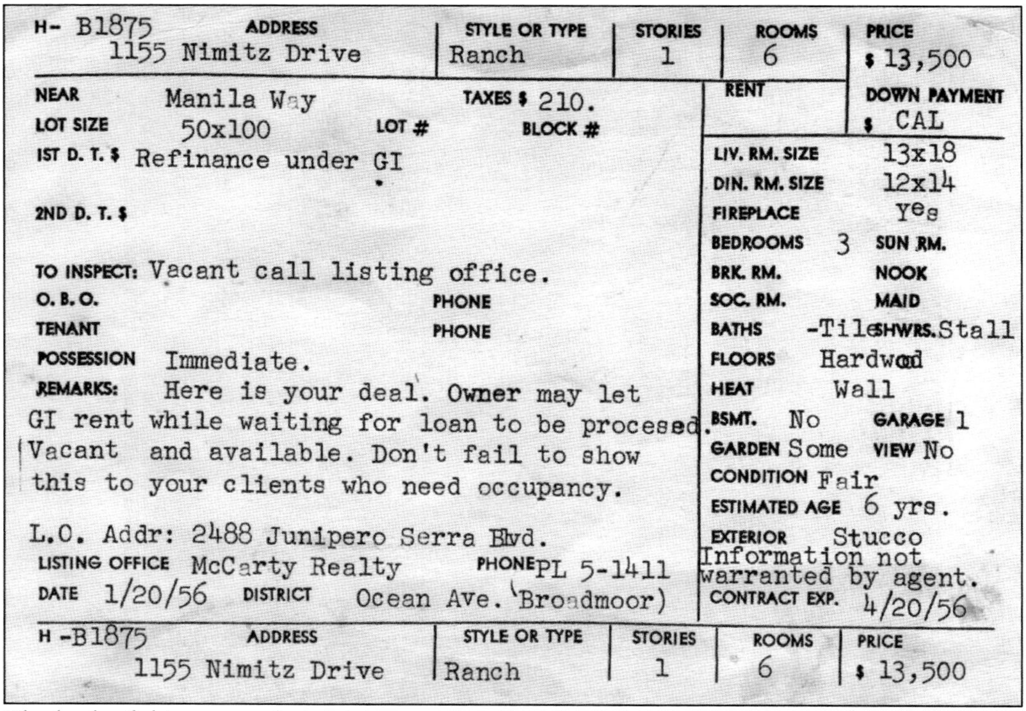

H- B1875 ADDRESS	STYLE OR TYPE	STORIES	ROOMS	PRICE
1155 Nimitz Drive	Ranch	1	6	$ 13,500

NEAR Manila Way TAXES $ 210. RENT DOWN PAYMENT $ CAL
LOT SIZE 50x100 LOT # BLOCK #
1ST D. T. $ Refinance under GI
2ND D. T. $
TO INSPECT: Vacant call listing office.
O. B. O. PHONE
TENANT PHONE
POSSESSION Immediate.
REMARKS: Here is your deal. Owner may let GI rent while waiting for loan to be processed. Vacant and available. Don't fail to show this to your clients who need occupancy.
L.O. Addr: 2488 Junipero Serra Blvd.
LISTING OFFICE McCarty Realty PHONE PL 5-1411
DATE 1/20/56 DISTRICT Ocean Ave. (Broadmoor)

LIV. RM. SIZE 13x18
DIN. RM. SIZE 12x14
FIREPLACE Yes
BEDROOMS 3 SUN RM.
BRK. RM. NOOK
SOC. RM. MAID
BATHS -Tile SHWRS. Stall
FLOORS Hardwood
HEAT Wall
BSMT. No GARAGE 1
GARDEN Some VIEW No
CONDITION Fair
ESTIMATED AGE 6 yrs.
EXTERIOR Stucco
Information not warranted by agent.
CONTRACT EXP. 4/20/56

H -B1875 ADDRESS	STYLE OR TYPE	STORIES	ROOMS	PRICE
1155 Nimitz Drive	Ranch	1	6	$ 13,500

The back of this postcard reveals yet another Broadmoor homeowner getting financing from a G.I. loan. Cal Harada was a veteran of the U.S. Army. Also pictured are the original dimensions of the house and the price. Condominiums are not even sold in this day and age for the price listed on this house in 1956. (Courtesy Mrs. Chiyeko Harada.)

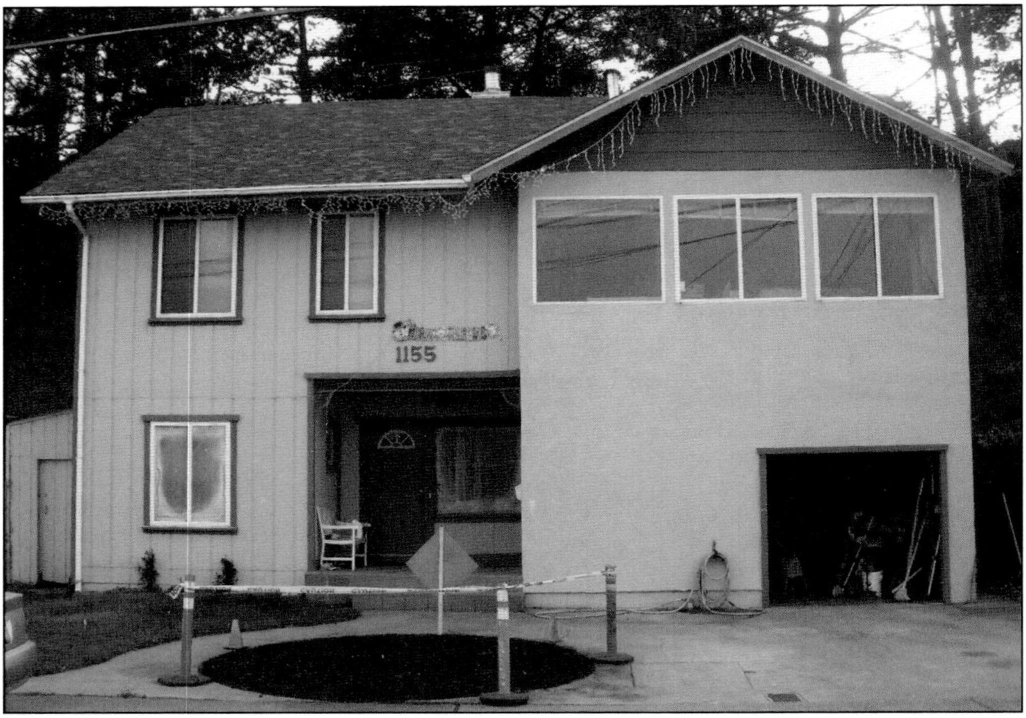

Pictured here is 1155 Nimitz Drive as it looks in 2010. A second story has been added along with new paint and windows. While most all of these Stoneson houses in Broadmoor have had to be upgraded and repaired, most have not suffered expansions like this one has. Despite all of this expansion, the garage still remains a place for only one car.

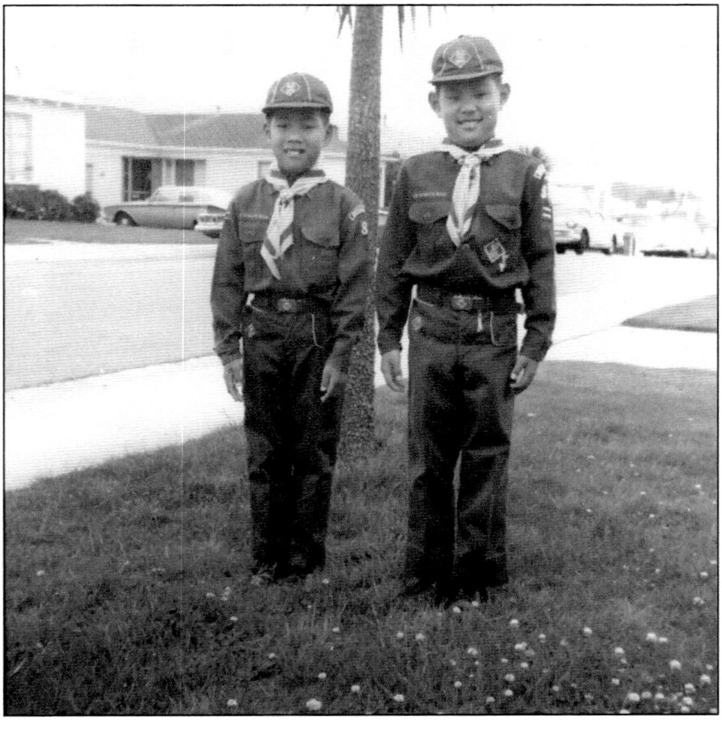

The Harada residence was also home to Cub Scout den No. 7 during the mid-1960s. Part of pack No. 84, it was the Broadmoor pack. Den meetings were held once a week with Mrs. Harada presiding as den mother. Pack meetings were held with the other dens once a month at the Broadmoor Presbyterian Church. Rival pack No. 259 was located in Daly City. (Courtesy Mrs. Chiyeko Harada.)

The Harada boys are pictured from left to right, as follows: Curtis, Craig (eldest), Clifford (second eldest), and the character in front is Clayton (the youngest). Curtis and Clifford are not only wearing their Cub Scout uniforms but also are holding sail boats made to perform in competition at the Scout-O-Rama that year. (Courtesy Mrs. Chiyeko Harada.)

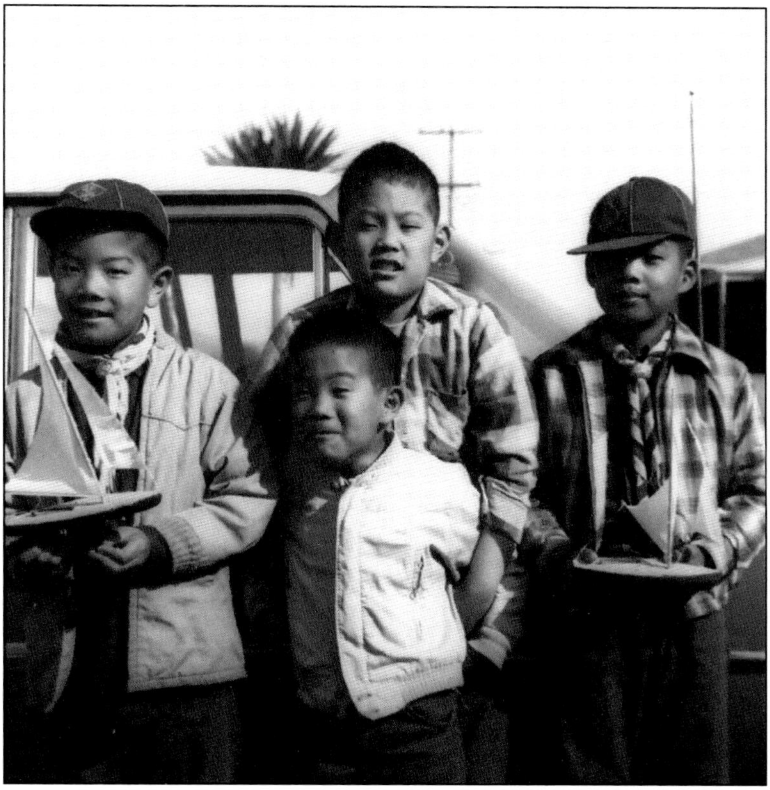

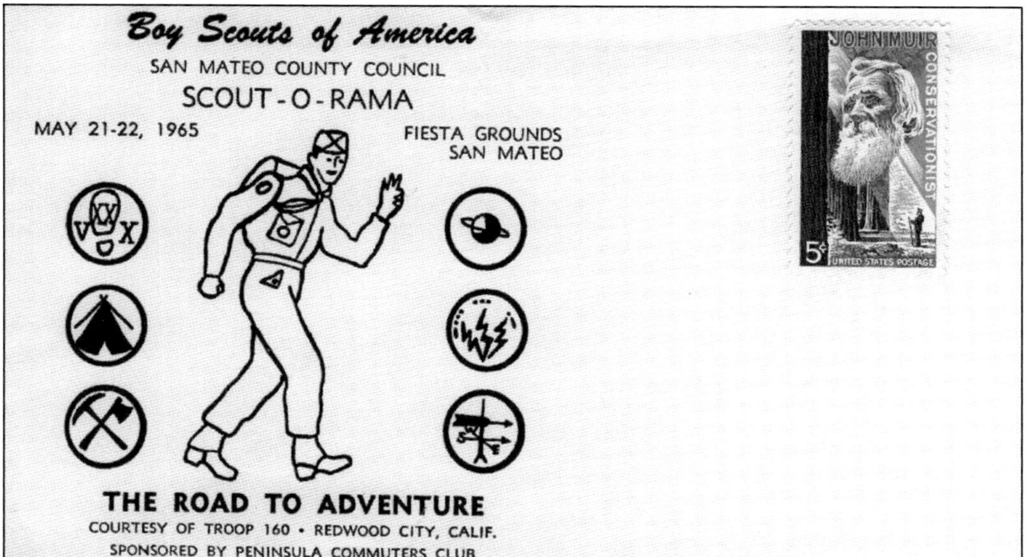

This is an invitation for the 1965 Scout-O-Rama. Usually held at the San Mateo County Fair Grounds, the annual event provided an opportunity for all local packs and dens to meet and compete for ribbons and prizes. Note the John Muir stamp on the envelope for 5¢ postage. (Courtesy Mrs. Chiyeko Harada.)

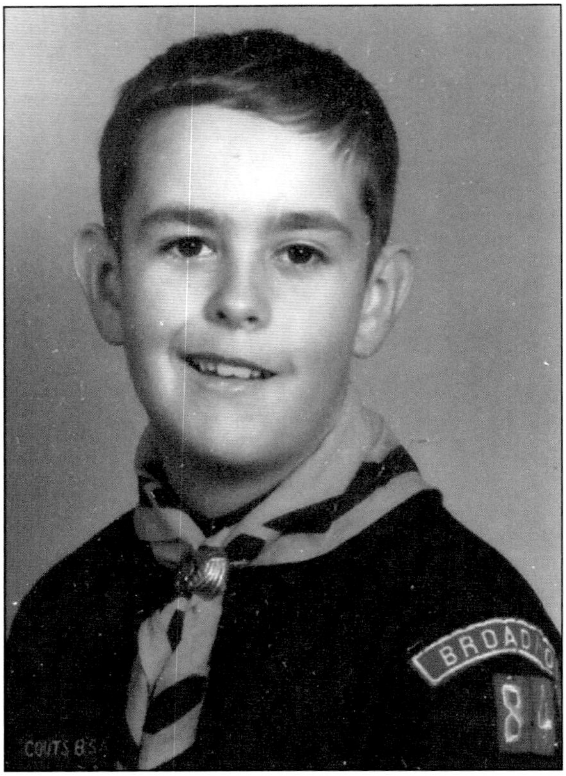

It was a short trek up the hill to the Harada's house for young Raymond and David Crapse. Here is David in his fourth grade class picture sporting his new uniform. Participating in Cub Scouts was just one of many activities provided for baby boomers in the little community of Broadmoor Village.

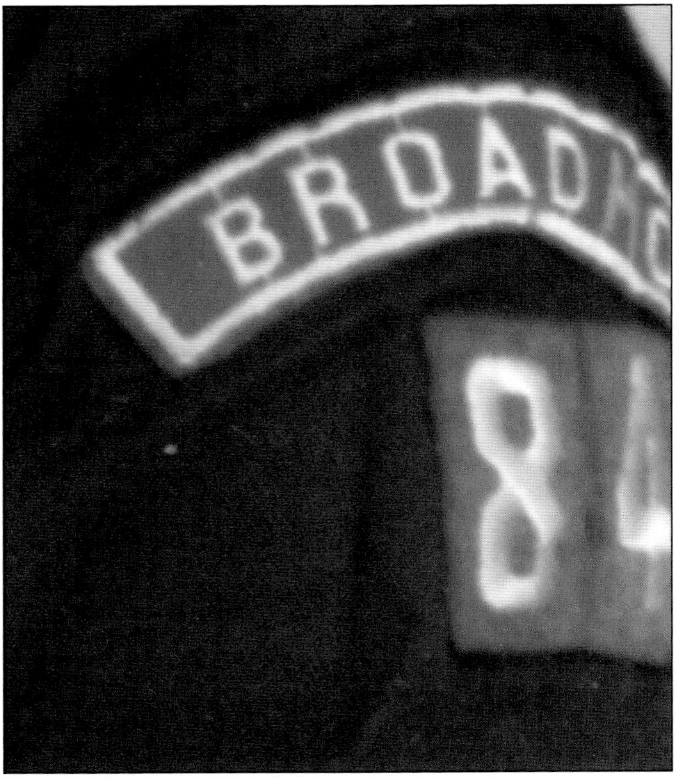

The rival pack was pack No. 259 in Daly City. The *Daly City Record* reported that Pack No. 259 was originally located in Broadmoor during the 1950s. No matter where they were, the troops of pack No. 84 were very aware of the fact that they were in Broadmoor and not Daly City.

Living almost on the corner of Eighty-seventh and Washington Streets in Broadmoor allowed the Carlson family a bird's-eye view of the parade from their front porch. Here is Cub Scout Pack No. 84 from Broadmoor marching with their pack colors. Right next door to the Carlsons is an empty lot that would eventually be home to the Broadmoor Community Center. (Courtesy Leif and Lauri Carlson.)

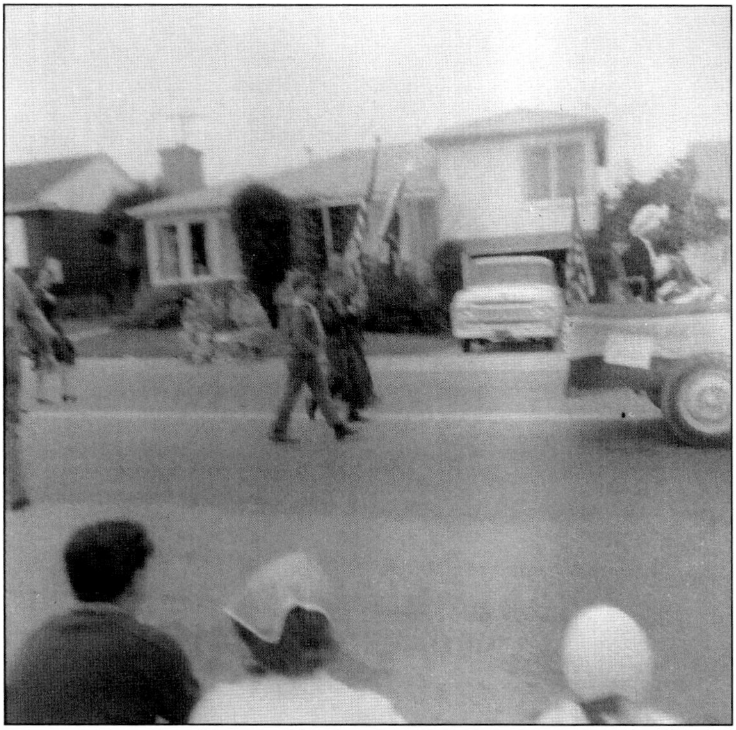

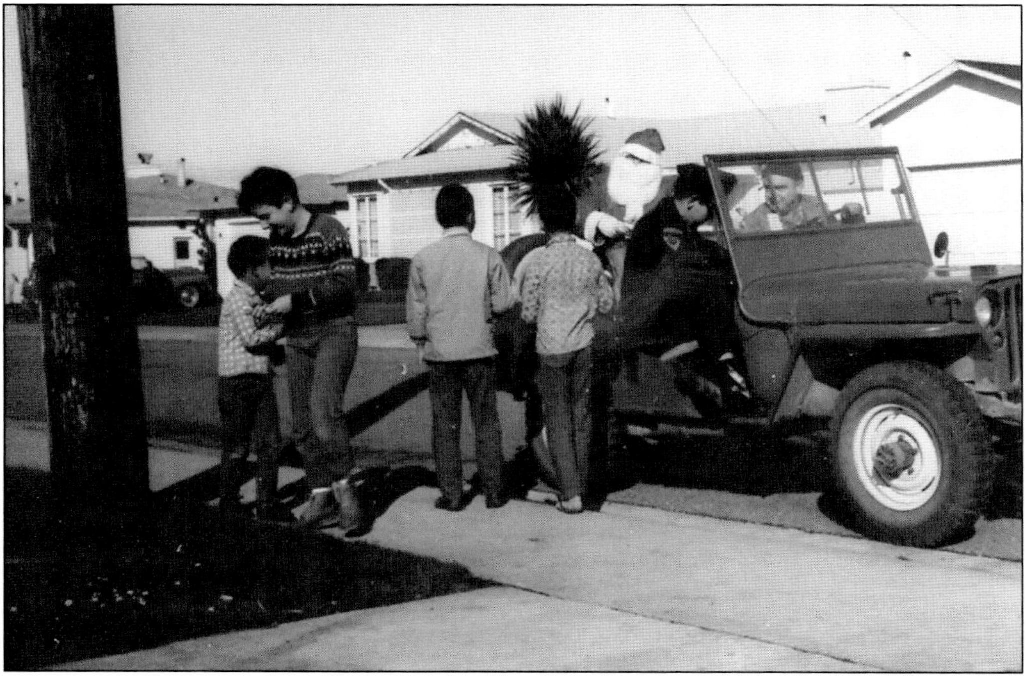

Christmas time did not bring parades to the streets of Broadmoor, but it did bring Santa Claus. Usually Santa would be riding on top of a Colma Fire Truck. For some reason, Santa came to town in a military jeep the year this picture was taken. Along with Santa is a Broadmoor police officer for protection. Here are the Harada boys getting their fair share of goodies. (Courtesy Mrs. Chiyeko Harada.)

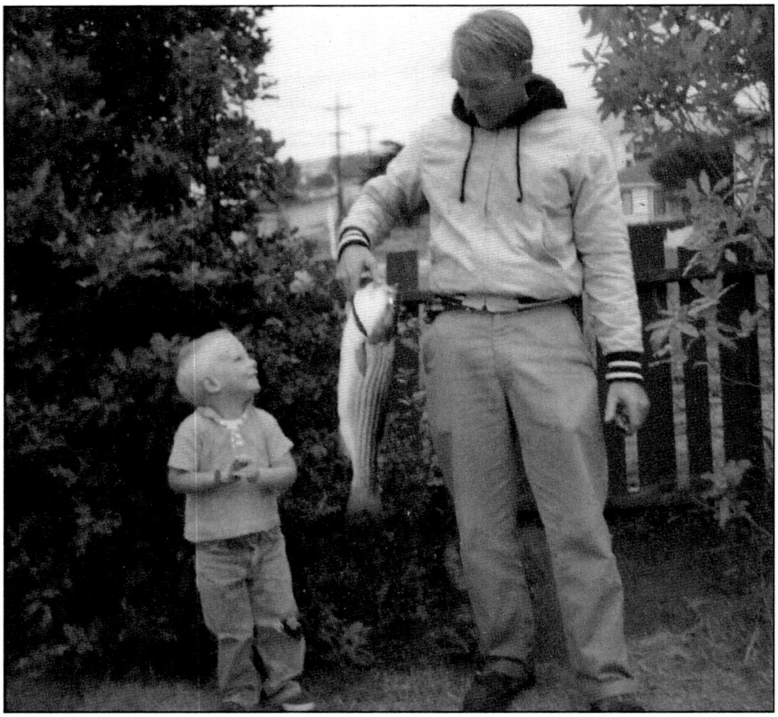

Here is little Leif Carlson and his dad, Glen, in their backyard after a good day of fishing. One could drive to nearby Lake Merced or the Pacific Ocean, which is just as close. Mom, Irma Jean Carlson, took this picture of the prized catch. (Courtesy Leif and Lauri Carlson.)

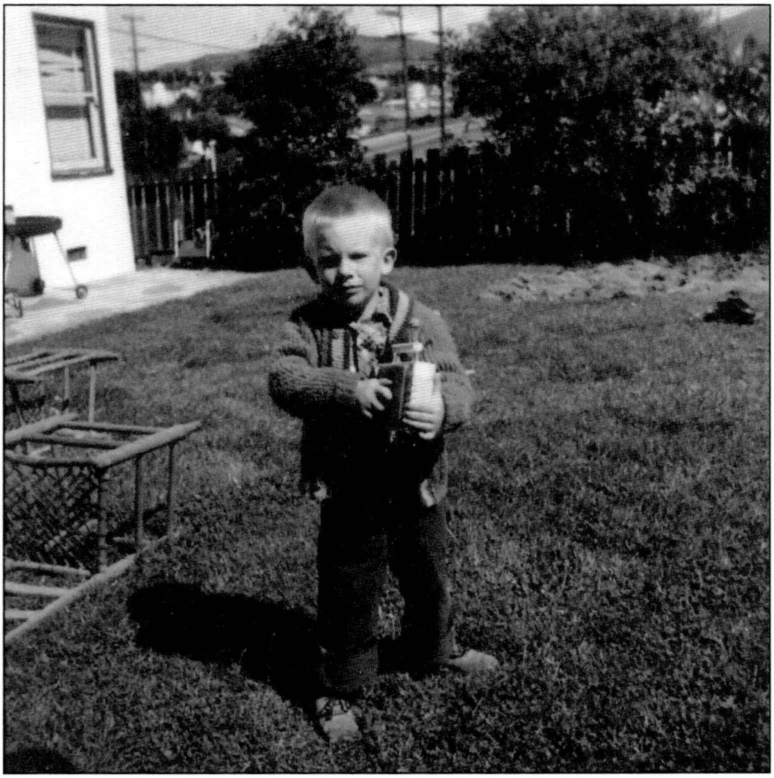

This is Leif playing in the family backyard. Behind him, to the east is San Bruno Mountain and, most notably, the vacant lot that will be the home for the new Broadmoor Community Center. Little sister Lauri cannot be found; perhaps she is inside playing with a doll or listening to a Beatles record. (Courtesy Leif and Lauri Carlson.)

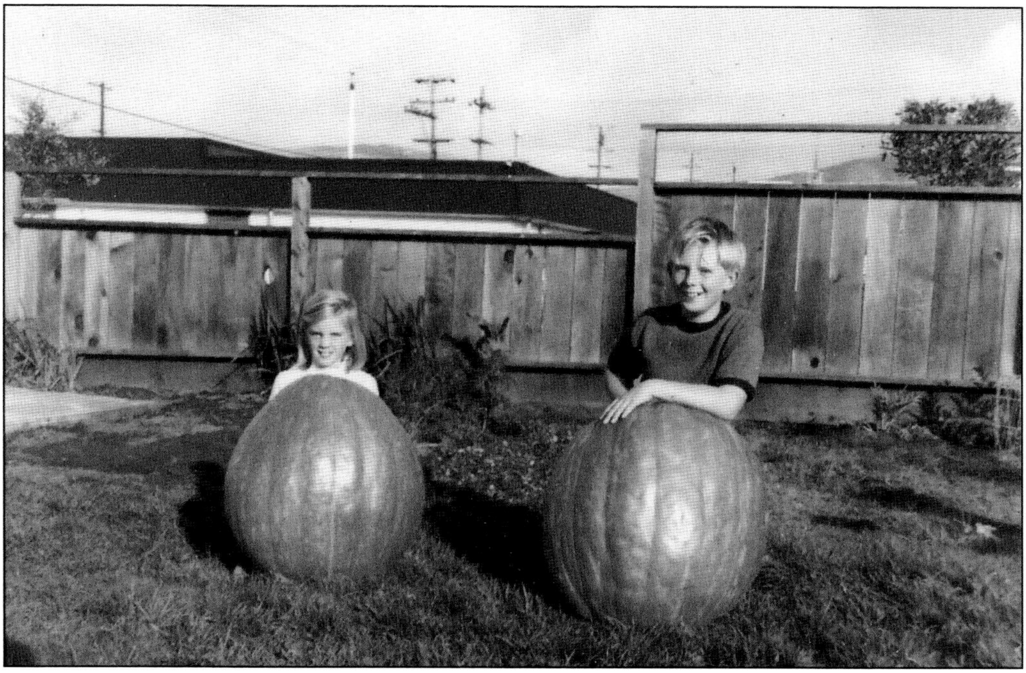

A few years later, the Great Pumpkin paid a visit to the Carlson house. This is another picture in their backyard facing east. There is a new fence and a new neighbor, the Broadmoor Community Center. Another new neighbor is Daly City. Across the street further east, lands on Eighty-seventh Street were annexed in 1963. (Courtesy Leif and Lauri Carlson.)

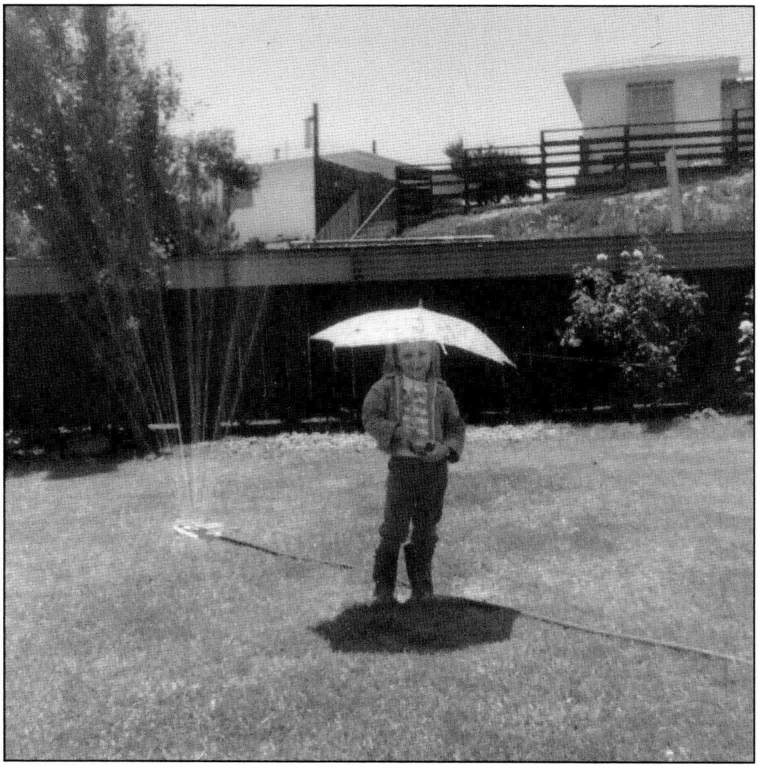

Kids in Broadmoor Village will say that there are not too many warm sunny days. So what is a kid suppose to do when the sun does come out? Break out the galoshes and the umbrella and pretend it's raining. One might say that this is working on one's tan, Broadmoor style. (Courtesy Leif and Lauri Carlson.)

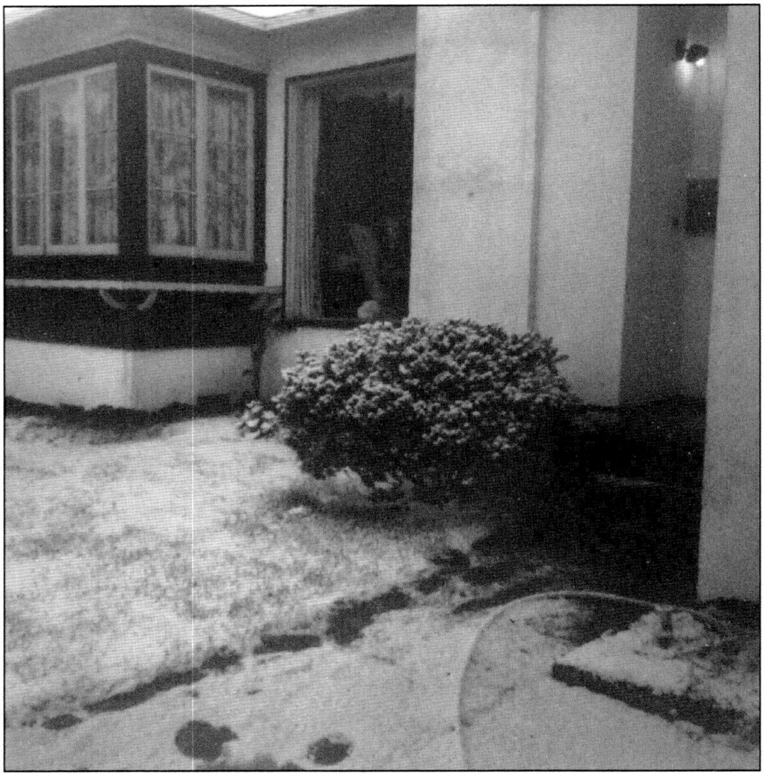

Snow, in Broadmoor? It has happened in the past. In January 1962, an artic blast created a winter wonderland in the unincorporated community. Here at the Carlson house on Eighty-seventh Street, the snow stuck around almost the entire day. White Christmas was a little late, or a lot early, depending on one's perspective. (Courtesy Leif and Lauri Carlson.)

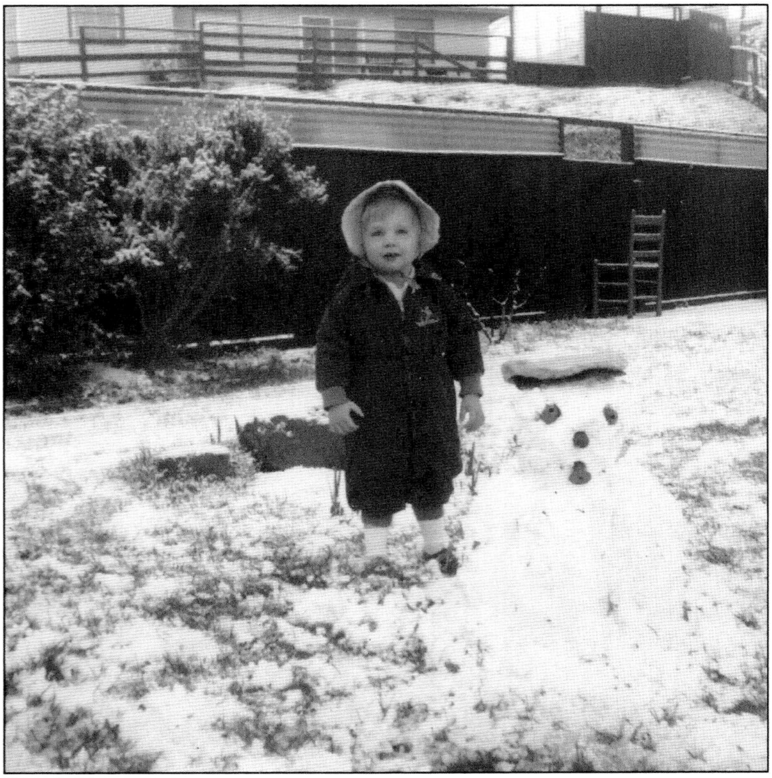

Here is little Lauri Carlson in the backyard with her very own "Frosty the Snowman" that she and the family made. Behind her is the house of Herbie Henderson and his family on Midway Avenue. It gets cold in Broadmoor, but thermal clothes are not really the normal attire. (Courtesy Leif and Lauri Carlson.)

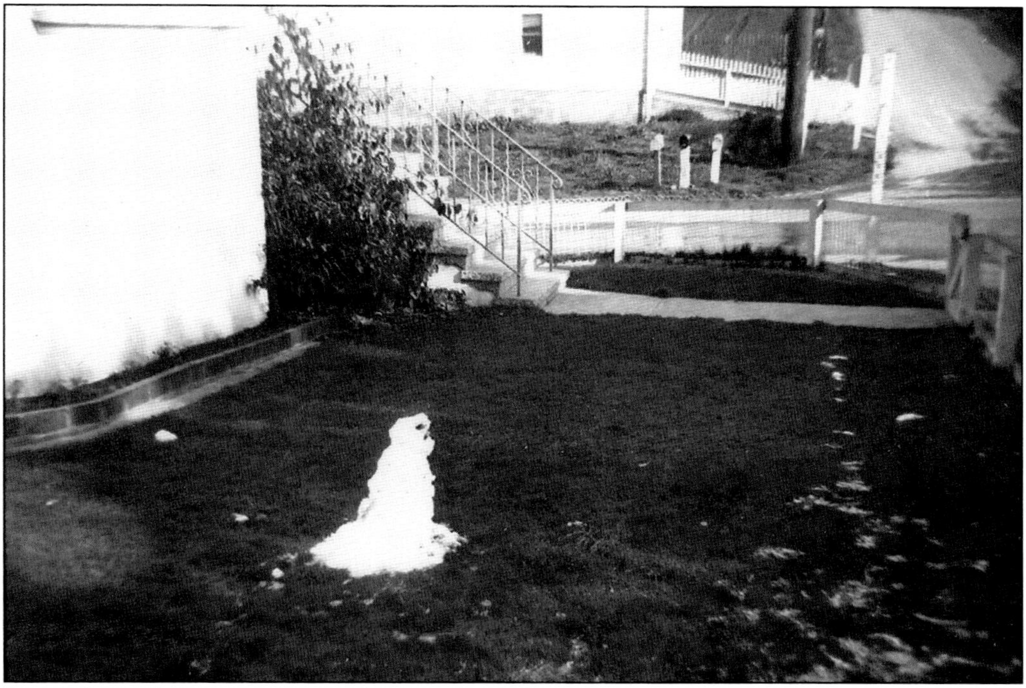

Frosty also made an appearance at the Wegscheider home on that day. Even though the Wegscheiders were only a few blocks away from the Carlsons, they were in Unincorporated Colma and not Broadmoor Village. Unincorporated Colma, however, does come under the jurisdiction of the Broadmoor Police Protection District. (Courtesy Mrs. Alvina Wegscheider.)

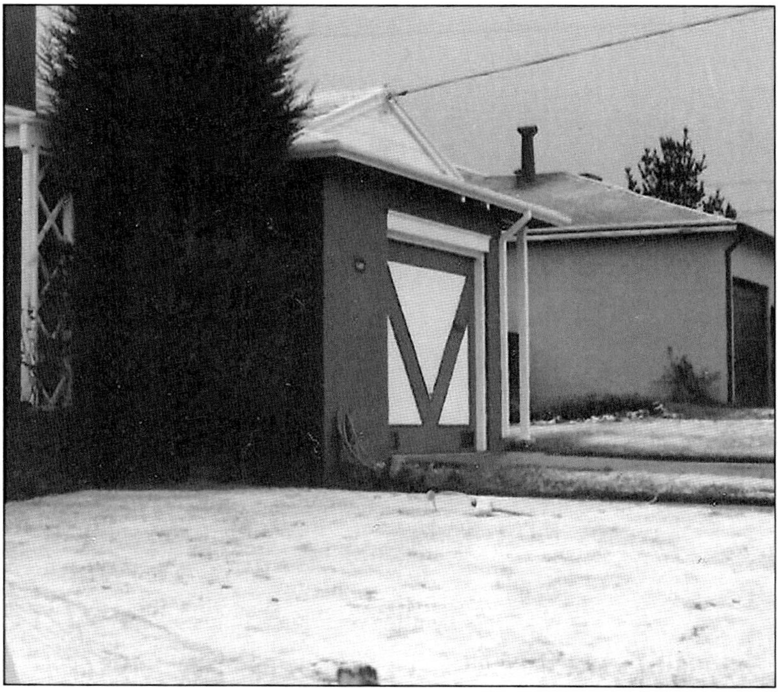

Snow made another appearance on the lawns of Broadmoor Village in February 1976. Here is the Medina residence at 1307 Sweetwood Drive. Walking in a winter wonderland could well have been the theme for this day as well. The snowfall on this day, as in 1962, only stayed on the ground for a day or so but was a topic of conversation for weeks afterward. (Courtesy Sue Medina-Larson.)

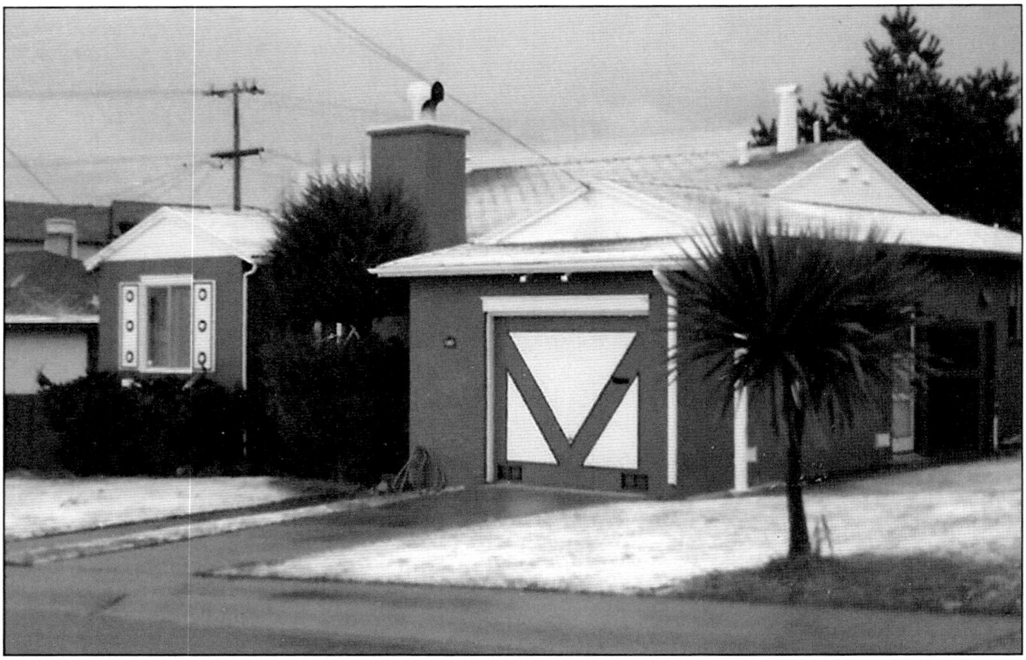

Here is another angle of Sue's house showing the snow on the roof and in the palm trees. One can also see, to the left of the picture, the apartments on Ninetieth Street. The land the apartments are currently on was once Unincorporated Colma and was annexed by Daly City in 1964. (Courtesy Sue Medina-Larson.)

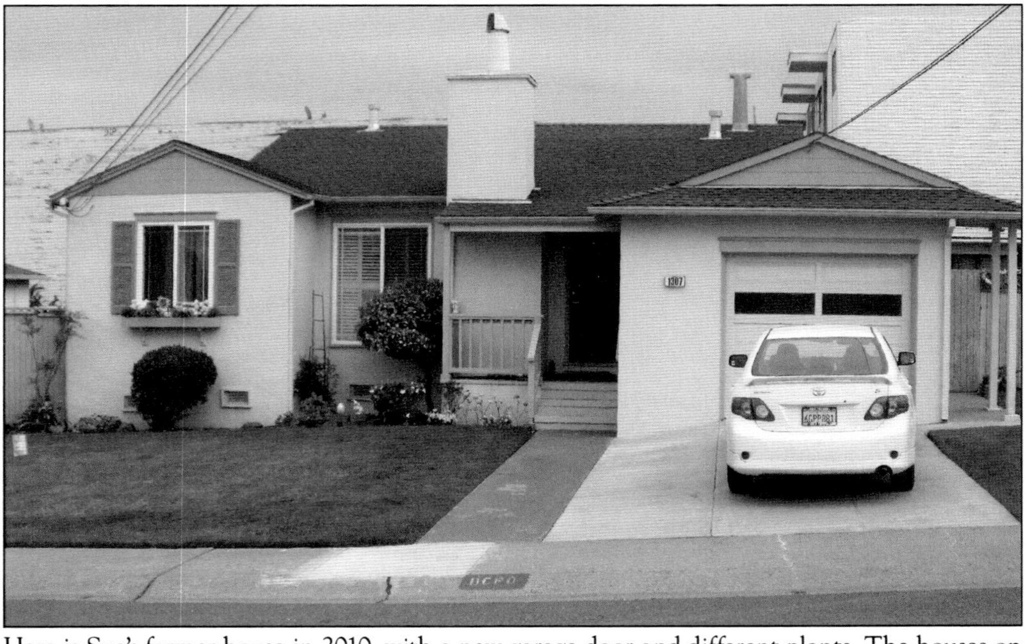

Here is Sue's former house in 2010, with a new garage door and different plants. The houses on this, the east side of Sweetwood between Ninetieth and Ninety-first Streets, were annexed by Daly City in 1978. So while these are Stoneson houses with round curbs on the sidewalks, they now have blue street signs not green. In other words, these houses were once in Broadmoor Village and are now in Daly City.

Three

Education, Broadmoor Style

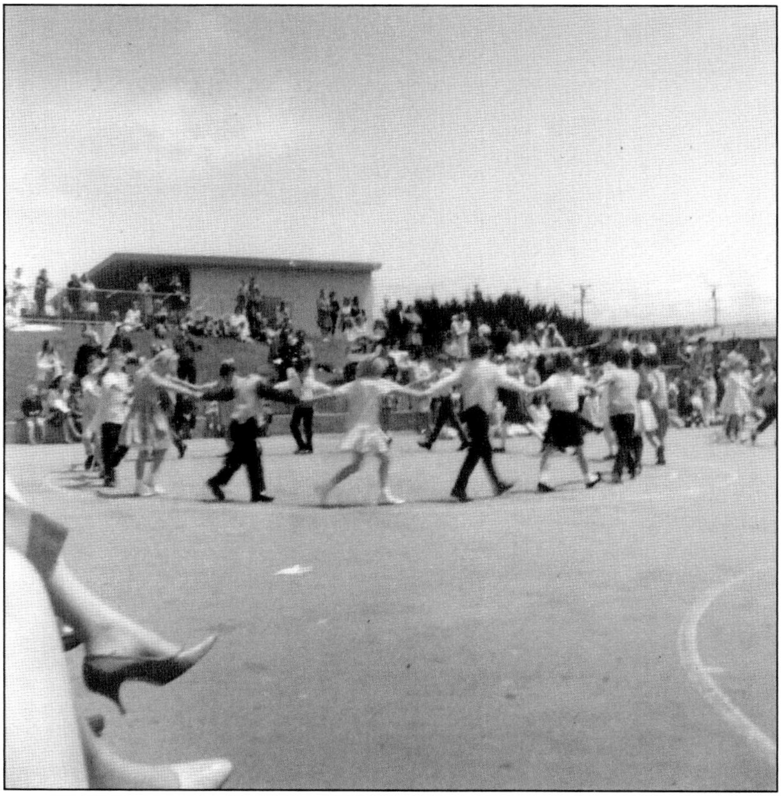

This scene is at Garden Village Elementary School; the event is the annual Mayday Dance that the whole school takes part in. Each class dresses up in colorful ribbons and costumes, and they do their best versions of "Ring Around the Rosie" and "The Hokey-Pokey." One year, in the 1960s, a rebellious class got to dance to a Beatles record, raising some parents' eyebrows. (Courtesy Leif and Lauri Carlson.)

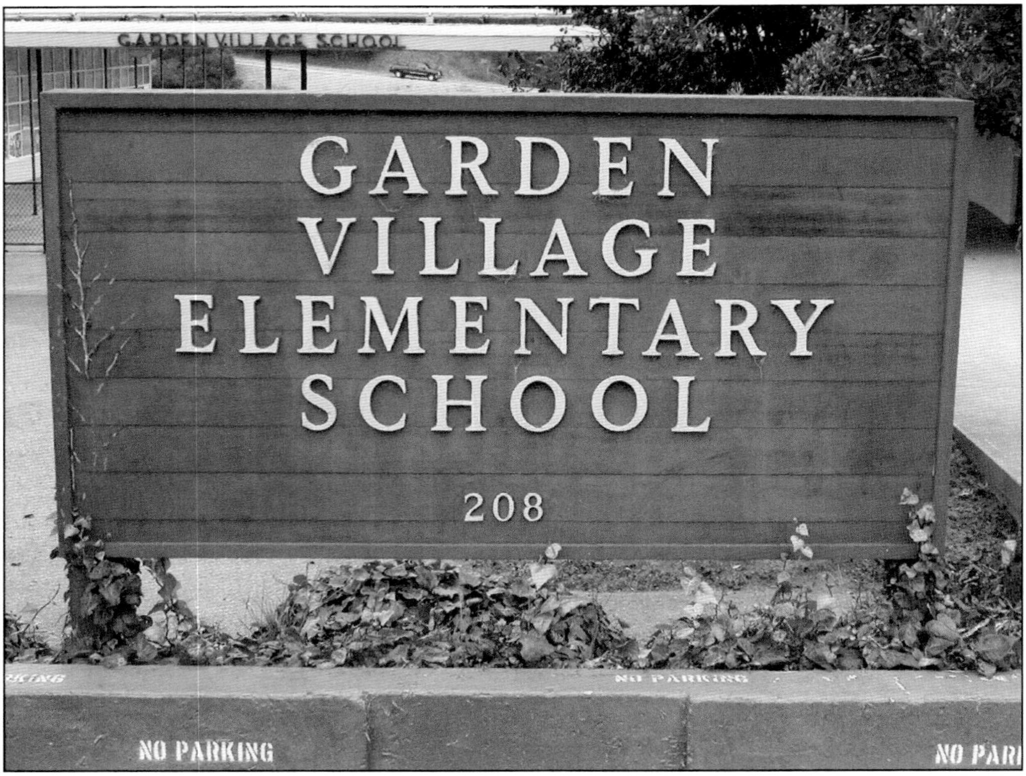

The first official school of Broadmoor Village, Garden Village Elementary School, opened in 1950 and was located at 208 Garden Lane. When Broadmoor homes were first being built in the late 1940s, parents needed schools close by for their children. Kindergarten and first grade were taught for a very short time at both the original Broadmoor Community Center and at the Broadmoor Presbyterian Church.

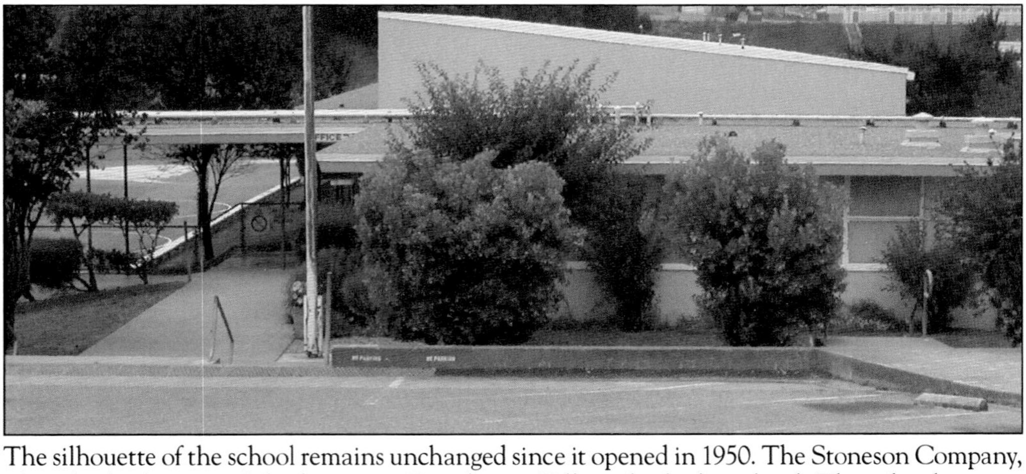

The silhouette of the school remains unchanged since it opened in 1950. The Stoneson Company, who also built most of the homes in Broadmoor Village, built the school. The school gets its name from the two closest streets, Garden Lane and Village Lane. These two main streets and several smaller connecting roads were actually a community unto itself know as Garden Village, separate from Broadmoor Village.

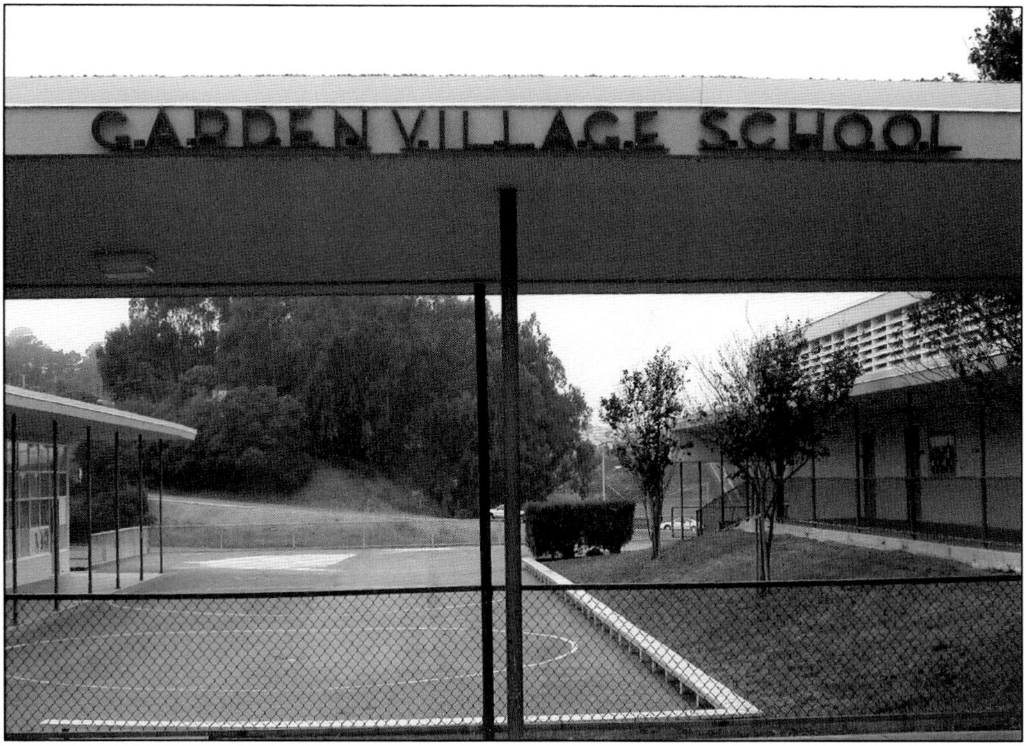

The original letters, the upper courtyard, the benches, and the wings containing school classrooms have all remained unchanged except for maybe being painted. All of the neighboring homes on Garden Lane and about two-thirds of the homes on Village Lane were actually built by the Paul Waters Company between 1938 and 1941, a few years before the Stonesons arrived to build Broadmoor.

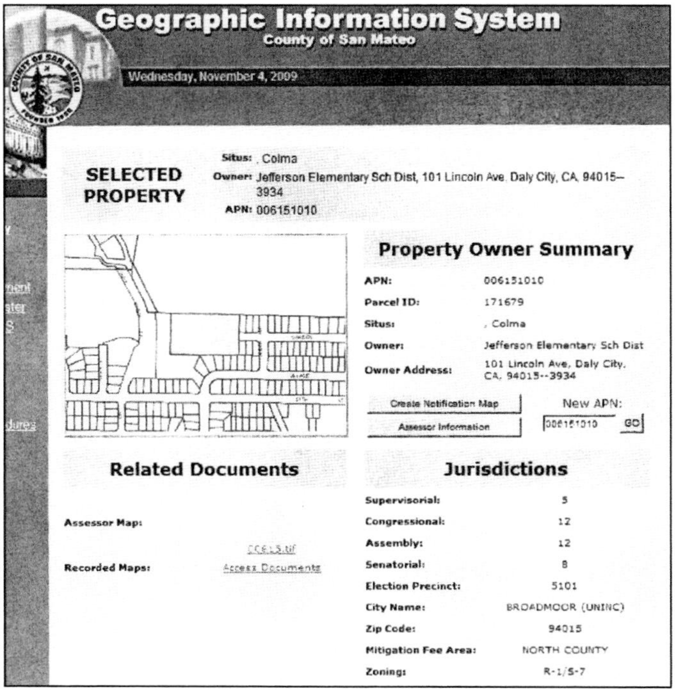

The school's proximity has always been an issue with locals as to whether the school is in Garden Village or Broadmoor Village. In an online search, the address on half of the pages states that it is in Colma, and the other half lists Daly City. The confusion ends when one makes a trip to the county public works. Look it up, and the city is listed as Broadmoor (unincorporated).

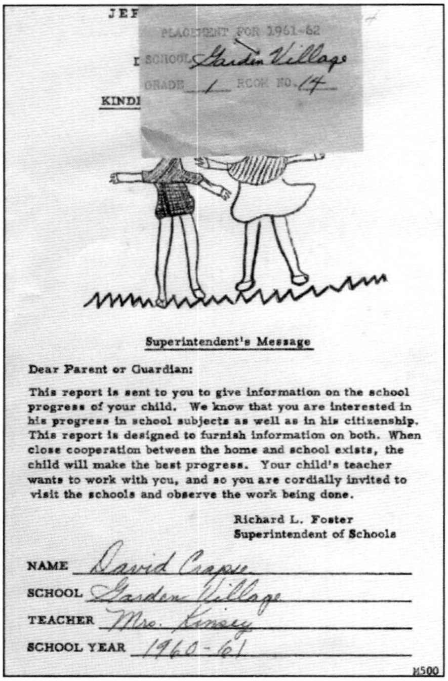

JEF

PLACEMENT FOR 1961-62
SCHOOL Garden Village
GRADE 1 ROOM NO. 14

KINDI

Superintendent's Message

Dear Parent or Guardian:

This report is sent to you to give information on the school progress of your child. We know that you are interested in his progress in school subjects as well as in his citizenship. This report is designed to furnish information on both. When close cooperation between the home and school exists, the child will make the best progress. Your child's teacher wants to work with you, and so you are cordially invited to visit the schools and observe the work being done.

Richard L. Foster
Superintendent of Schools

NAME David Crapse
SCHOOL Garden Village
TEACHER Mrs. Kinsey
SCHOOL YEAR 1960-61

M500

This is a 1960 report card from Garden Village. The stick figures are a long way from the digital methods of keeping grades today. Grades that were issued in the day were "X" for excellent, "S" for satisfactory, and "U" for unsatisfactory. In that era, the hardest subject in kindergarten was singing "Row Row Row Your Boat"

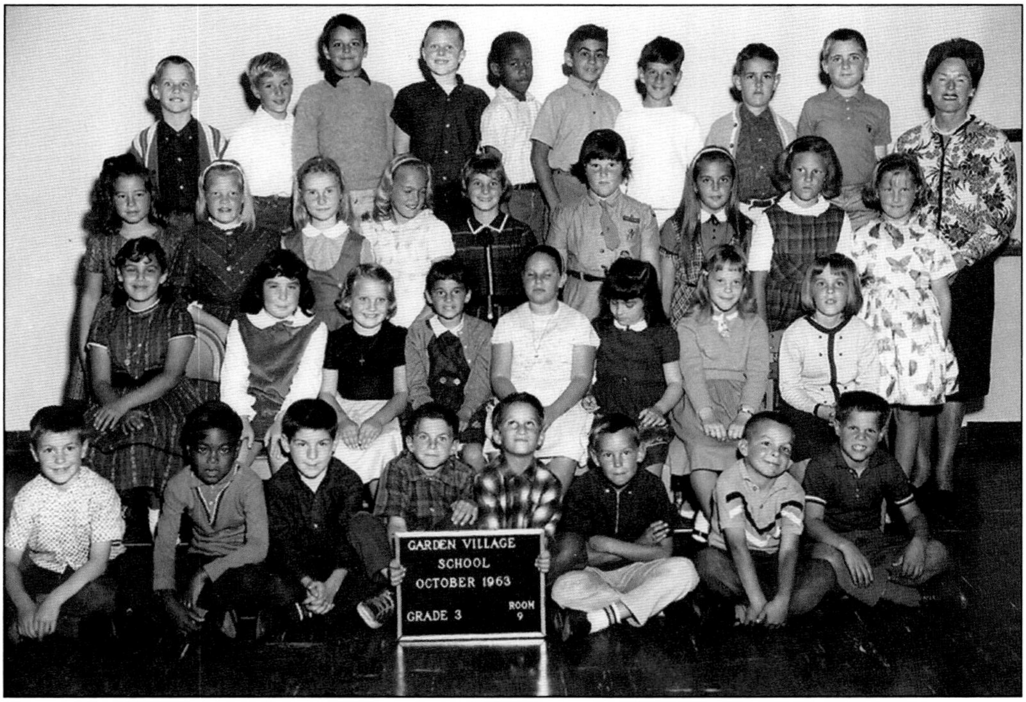

Mrs. Lewis's third grade class is pictured here. From left to right, in the first row are Alan Henley, unidentified, John Gerhardt, unidentified, John Chiosso, Brad Cloonan, Louis Medrano, Mark Sanguinetti; (second row) Kim Clifford, all others unidentified; (third row) Lisa Reeser, unidentified, Laura Biagini, Twila Hentorn, unidentified, Pam Proctor, unidentified, unidentified, Karen Fleische; (fourth row) unidentified, unidentified, Eugene Gelerduchi, Mark Haymaker, Fred Brown, unidentified, unidentified, David Crapse, Jim Katapodis, and Mrs. Lewis

Many schools have block programs where one can earn the school letters for a jacket or sweater. Such was the case at Garden Village Elementary School in the 1950s and 1960s. The colors were white for the background and red for the letters. One could earn points towards getting the school block or letters through extracurricular activities. More recently, the school adopted the roadrunner as its mascot.

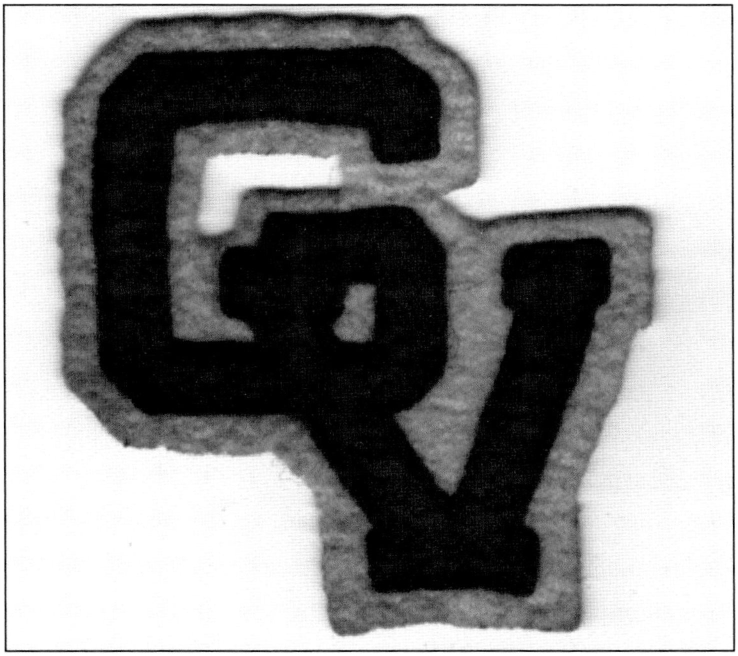

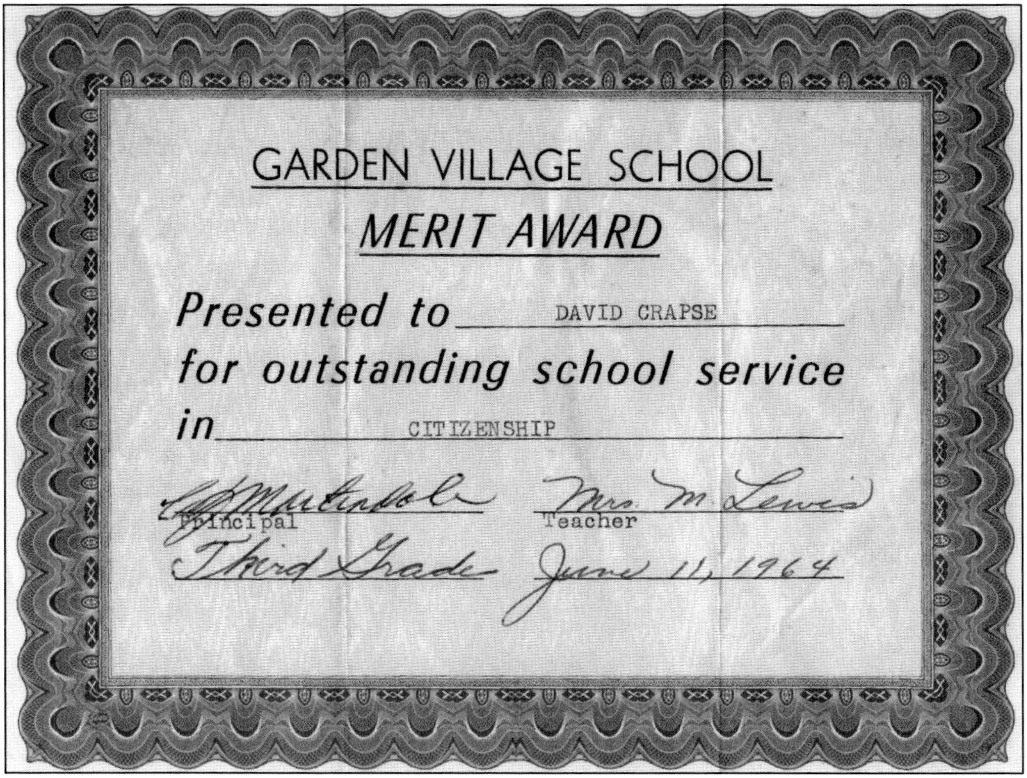

Merit awards like this one were given to students for extracurricular activities while they were adding up points towards the school block or letters. These awards were given for a variety of activities such as good citizenship, cafeteria helper, student service, milk monitor, library monito, and other duties.

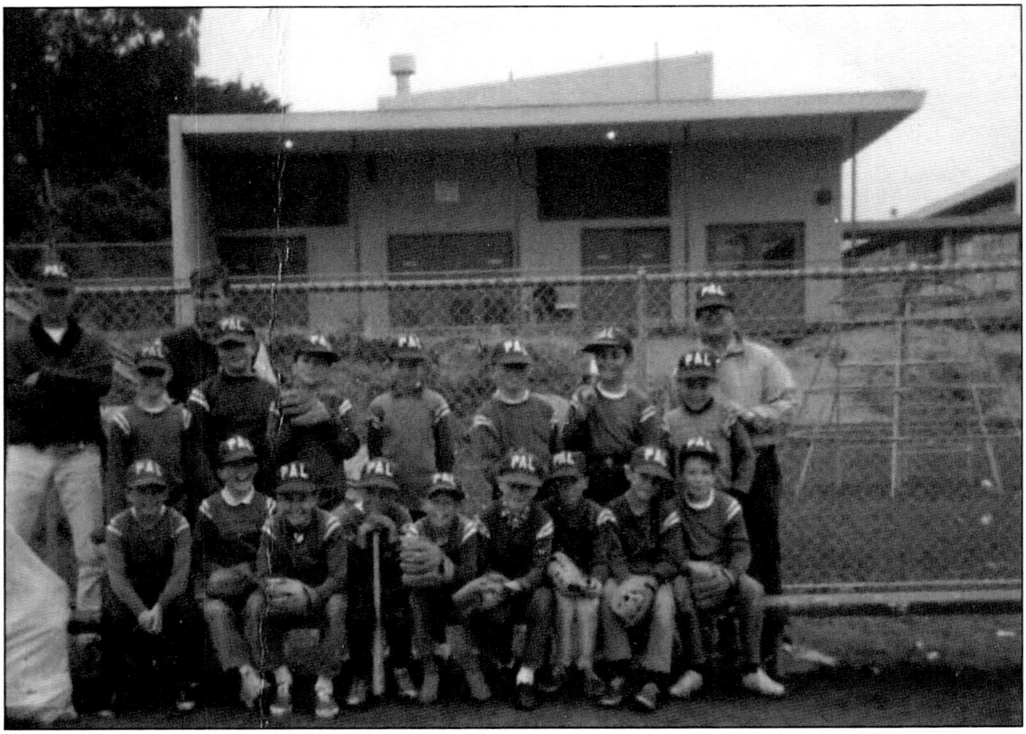

Here are the PAL Bobcats around 1963. During the summertime Little League Baseball was a common hobby and pastime. The Bobcats were in the Pee Wee division for local play. Practice was held twice a week at the playground at Garden Village School. Games were played on the weekends. (Courtesy Mark Sanguinetti.)

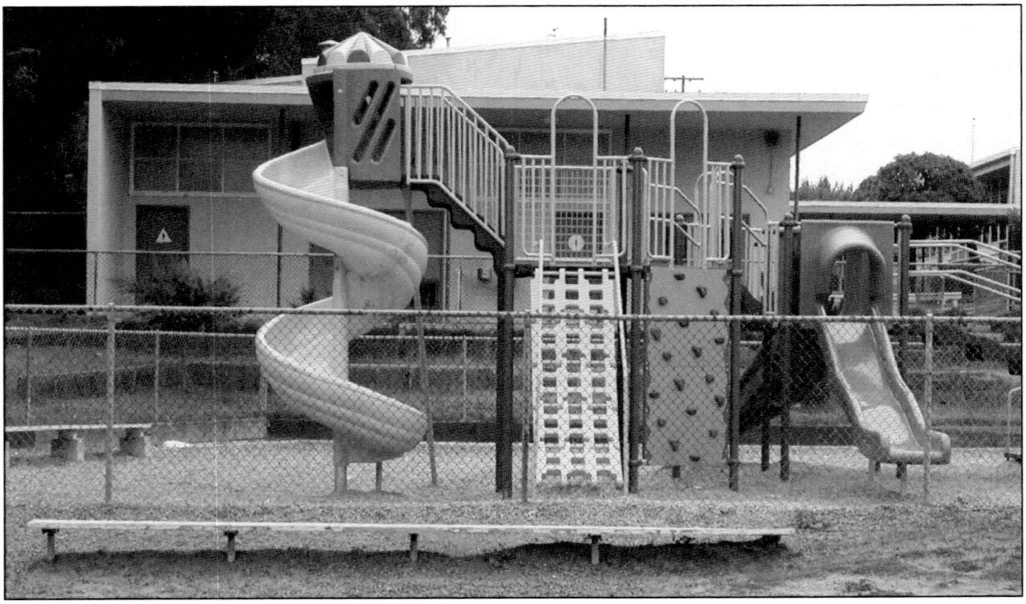

The same bench that the Bobcats posed on in 1963 is still on the field in 2010. The school building looks the same except for the international signs on the restrooms, and the monkey bars and slides on the tan bark have been replaced. The gophers still take up residence in the outfield as well.

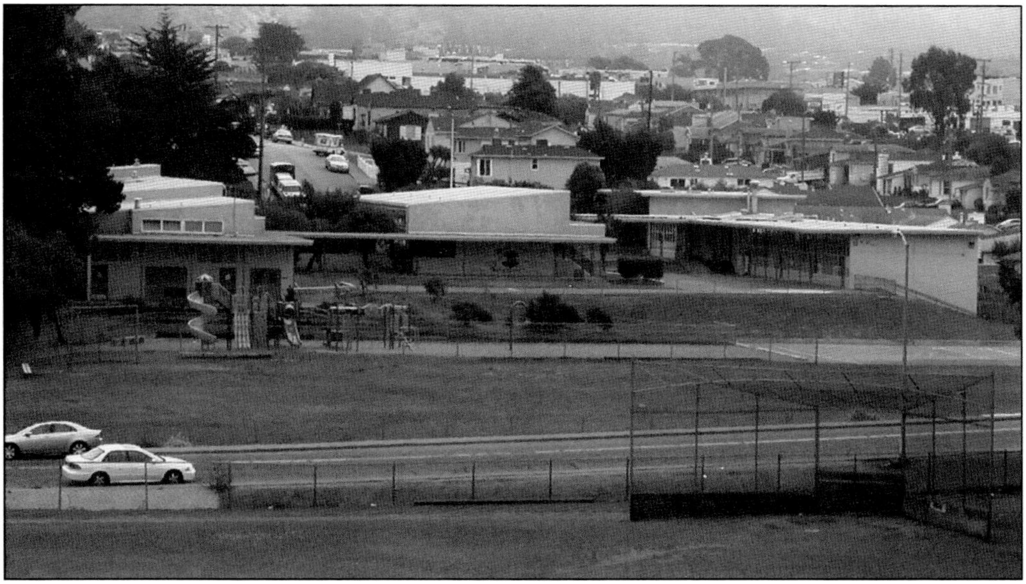

This is the view of Garden Village from across the field at Ben Franklin Junior High School. Behind the school, on the left is Garden Lane and to the right is Village Lane. In the foreground of the picture is the backstop for the main baseball diamond at Ben Franklin. Also in the foreground is the extension for Park Plaza Drive, which now separates the two schools.

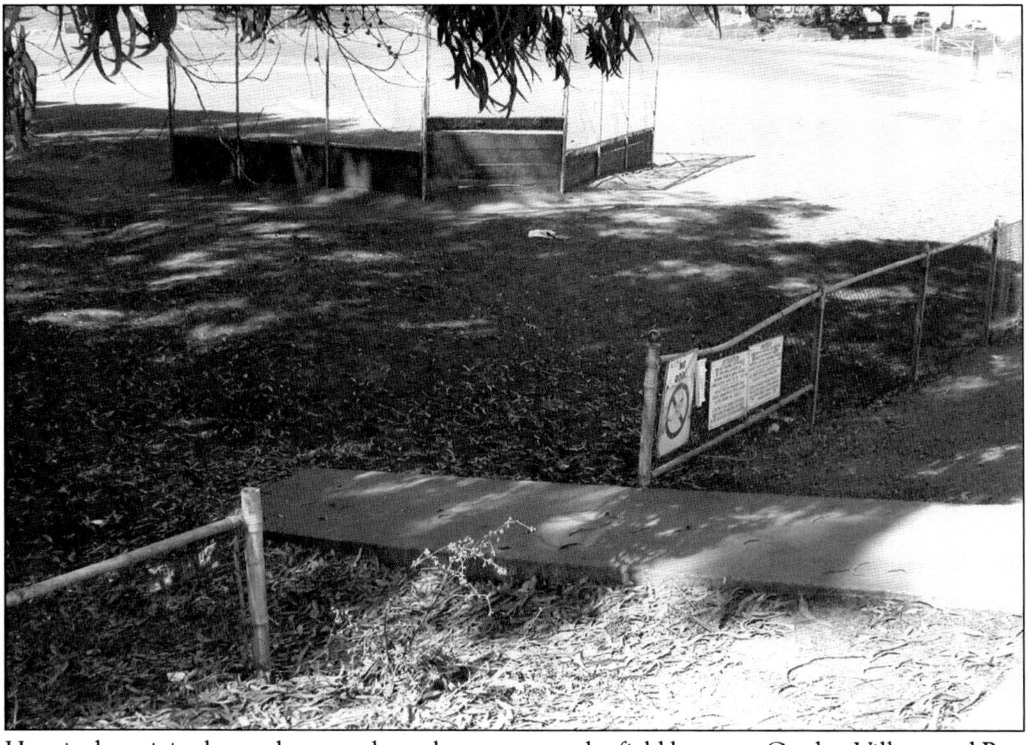

Here is the original gate that was the only passage on the field between Garden Village and Ben Franklin. The extension for Park Plaza Drive was built in 1964; before that, the chain link fence separated both schools. A ramp was built and put at the spot of the original gates to allow little leaguers better access to the baseball diamond.

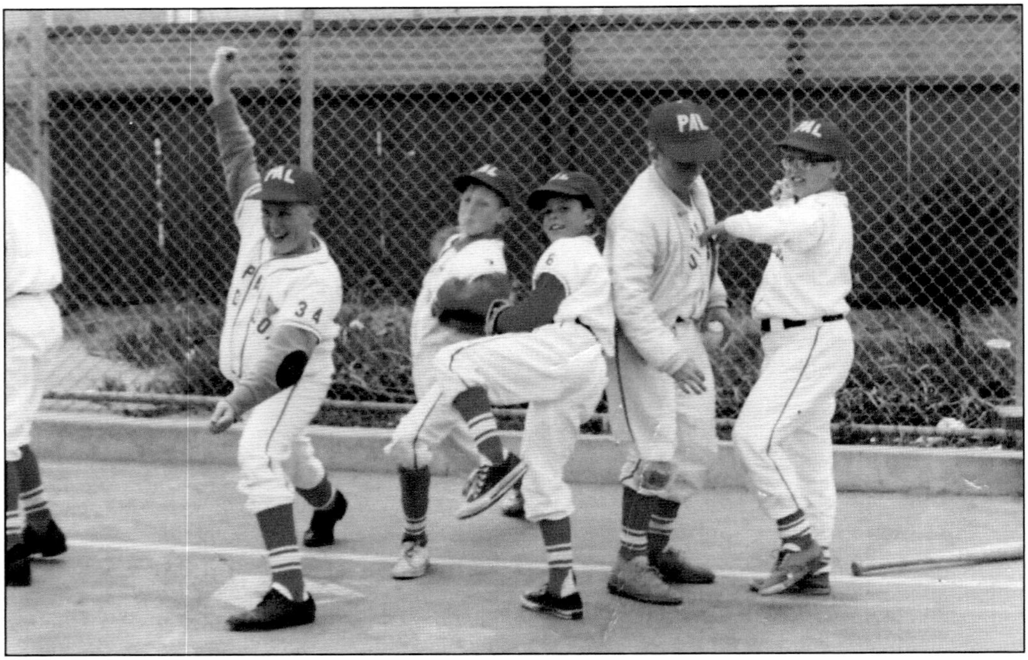

Speaking of baseball, the PAL Bobcats started growing up, as all children do, and moved on to the midget league. Along with the new league came new uniforms and a name change to the PAL Red Sox. Homefield was in Westlake just down the hill from Pips drive-in, later A&W then Burger King. (Courtesy Renny Wright.)

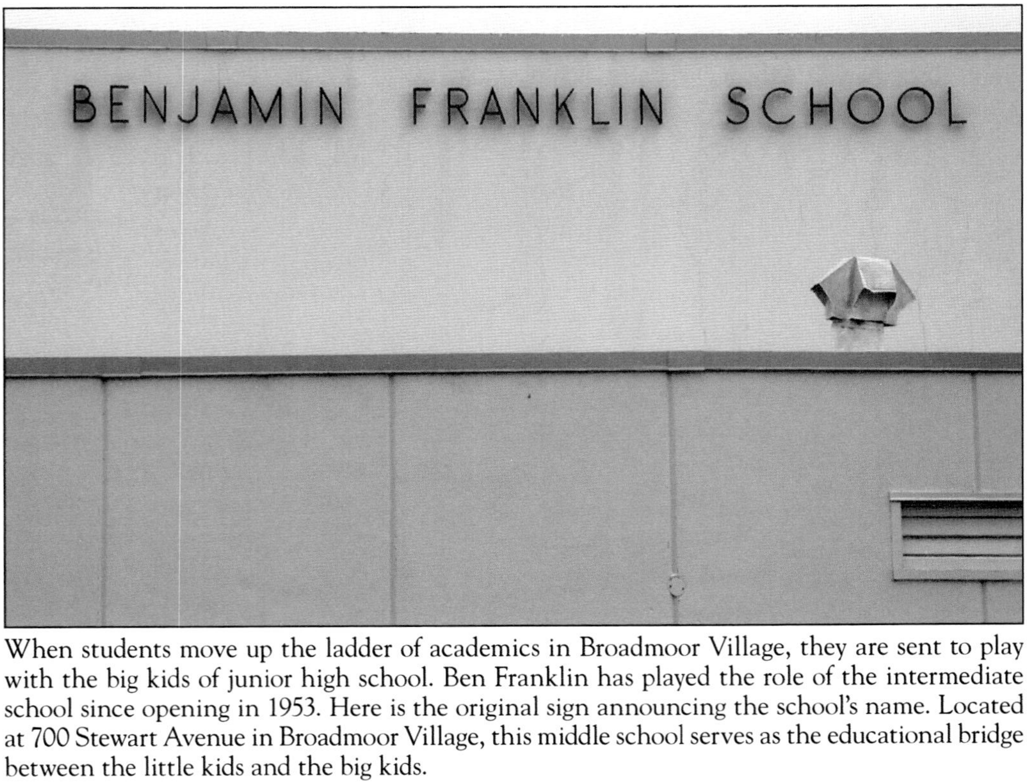

When students move up the ladder of academics in Broadmoor Village, they are sent to play with the big kids of junior high school. Ben Franklin has played the role of the intermediate school since opening in 1953. Here is the original sign announcing the school's name. Located at 700 Stewart Avenue in Broadmoor Village, this middle school serves as the educational bridge between the little kids and the big kids.

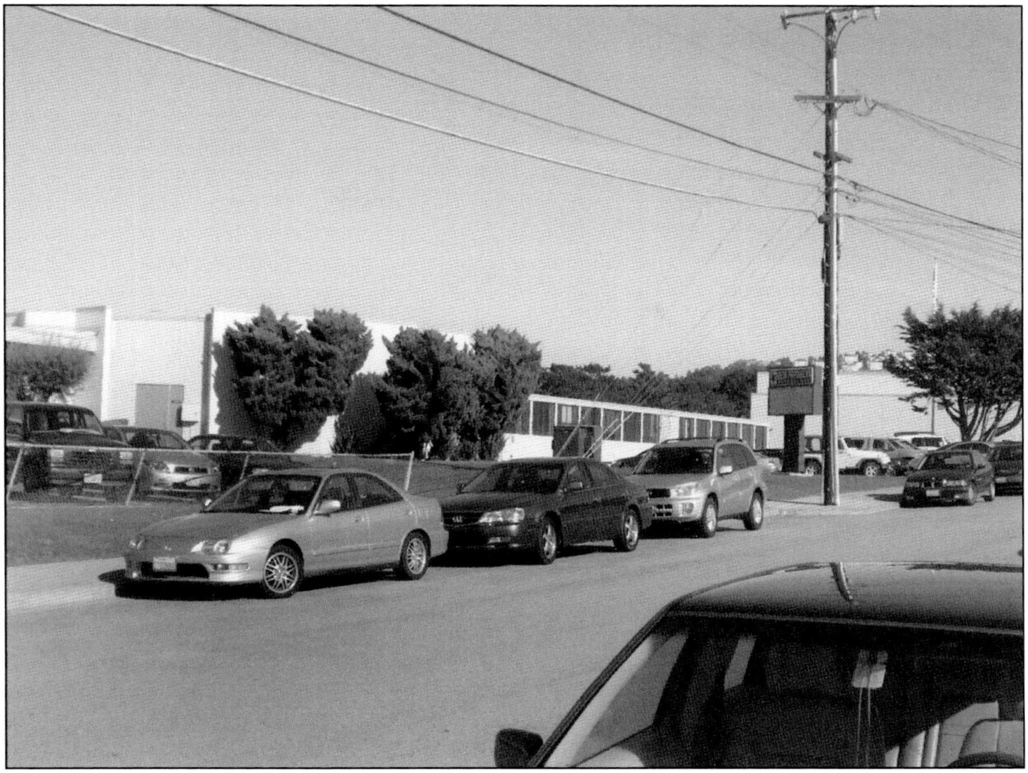

This is the front of Ben Franklin Junior High School as seen in 2010 on Stewart Avenue. The music room is to the left. This is where the choir and the band rehearse. Ben Franklin has been home to the Falcons since the opening. The school has fielded basketball, flag football, baseball, and track in the past. The teams have all been competitive and successful.

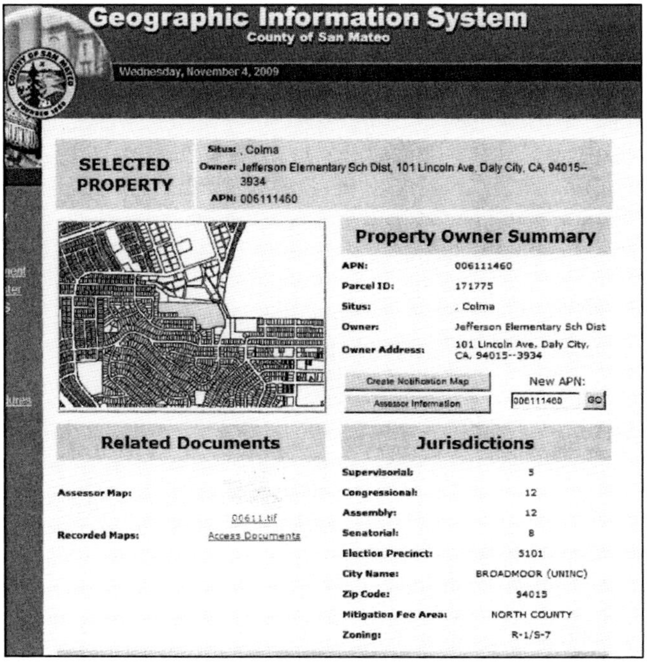

The controversy and confusion again swirls around the issue of the location of this school. When one does a web search for Ben Franklin Junior High, several Ben Franklin schools show up. The nearest one to Broadmoor is in San Francisco. The Broadmoor version is listed as Daly City, but again, a trip to the San Mateo County Public Works Department verifies it being in Broadmoor (unincorporated).

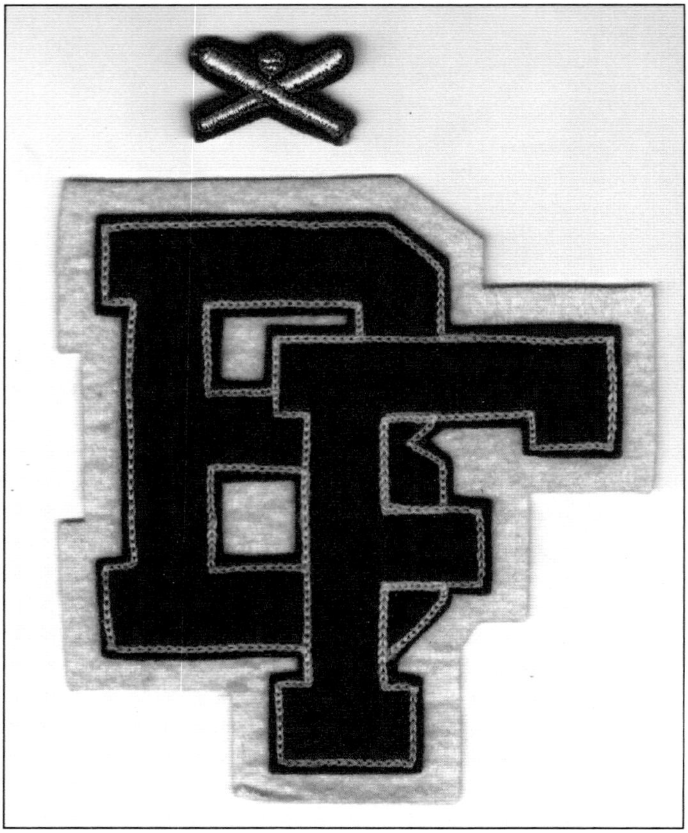

Ben Franklin Junior High School also had a school letter awards system. One got points, again with extracurricular activates such as rally boy, library monitor, sports, choir, and band. In sports, one also got the small award as well, that designated the particular sport one played. Above the "BF" block is the award for being on the baseball team. Ben Franklin's blocks had white backgrounds with green letters.

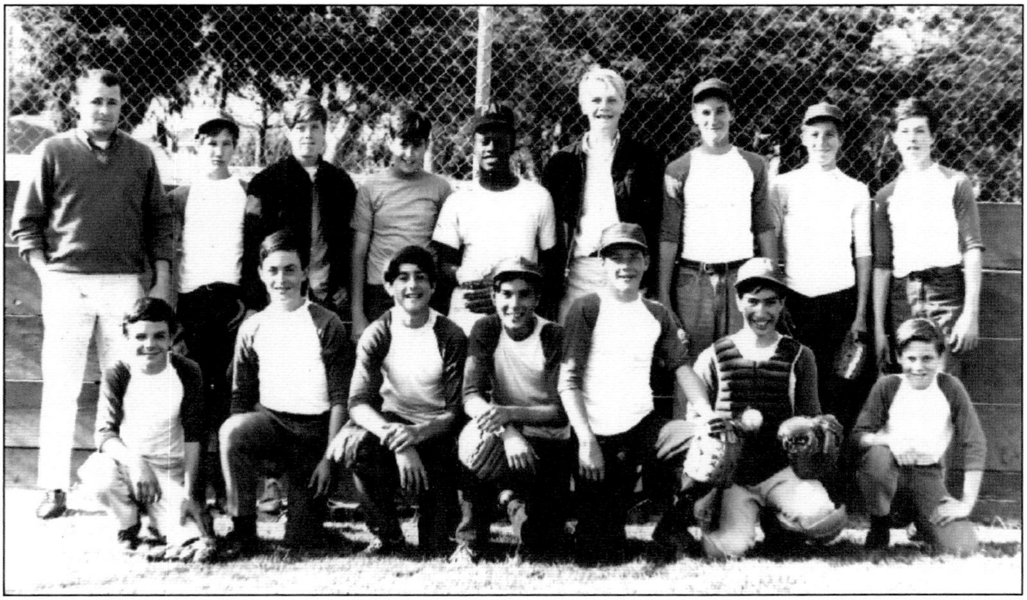

Here is the Ben Franklin baseball team from 1969. Though they did not take the championship, they did have a winning season. In the second row, third from the right, is Gavin Long, who went on to play professional baseball for the Detroit Tigers. Also in the second row, fourth from the right next to Gavin is Leo Biedermann who played professional football for the San Francisco 49ers.

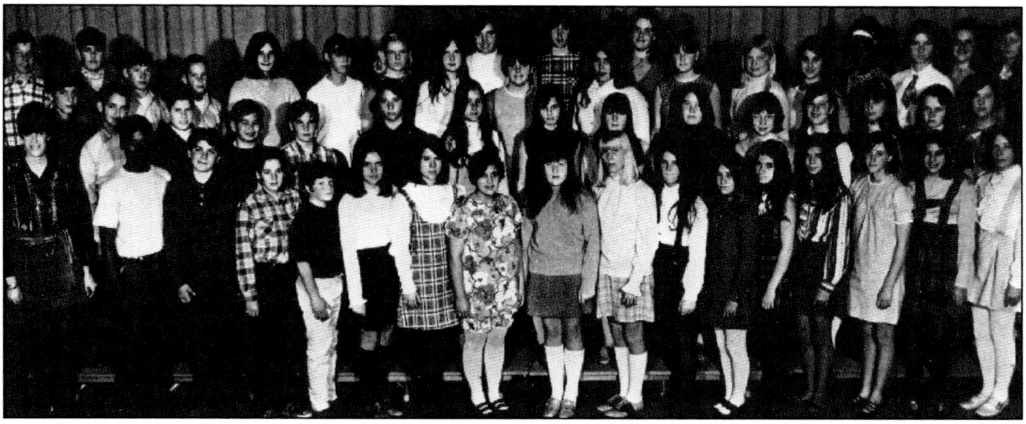

Here is the Ben Franklin eighth grade choir of 1968–1969. Under the direction of Mrs. Schwartz, they took first place in the San Mateo County competition held at Crestmoor High School. Note this is not a typo. Westmoor is in Daly City, while Crestmoor High School was in San Bruno, California. Crestmoor was closed in the 1980s like many schools due to the shrinking population of children in the area.

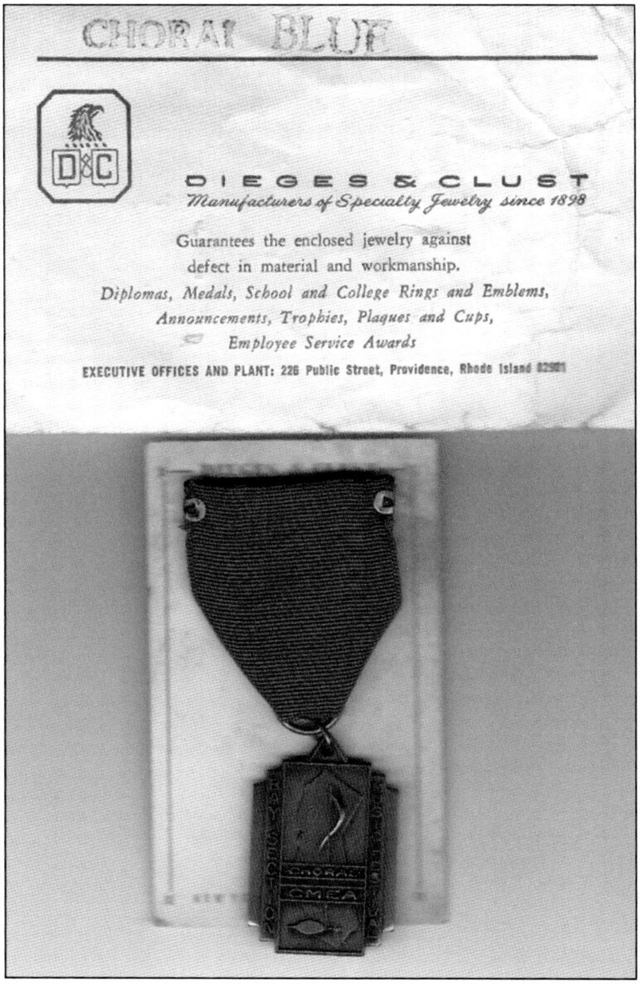

This photograph shows the first-place blue ribbon and medal that Mrs. Schwartz's choir earned. The choir's repertoire was rather on the cutting edge for the day. Mrs. Schwartz made sure that popular songs of the day were sung. Some of the songs, like "Black Day in July" by Gordon Lightfoot, "By the Time I Get to Phoenix" by Glen Campbell, and "Both Sides Now" by Judy Collins, made parents a little uneasy.

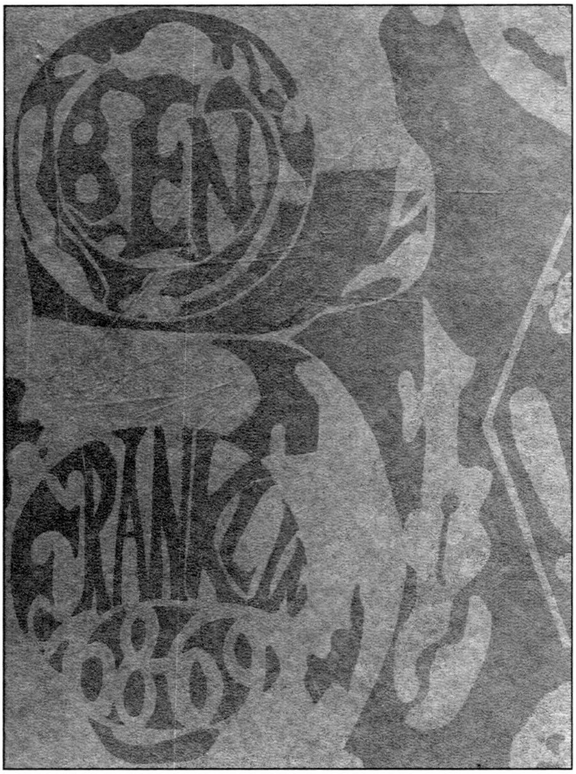

Looking very hip and psychedelic for the times is Ben Franklin's yearbook from 1969. Where it is dark is a very dark green, and the light gray is actually purple. One should note that this was an era of paisley and protest. The demonstrations at San Francisco State University were only a few miles away from little Broadmoor Village.

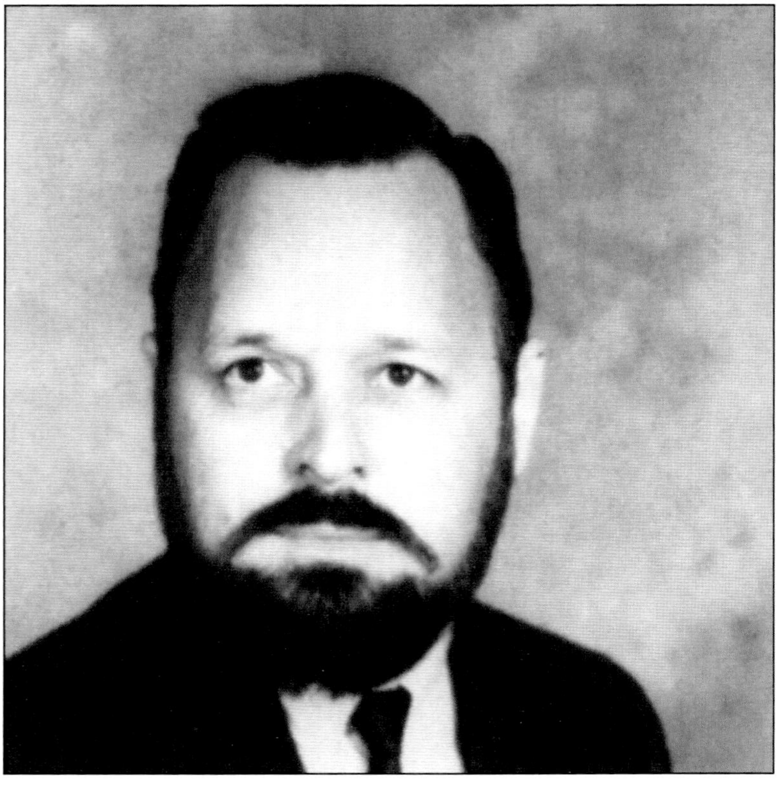

Mr. James Love was one of the many great teachers at Ben Franklin Junior High School. Mr. Love is the first of three generations to serve the Broadmoor community. His granddaughter will grow up to work as a police clerk for Broadmoor Police Department. His son, Greg Love, will inherit the position, chief of police for the Broadmoor Police Department.

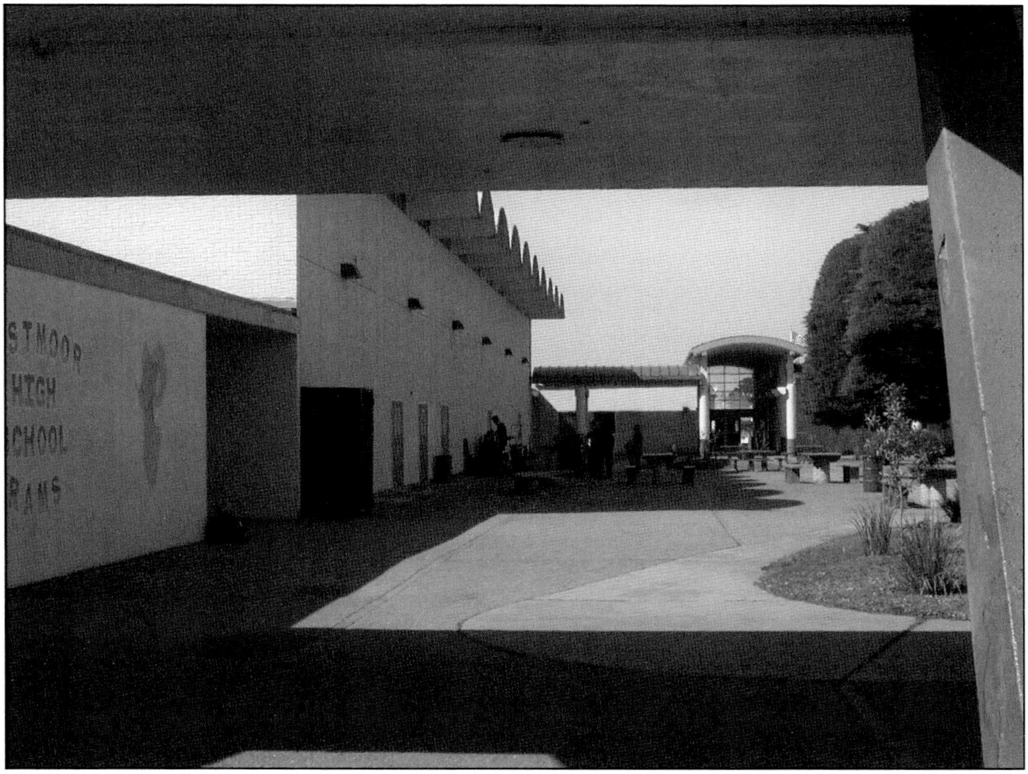

Westmoor High School in Daly City, California. The school is the final academic destination for a lot of folks. There were rumors that the name Westmoor comes from the words Westlake and Broadmoor as it took in students from both areas. Mark Fontana whose father Elio was on the school board in 1957 confirmed this rumor. It was actually Elio's idea to combine the two words. (Photograph Sharon Caren-Crimmen.)

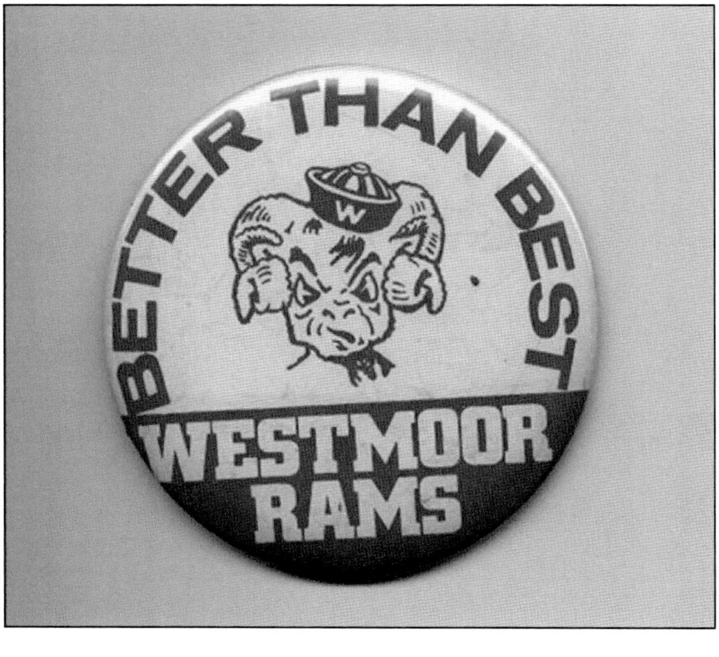

Students from Pacifica, California, went to Westmoor as well when it first opened in 1957. Terra Nova and Oceana High Schools were built in the early 1960s, which left Westmoor to provide for Broadmoor and Westlake solely. Seeing that Broadmoor was built before Westlake and even Westmoor, perhaps the school should have been called Broadlake High School—food for thought. (Courtesy Pat Stark Westmoor Alumni.)

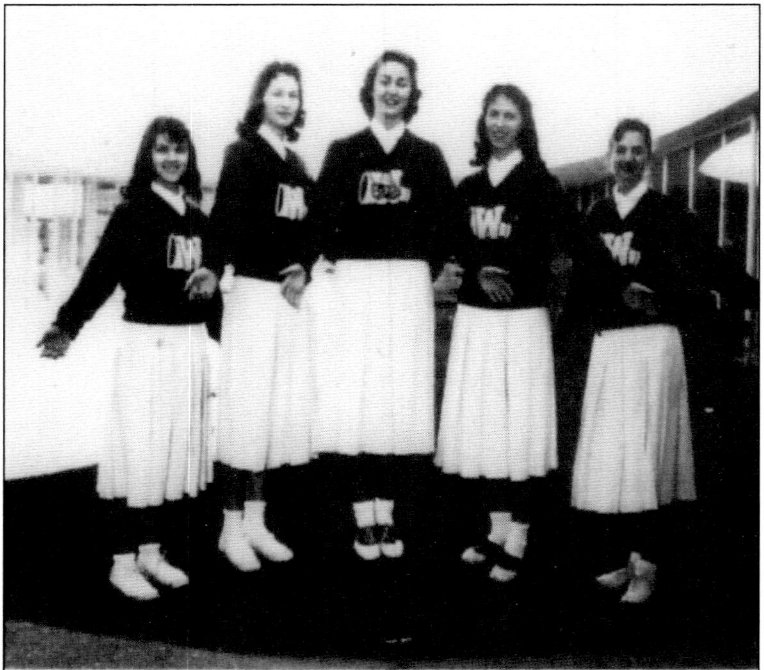

Left to right: Sandy Smith, Carole Finch, Arlene Anderson, Louise Battagalia, Sue Damon.

The 1958 Westmoor cheerleaders, from left to right, are Sandy Smith, Carole Finch. Arlene Anderson, Louise Battagalia, and Sue Damon. Being a cheerleader at Westmoor was not all glamour and glory. On game day for the varsity football team, they would get up as early as 3:00 a.m. and go to every player's house and leave cupcakes and signs with sayings like "Beat Jefferson." (Courtesy Kathleen Manning, Pacifica Historical Society.)

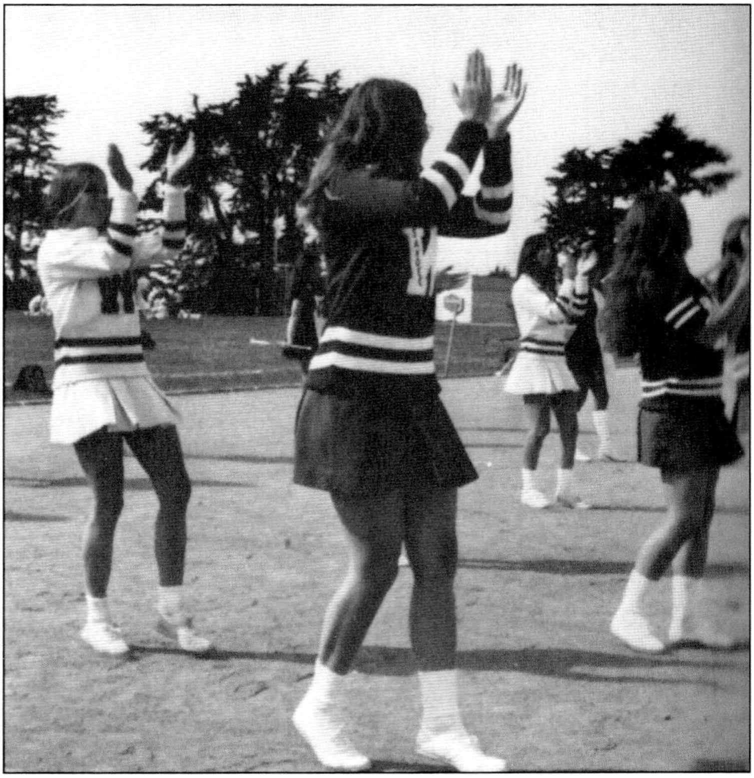

Pictured here are the Westmoor cheerleaders in 1972. The skirts got a little shorter and the hair got a little longer. The glory, signs, decorations, and cupcakes stayed, however. Janine Parokian, Janet Pierce, Donna Smith, Sandee Madsen, Noreen Murphy, Karen Neugabauer, and Paula Papageorge made up the squad that year. (Courtesy Darold Fredricks, San Bruno Historical Society.)

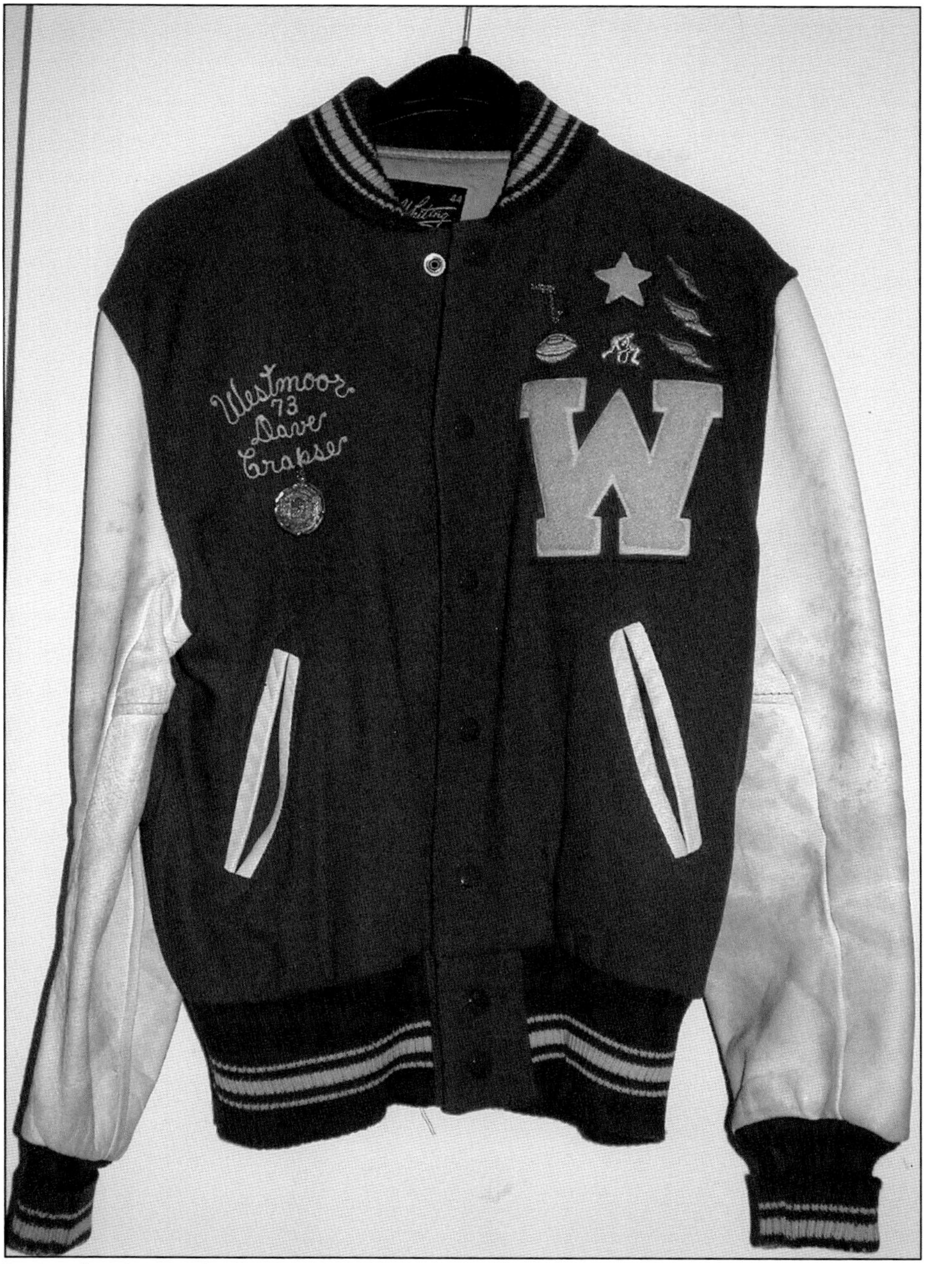

The high school named, in part, after Broadmoor has not done poorly for itself in the academic fields, especially music. One graduate of Westmoor High School is Greg Adams, founding member of the funk and R&B band Tower Of Power. Dave Sholin is another Westmoor graduate who did well in the music field. Known as Dave "Your Duke" Sholin, he was a popular disc jockey on KFRC, KLIV, and KGO radio stations. He went on to be a program director and also got to interview folks like John Lennon, Michael Jackson, and Paul McCartney. Here is the block "W" jacket of Dave Crapse, class of 1973. Like Ben Franklin Junior High, the school colors were kelly green and white. The colors are reversed though from Ben Franklin with white letters on a green background. Kids could wear their awards on sweaters, but the jackets were taking over as the hip vehicle in the 1970s.

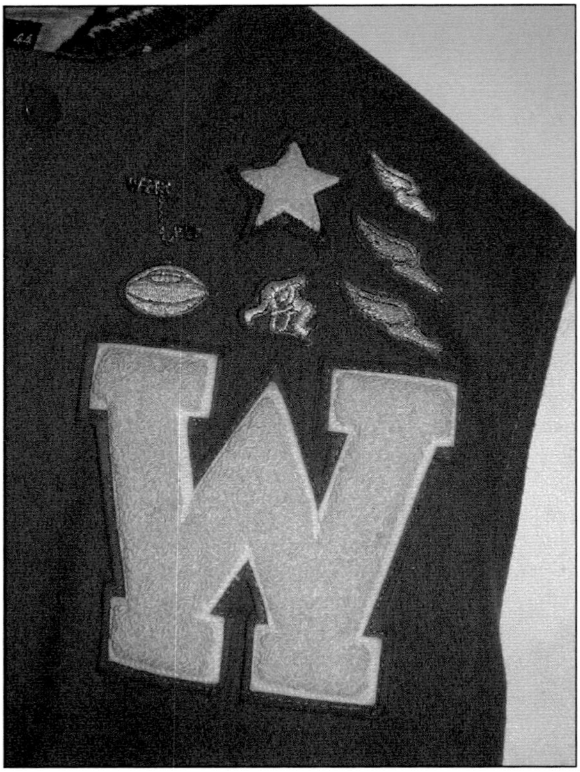

Individual sports for freshmen, sophomores, and junior varsity were represented on the block jackets above the block "W." Varsity awards were put on the block "W" itself. Pictured here are awards for football, wrestling, and track. Two of the three track awards were for varsity, but Dave felt it looked better organized in this fashion. The star is for "Sergeant at Arms." The class of 1973 pin completes the scene.

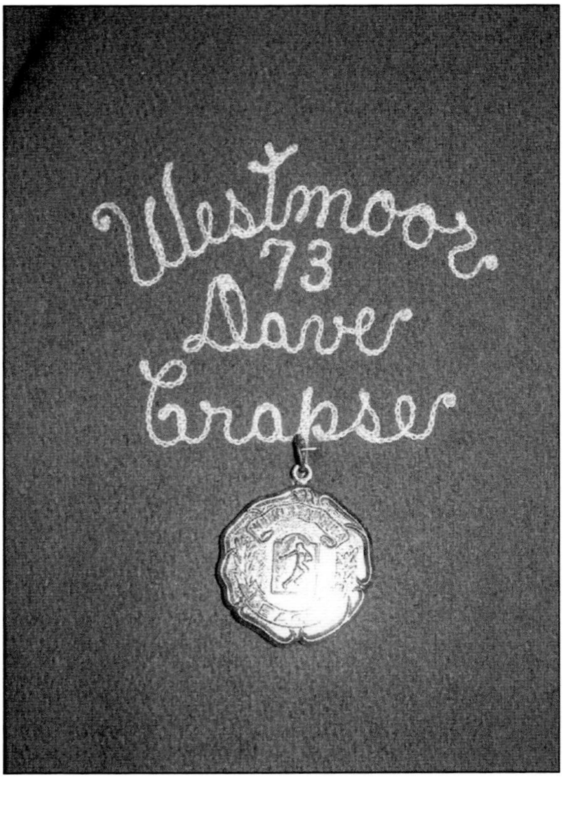

The gold medal is for Westmoor's sophomore football championship in 1970. The coaches were Harry Weidner and Marc Mallinger. As seniors, the class of 1973 would again win the football championship under coaches Bob Lotti, Rod Losberger, and Pete Matisi. Bob Lotti Jr., the coach's son, grew up to become chief of the Colma Police Department.

Four

Broadmoor's Police Department

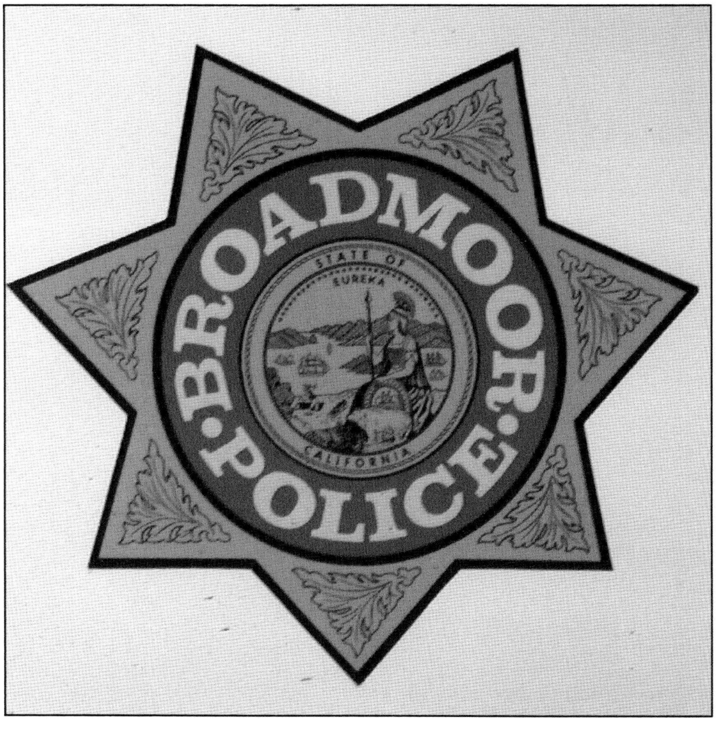

The thing that makes Broadmoor different from other unincorporated districts in California is the Broadmoor Police Protection District. Broadmoor was under the jurisdiction of the San Mateo County Sheriff's Department, because it is unincorporated. The sheriff's department however is in Redwood City, and there were no freeways in 1947 causing response times to be about 30 minutes. In 1948, the citizens petitioned San Mateo County to create their own force.

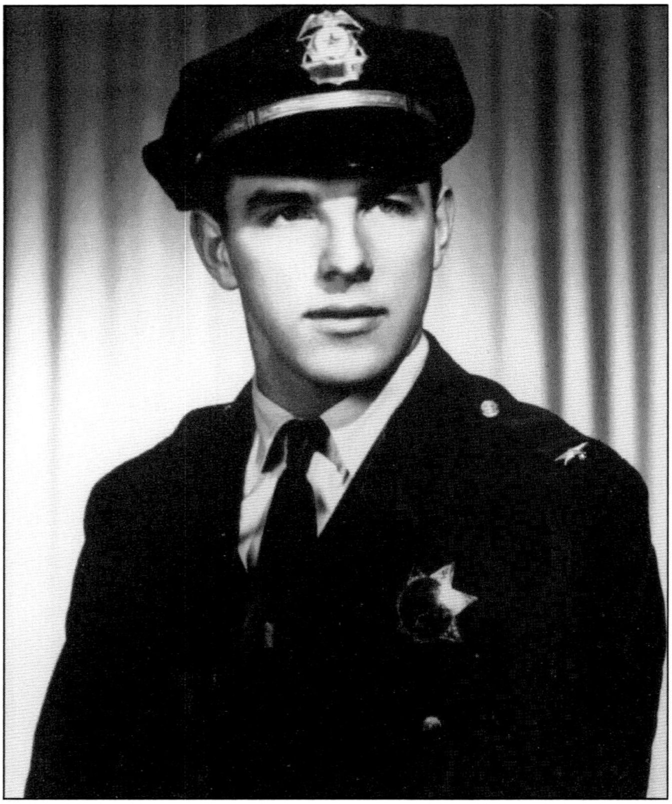

The county board of supervisors granted the request (resolution No. 3792) on December 21, 1948. Here is Chief Paul Scmidt, first police chief of the Broadmoor Police Protection District. It is reported that, at the age of 24, he was one of the youngest police chiefs in the world. He served as chief from 1949 to 1953. (Courtesy Chief Love, Broadmoor Police Department.)

Vet, 24, Named Police Chief At Broadmoor

Paul S. Schmidt, 24-year-old army veteran, became one of the youngest police chiefs in the state last night when he was appointed top officer of the Broadmoor Police District by the Broadmoor board of police commissioners.

Schmidt, who had been acting as chief since the police district was authorized by the San Mateo County Board of Supervisors in early summer, was officially given the post by unanimous vote at last night's meeting.

The three-man police commission is made up of Jack Gordon, chairman; Armando Ferraris, secretary, and M. D. Peterson, treasurer.

The police district embraces three communities: Garden Village, Broadmoor and part of Colma—and is the newest police district in the state.

After his appointment, Chief Schmidt said: "I will carry out the duties of chief of police and uphold law and order and make the Broadmoor district a safe and protected district at all times."

Schmidt is the son of Fred H. Schmidt, chairman of the police board of Brisbane, and is a graduate of Brisbane Grammar School, Jefferson High School, Daly City, and the Oakland Police Academy. His previous experience includes a year as deputy sheriff in Woodside, and a year as night sergeant in Brisbane. In the army he was a sergeant instructor in the officer candidate infantry school at Fort Benning, Ga.

Circa 1949

This clipping is from a local newspaper in 1949. It is the confirmation of the first chief of police for the Broadmoor Police Department, Paul Schmidt, yet another veteran from World War II. He handled the post well until Ray Savage took over. The Broadmoor Police Protection District initially was made up of Chief Schmidt and two or three officers. (Courtesy Chief Love, Broadmoor Police Department.)

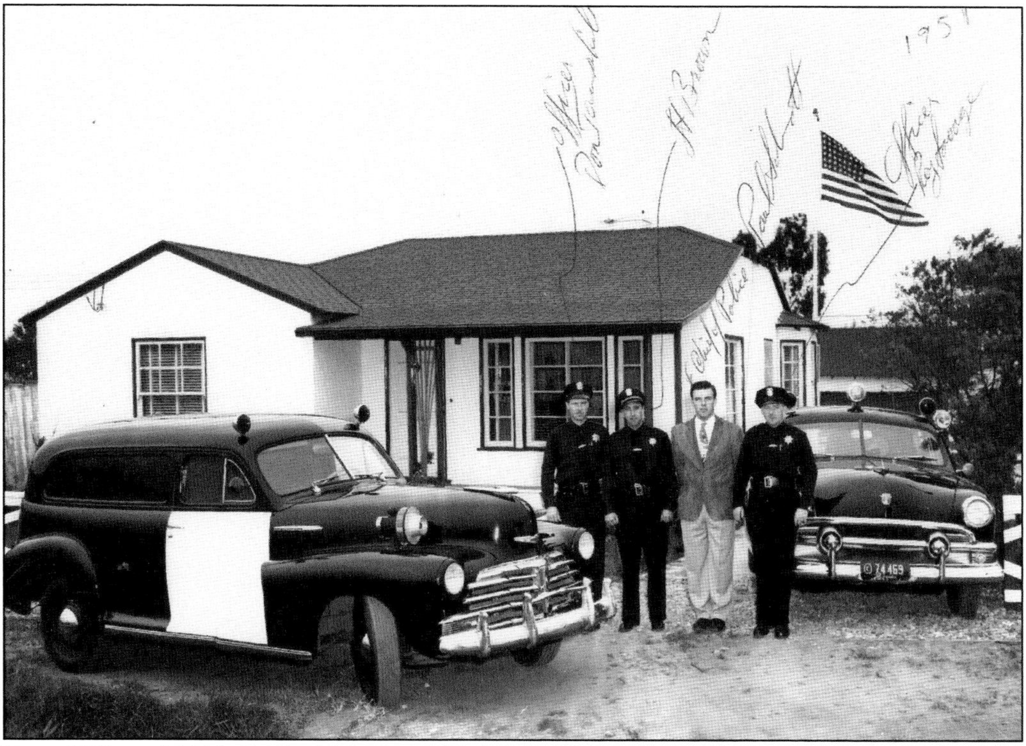

From 1952 until 2003, this building at 388 Eighty-eighth Street was the home of the force. For the strictest definition of where Broadmoor is, one can only say that it was, at the time, the subdivision of houses created by the Stoneson Company. This house then was east of the subdivision, and thus it is in Unincorporated Colma and not Broadmoor. (Courtesy Chief Love, Broadmoor Police Department.)

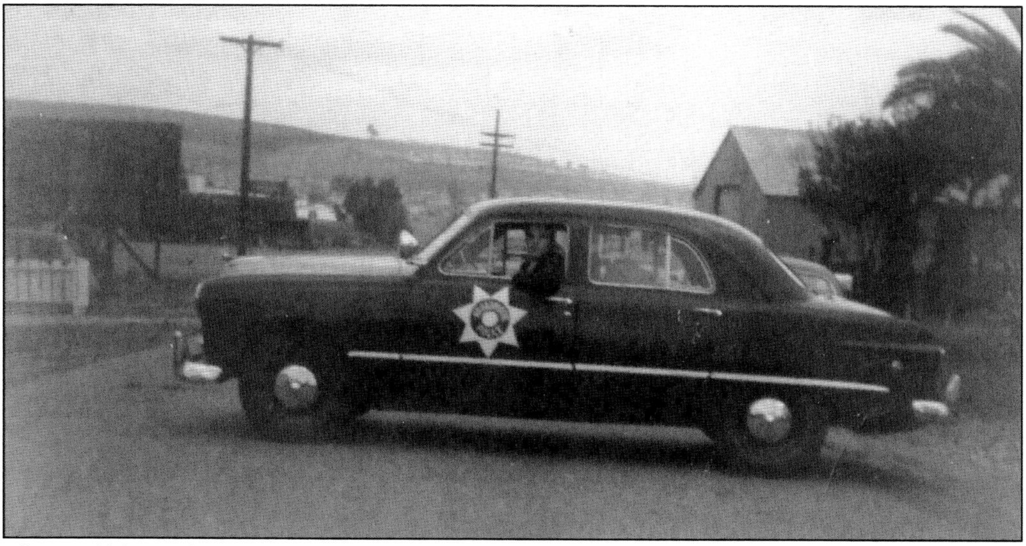

The small force also ran an ambulance service for the area. Before many of the annexations by Daly City, the officers of Broadmoor Police Department covered an area of roughly 10 square miles with approximately 5,000 residents. Here is the first police car used for patrol by the Broadmoor Police Department. It is a 1949 Ford Sedan. This picture was taken on September 5, 1949. (Courtesy Chief Love, Broadmoor Police Department.)

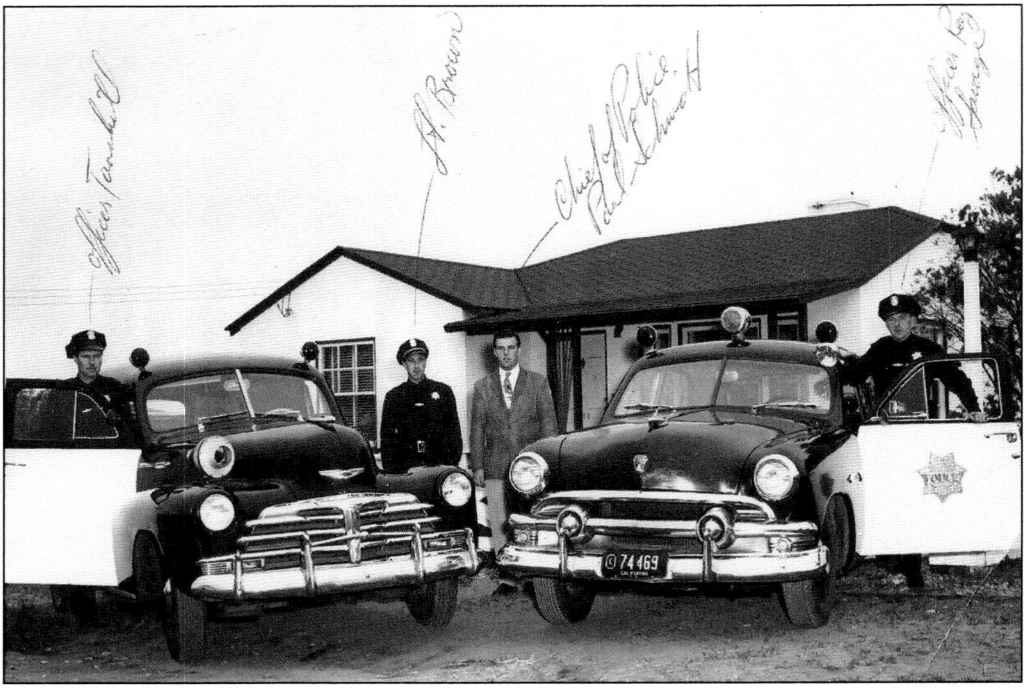

The first headquarters were in a basement of the farmhouse of Armando Ferraris, a police commissioner, on Ninetieth Street. Here are the squad car and the ambulance in front of what was then the new police station. The house was purchased on June 13, 1952, from Louis and Gladys Martines for $11,300. It was originally part of the "$75 Lot Homestead Association." (Courtesy Chief Love, Broadmoor Police Department.)

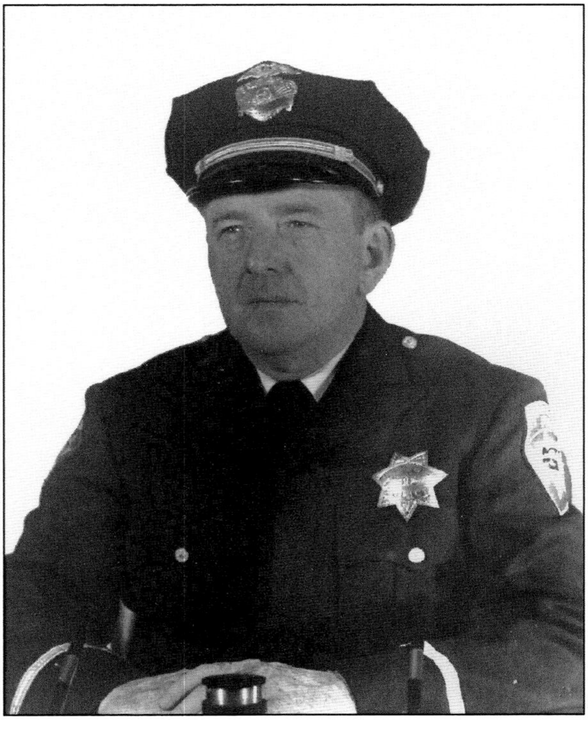

Broadmoor chief of police Ray Savage had the longest tenure of any chief in the department. He served from 1953 until 1975. There is the story of giving little Bobby Wright (two years old) a ride home from the Mayfair market after he had wandered off looking for milk. The chief called Mrs. Wright personally—the ultimate punishment, a phone call to one's parents. (Courtesy Chief Love, Broadmoor Police Department.)

Here is officer Charles Manning, the only Broadmoor officer ever killed while on duty. On Monday, January 6, 1964, Manning was investigating a parked vehicle at 1111 Hillside Boulevard when he surprised a suspect. The man, Timothy Silva, shot officer Manning six times. Manning returned fire but died at the scene. Officers from Daly City Police Department, including officer Ralph Warren, arrived and arrested Mr. Silva, who was convicted. Manning had been with the department for nine years when he was shot. (Courtesy Chief Love, Broadmoor Police Department.)

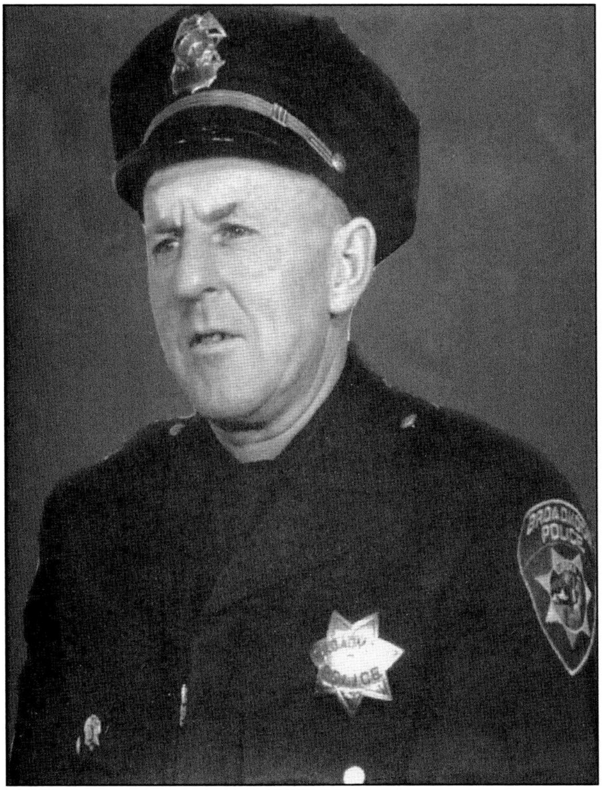

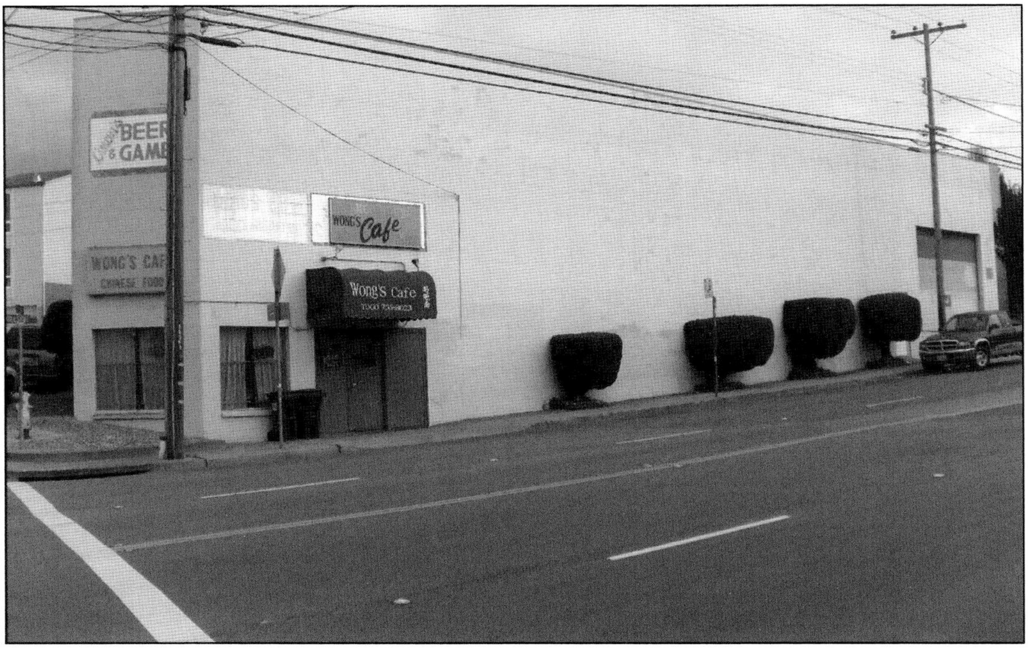

The building where officer Manning was mortally wounded is pictured here in 2010. The warehouse was home to New Mission Heating Company but is now home to Wong's Chinese Restaurant. This is in a section of Unincorporated Colma that is east of U.S. Interstate 280; thus, the zip code is 94014, whereas Broadmoor's zip code is 94015 due to the fact it is west of the freeway.

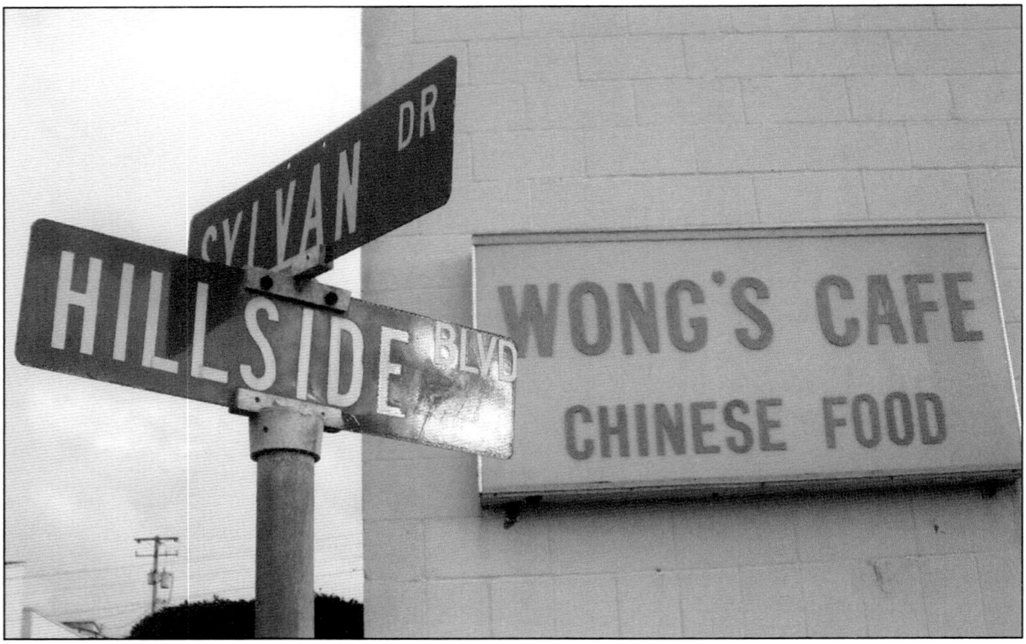

The building is on the corner of Hillside and Sylvan. Note that the street signs are green, making it Unincorporated Colma (county) land and not blue with a seagull logo making it Daly City. This unincorporated area is still the jurisdiction of the Broadmoor Police Force.

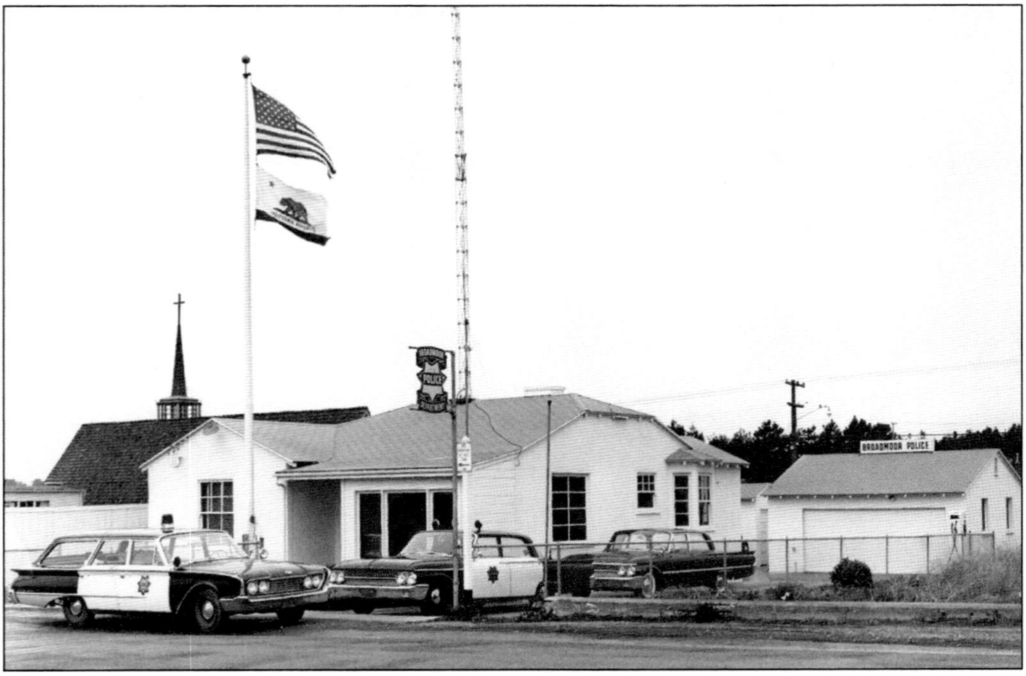

The Broadmoor Police Department headquarters is pictured as it looked in Chief Savage's time with new paint and newer cars. This confusion of what Broadmoor is and where it is will be exacerbated in September 1963, when the lands that the police station and the Broadmoor Presbyterian Church are on will be annexed by Daly City. (Courtesy Chief Love, Broadmoor Police Department.)

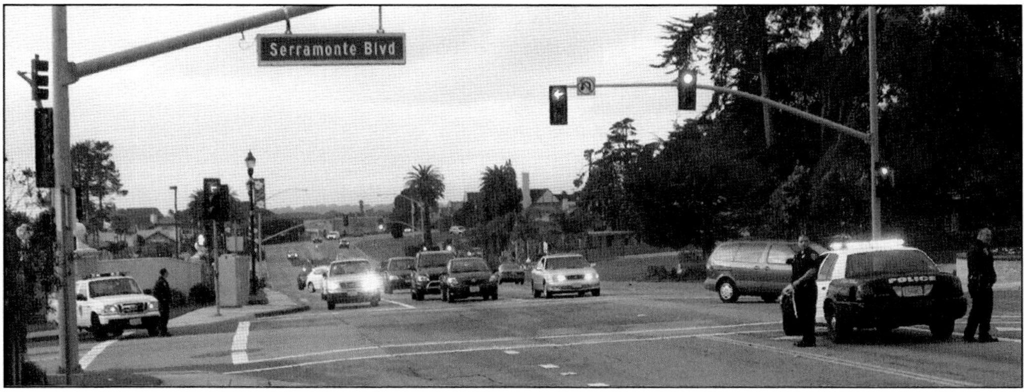

The Broadmoor, Daly City, and Colma Police Departments often work together on automobile collisions. Here on the corner of Serramonte Boulevard and Hillside Boulevard is a classic example. On Monday, January 11, 2010, everyone got a piece of the action. On the right are two Broadmoor Police officers; on the left is a Daly City police officer.

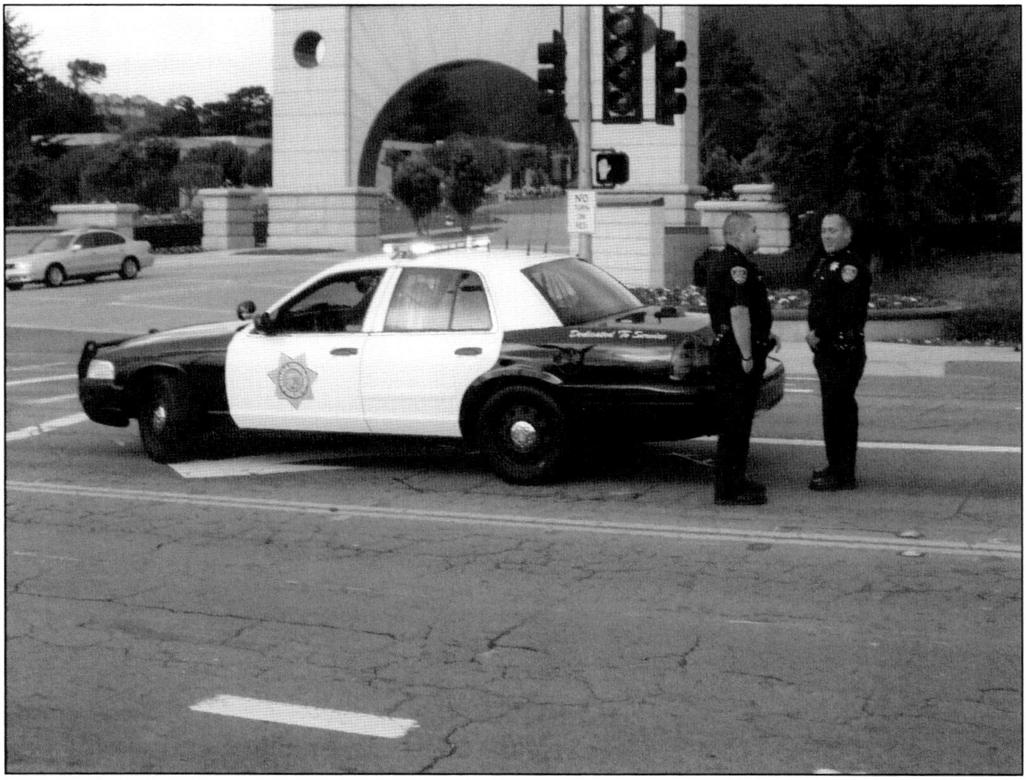

Here is a little better view of the officers and one of the Broadmoor police cars used that day. Emergency lights were flashing on both of the Broadmoor vehicles these officers used, and both were helping block the left turn lane so motorists heading north would not turn onto Serramonte Boulevard.

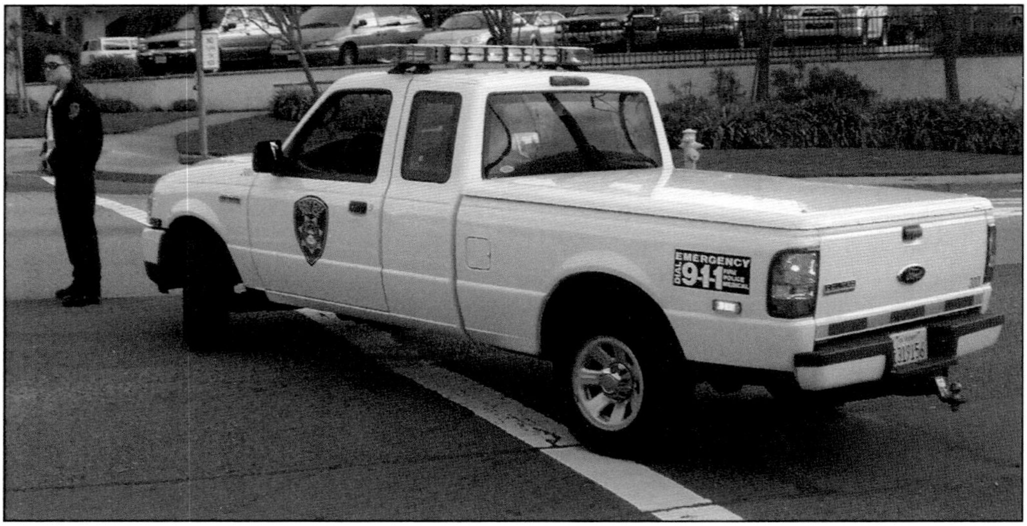

Looking south on Hillside Boulevard is the Daly City police officer also assisting with the issue at hand. Behind him is the Lucky Chance Casino located at 1700 Hillside Boulevard in Colma—the incorporated town, not Unincorporated Colma that is just to the north of here.

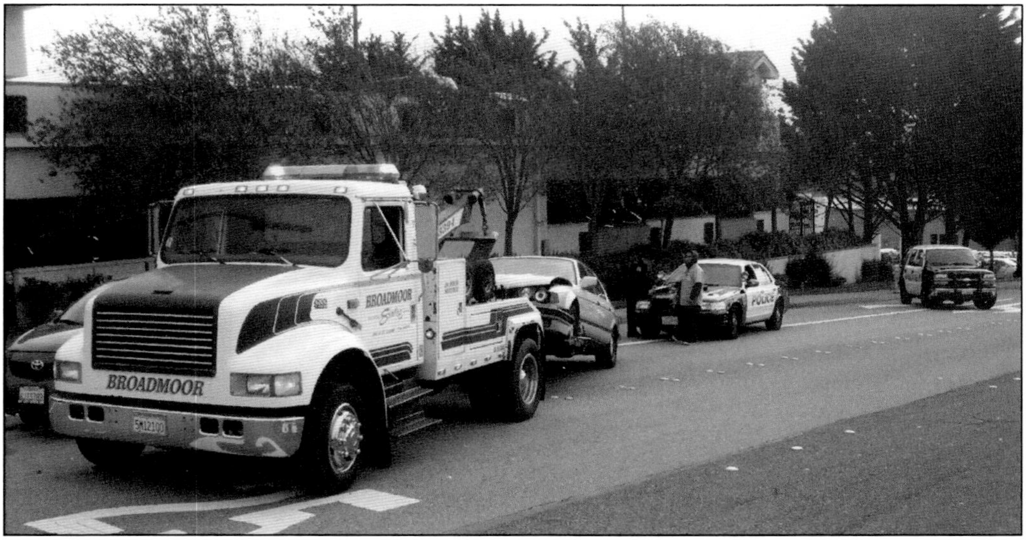

Looking west, down the hill from Hillside Boulevard is the reason for all the fuss. In broad daylight, someone was not watching where they were going. One might say their luck ran out at the Lucky Chance. Because the collision was within city limits of Incorporated Colma, it was Colma's jurisdiction; thus, they were the ones to handle the details while Broadmoor and Daly City took the role of assisting.

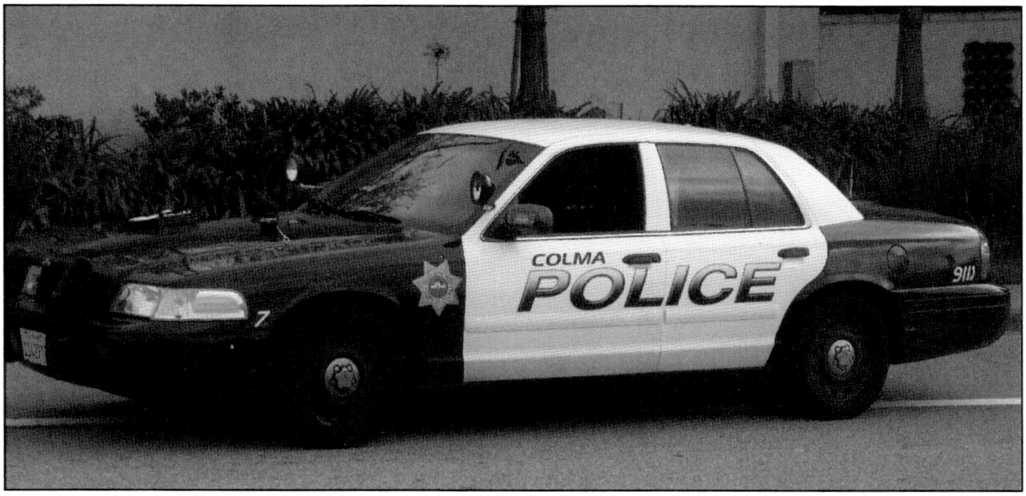

Here, completing the *ménage à trois*, is the Colma Police Department. The proximity of all three jurisdictions creates a situation where playing leapfrog by the departments is an everyday occurrence. The positive side to this is that not only does the public get better and quicker service, the officers get back up from their own department and the two neighboring ones, making a safer situation for all.

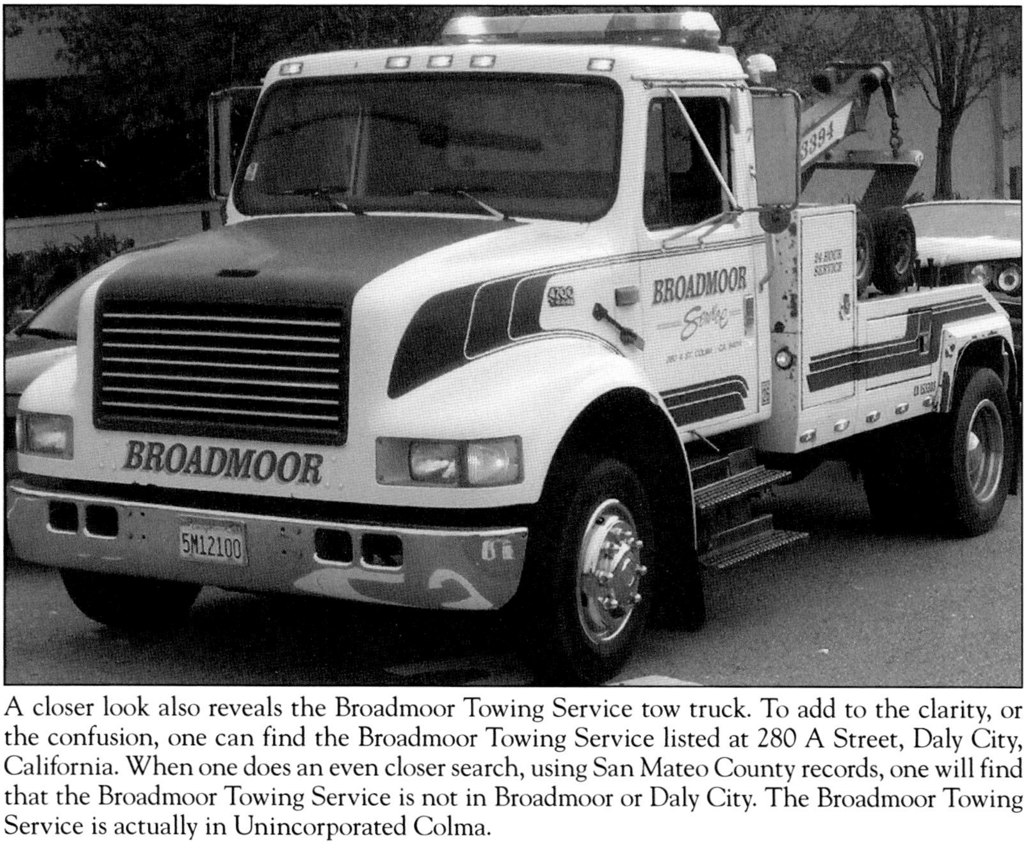

A closer look also reveals the Broadmoor Towing Service tow truck. To add to the clarity, or the confusion, one can find the Broadmoor Towing Service listed at 280 A Street, Daly City, California. When one does an even closer search, using San Mateo County records, one will find that the Broadmoor Towing Service is not in Broadmoor or Daly City. The Broadmoor Towing Service is actually in Unincorporated Colma.

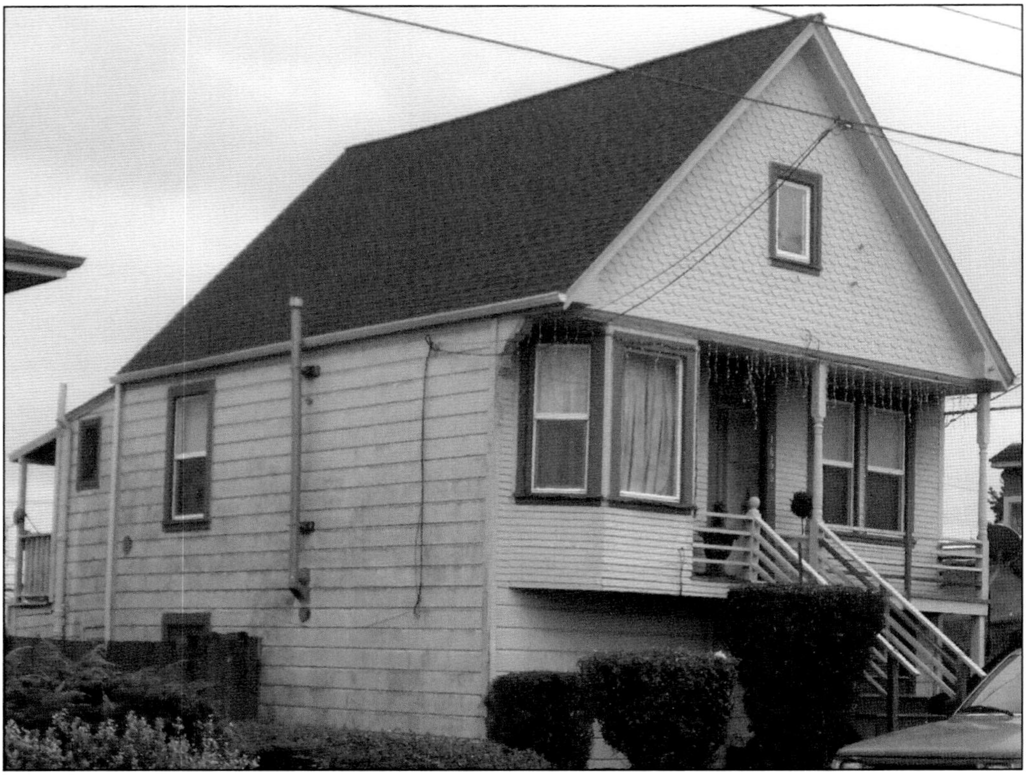

On Annie Street, Edgeworth Avenue, Bryant Street, and Pierce Street, there are still the two-story Victorian style farmhouses that were common when this area was all farmland. It is this style of house that was the first headquarters for the Broadmoor Police Department. It is described as being housed in a remodeled basement of a two-story farmhouse located on Ninetieth Street belonging to police commissioner Armando Ferrais.

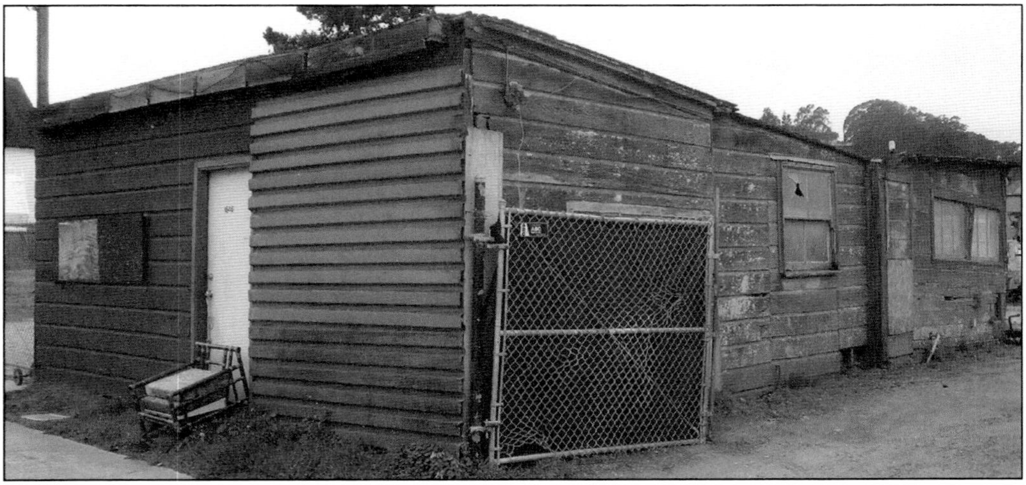

The second home to the Broadmoor Police Department still exists in 2010 and is located at 1546 Annie Street. This is the north side and was actually a construction shed used by the Stoneson Company. The farmhouses and the shed, however, are not built by the Stoneson Company and are all east of the Broadmoor subdivision. Thus, these houses were all in Unincorporated Colma but not in Broadmoor.

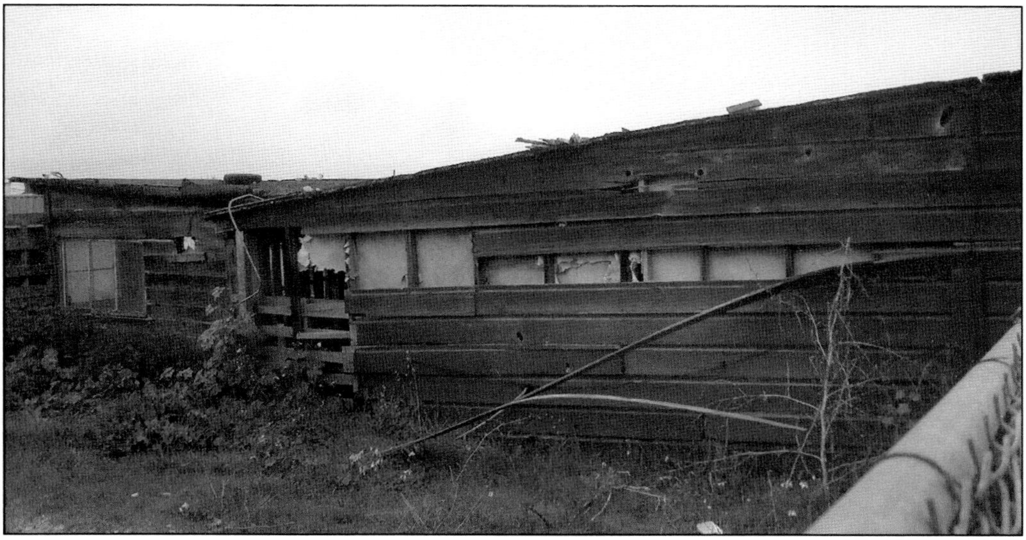

Here is the south side of the building. It has boards falling off of it, and one can see daylight through the walls. It is hard to imagine the work conditions the officers faced using this building. An adult standing at 6 feet could barely stand up straight in it. It is hard to tell if it is being used at all for any purpose.

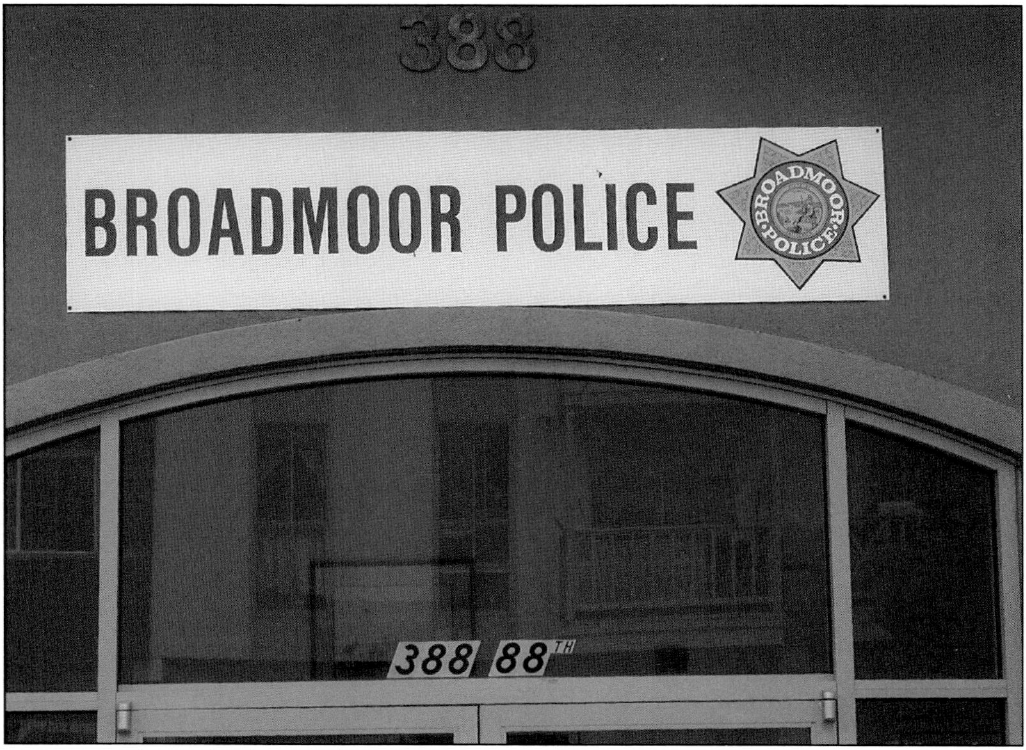

The current home for the Broadmoor Police Department was built in 2001–2002. The address of the Martines house of 388 Eighty-eighth Street was retained. The house was torn down in October 2001 to make room for a new state-of-the-art building. The officers took up residence in 2003. Police protection districts were abolished in 1959. In 1977, liability insurance was unavailable, but the department still survives.

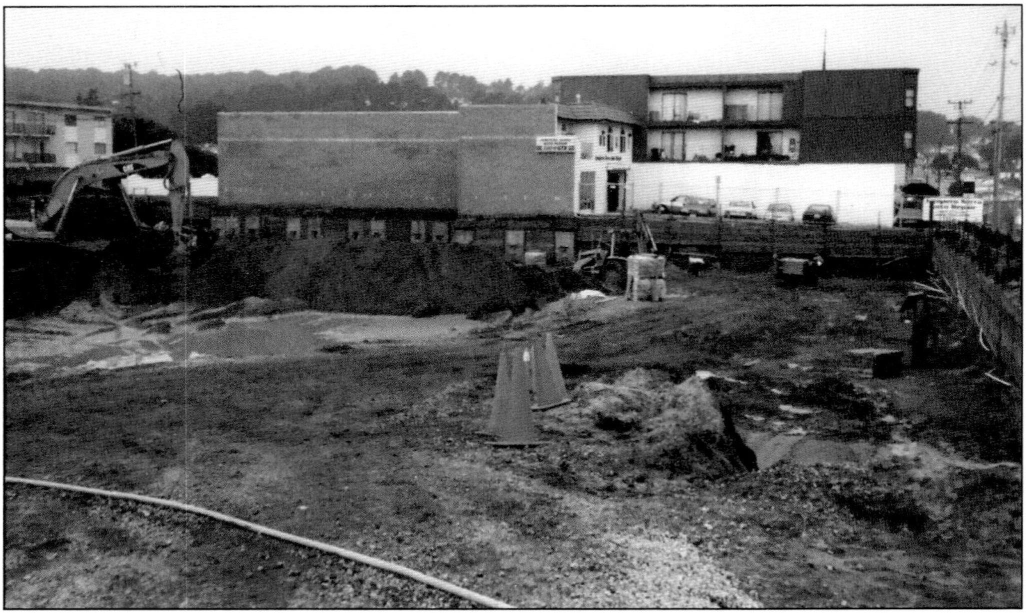

Here everything is torn down that was there before, including the Martines house, so work could begin on building the police department's new home. This is a scene looking west at an automobile repair shop and apartments on land annexed by Daly City. These buildings also block the view of the church. (Courtesy Chief Love, Broadmoor Police Department.)

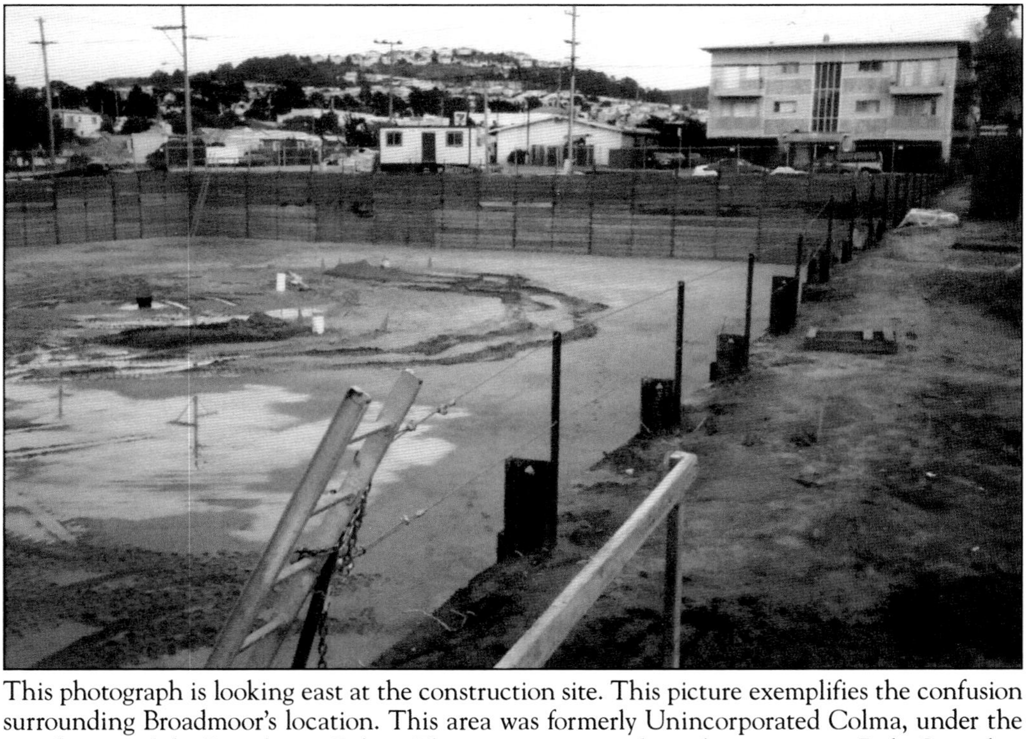

This photograph is looking east at the construction site. This picture exemplifies the confusion surrounding Broadmoor's location. This area was formerly Unincorporated Colma, under the jurisdiction of the Broadmoor Police. The apartments on the right are now in Daly City; that land was annexed in June 1960. County records list the 7-Eleven store, left of the apartments, as being in Broadmoor Unincorporated. (Courtesy Chief Love, Broadmoor Police Department.)

Through Chief Love's efforts with the postal service, the department has been able to retain the word Broadmoor for the mailing address by using the zip code 94015-1717. The department was losing many time-sensitive documents to miss deliveries due to the confusion of the borders between Broadmoor and Daly City. It should be noted that while the new station is in Daly City, the Broadmoor Police Department owns the building.

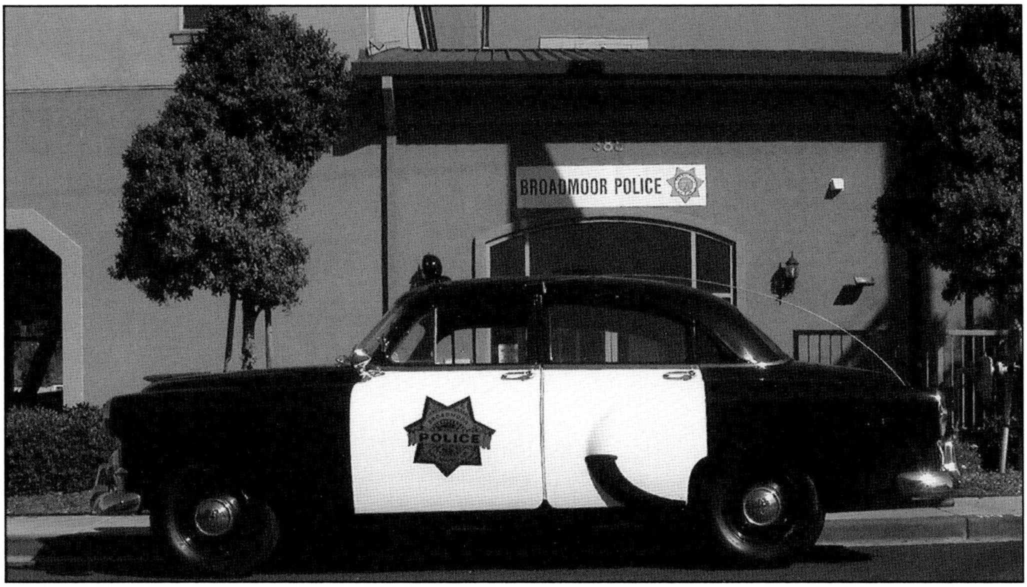

Here is the pride of the Broadmoor police force, a completely restored 1953 Chevy. Seen here in front of the new Broadmoor Police Department building, the Chevy is brought out for parades and special occasions. Officer Gus Vasquez was even able to find authentic Chevy hubcaps for this baby. The car even sports a California historical license plate.

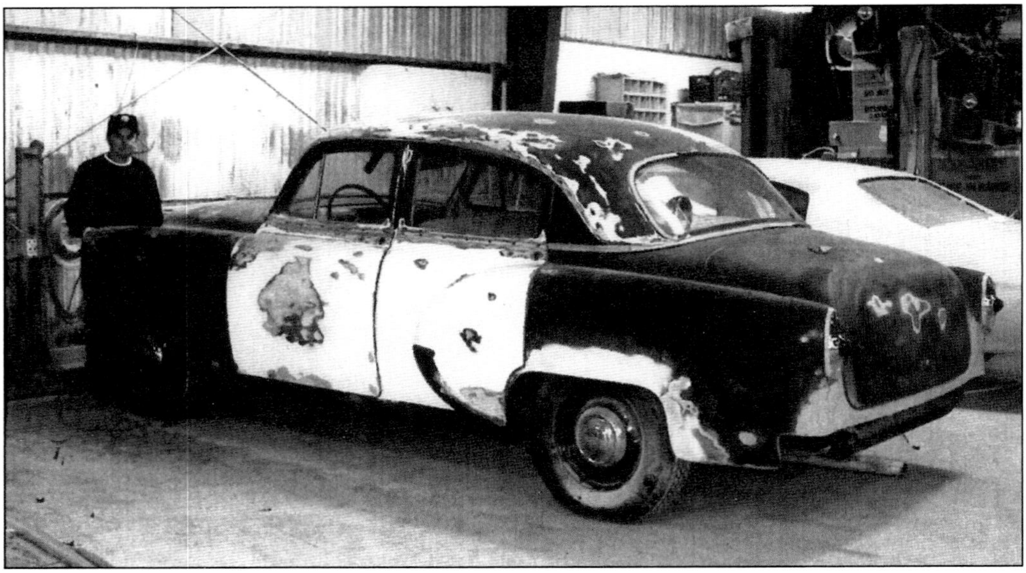

Here is what the old gal looked like before she was gussied up. The father of officer Mike Sullivan originally owned it. The car was then donated to the department but left in the driveway. Officer Gus Vasquez took a personal interest and decided to restore the vehicle. Officer Vasquez is pictured here just before the car's surgery. (Courtesy officer Gus Vasquez, Broadmoor Police Department)

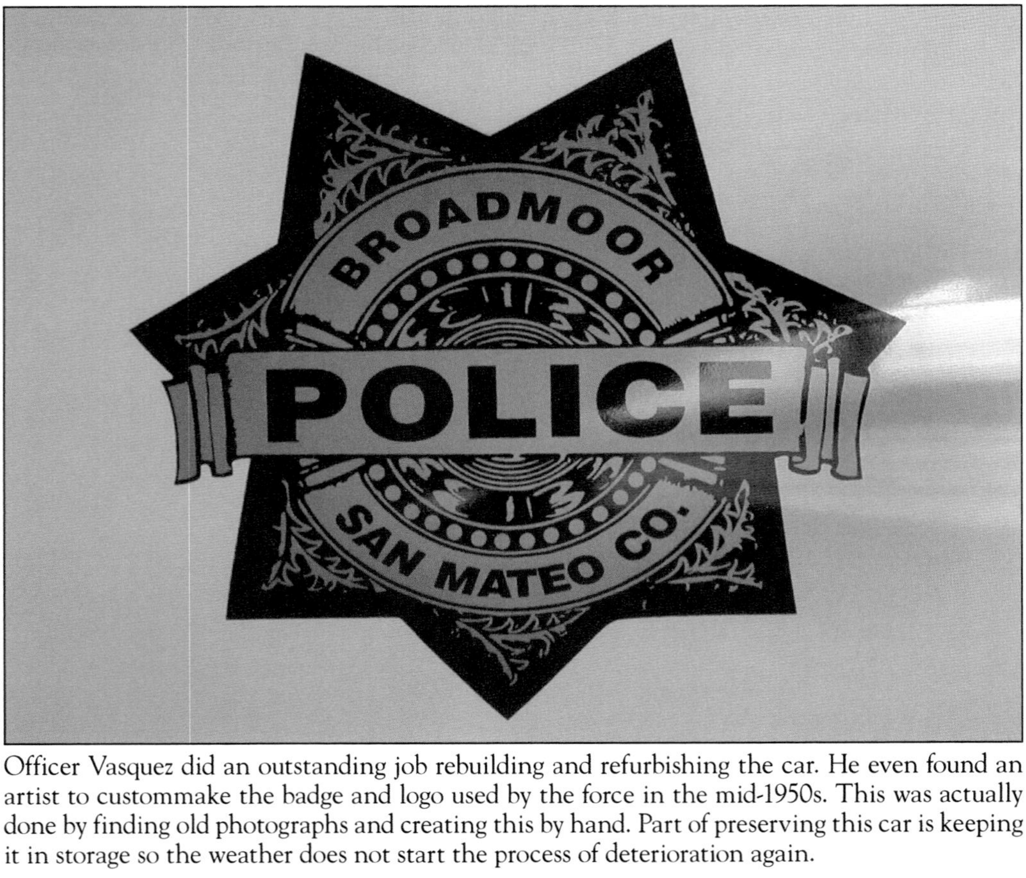

Officer Vasquez did an outstanding job rebuilding and refurbishing the car. He even found an artist to custommake the badge and logo used by the force in the mid-1950s. This was actually done by finding old photographs and creating this by hand. Part of preserving this car is keeping it in storage so the weather does not start the process of deterioration again.

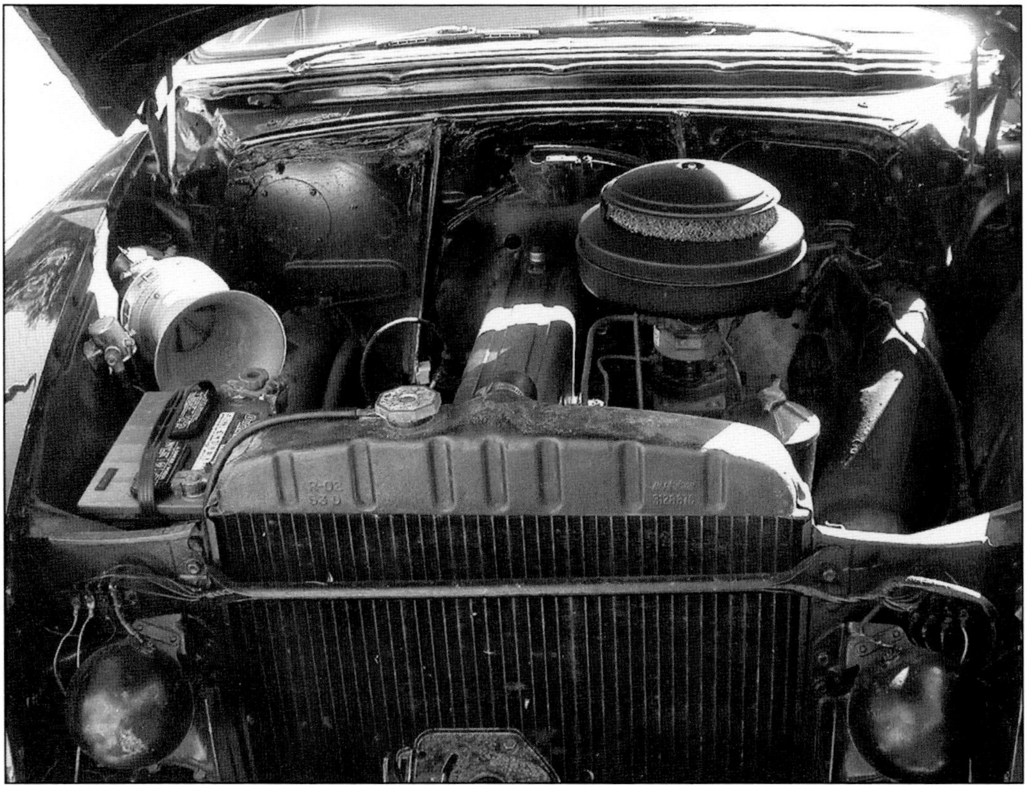

The rebuilding of this 1953 beauty is so authentic that Gus even kept the oil bath air filter in it. Finding parts for this antique is not easy. Lots of things have to be custom made, as this car is over 50 years old. It had just gotten back from a parade the day these photographs were taken.

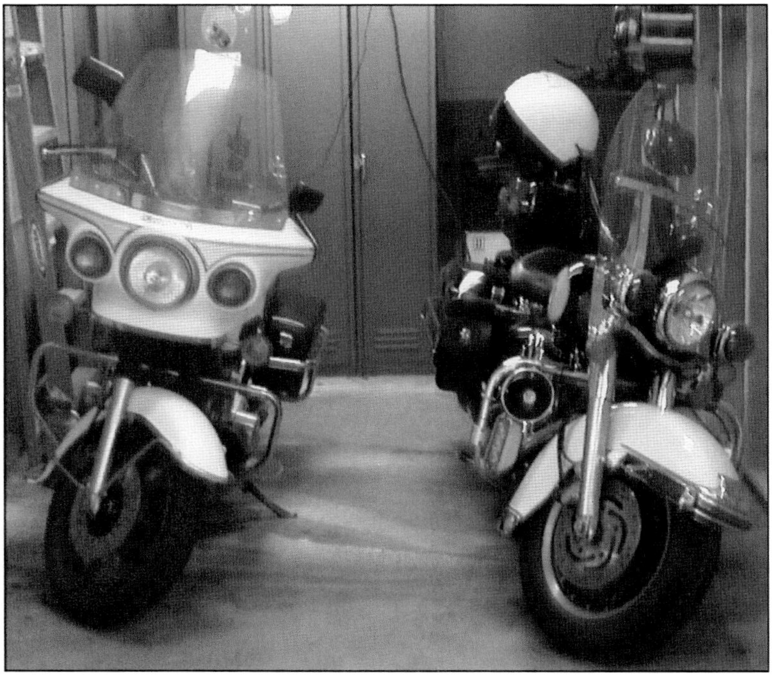

Broadmoor Police Department also has a complement of motorcycles. It was Chief Love's idea in the 1980s. He was then an officer but loves motorcycles. He has some friends on the California Highway Patrol and was able to have the Harley purchased from them. The Broadmoor Police Department logo is proudly displayed on the gas tanks, and they are mostly used for traffic control.

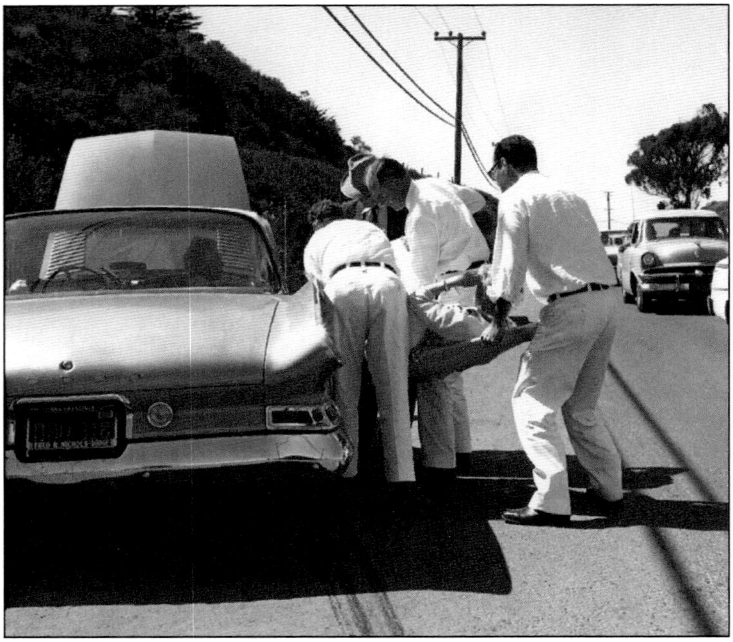

This photograph from the police department archives was taken on Junipero Serra Boulevard facing north. Up the hill to the right in this photograph is a billboard for one of the cemeteries in the area. Just below the billboard is the road that took one to the dump. This was at Junipero Serra Boulevard and Chinese Cemetery Road, just south of what is now Southgate Boulevard. (Courtesy Chief Love, Broadmoor Police Department.)

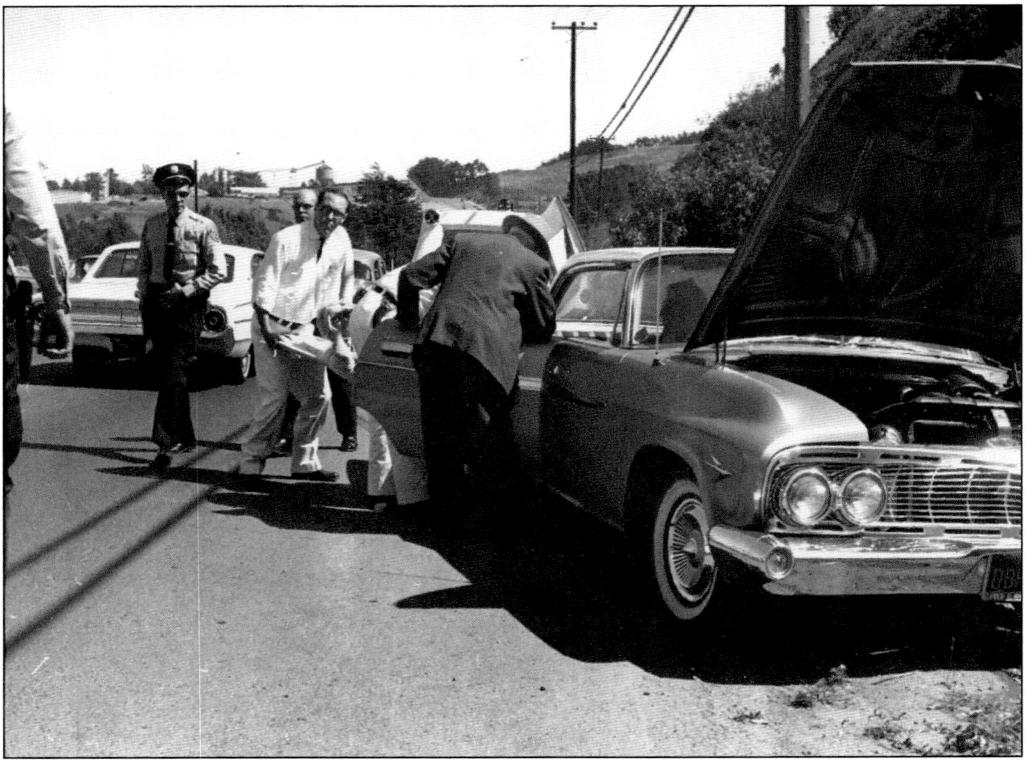

This is the same collision looking south. On the left side is the dump and on the right dairy farms that will eventually become Serramonte Center. This area used to be under the jurisdiction of the Broadmoor Police Protection District, but due to some 52 annexations by Daly City, the area once covered by Broadmoor Police Department has decreased by approximately 80 percent, if not more. (Courtesy Chief Love, Broadmoor Police Department.)

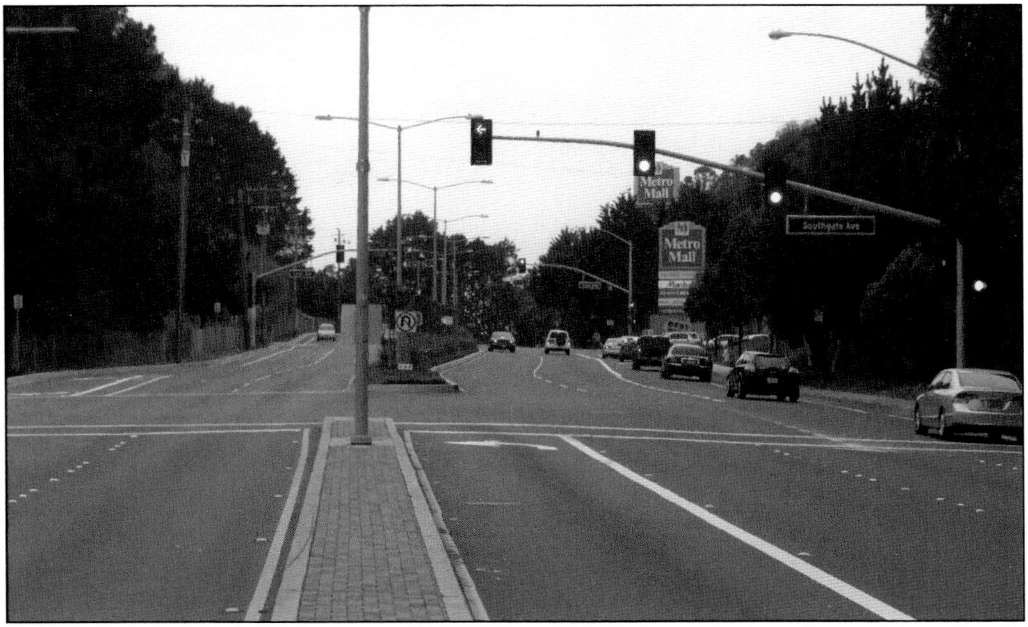

This image shows northbound Junipero Serra Boulevard in 2010. It is hard to approximate the exact spot, because there are now six lanes of traffic where there used to be two. In the background on the right, the billboard is now the Metro Mall sign. The road now goes to the mall and Home Depot that was built over the garbage dump.

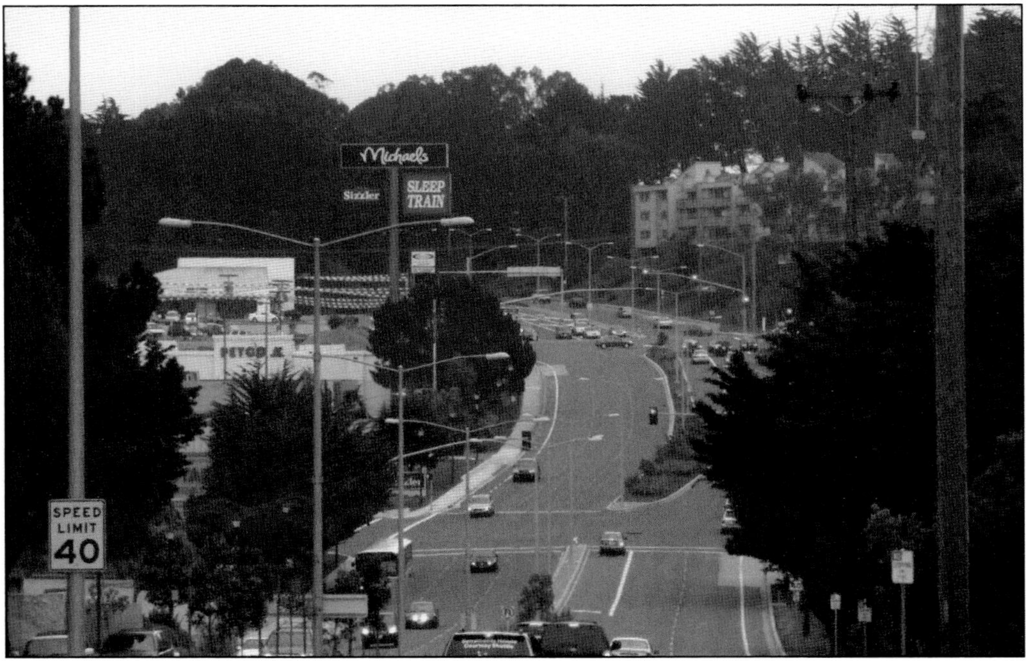

Here is Junipero Serra Boulevard southbound in 2010 from close to the same position. In the background on the hills to the right (west) are now apartments where once dairy cattle grazed. On the left (east) side is mall that is home to Target. The east side of Junipero Serra Boulevard is now the town of Colma. The west side of the street is U.S. Interstate 280 and beyond that is now Daly City.

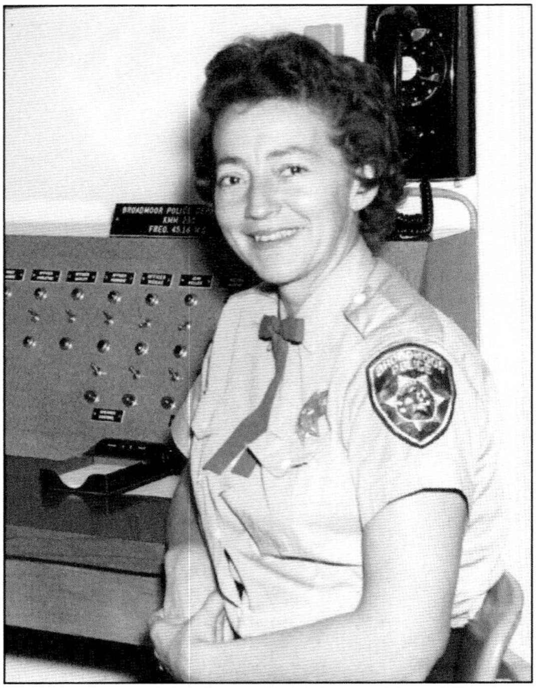

The history of the ladies of Broadmoor Police Department goes all the way back to the beginning of the department. Here is Jean Keller, police dispatcher, who started with the department in the early 1950s and stayed on until the mid-1970s. She then transferred to South San Francisco Police Department. (Courtesy Chief Love, Broadmoor Police Department.)

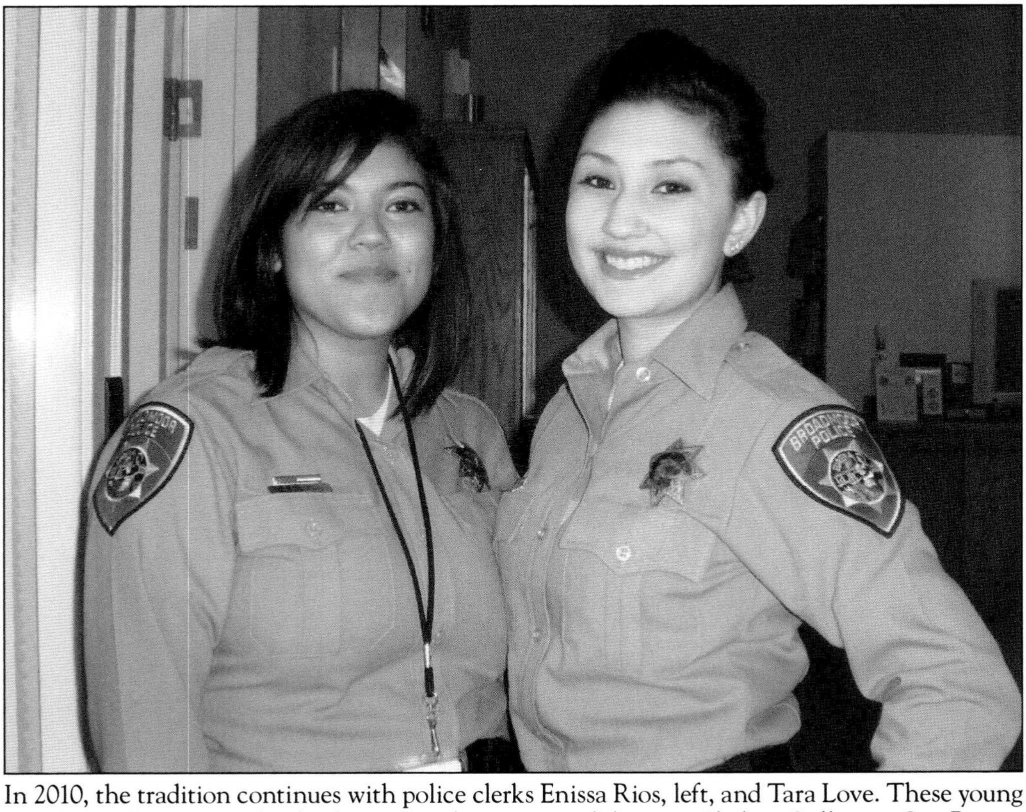

In 2010, the tradition continues with police clerks Enissa Rios, left, and Tara Love. These young women work part-time for the force once they get out of classes at Skyline College in San Bruno. Tara is the third generation of the Love family to serve Broadmoor Village.

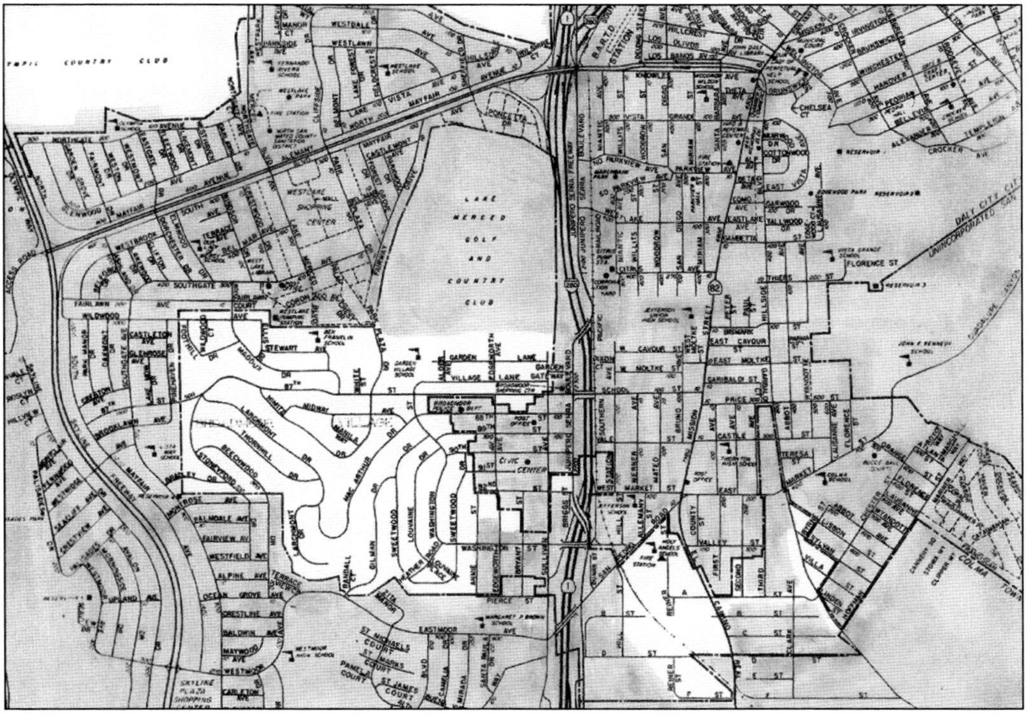

After the annexations, what is left of the Broadmoor Police Protection District is shown in the non-shaded areas. On the right of Junipero Serra Boulevard, Unincorporated Colma; in the middle, the apartments at Ninety-second and Sullivan Streets; and left is the main island including the original subdivision of Broadmoor Village, Garden Village, and parts of Eighty-seventh Street. The main island is now considered by the county public works to be Broadmoor.

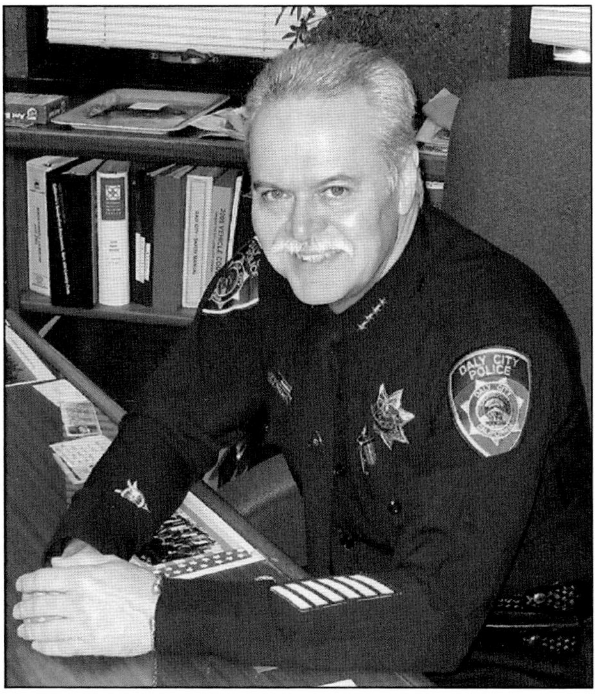

A former Broadmoor resident, retired Daly City police chief Gary McLane worked in concert with Broadmoor to help put a stop to the aggressions. It should be noted that the chief of Broadmoor Police Department lives in Daly City and the chief of Daly City Police Department lived in Broadmoor. (Courtesy Chief Gary McLane.)

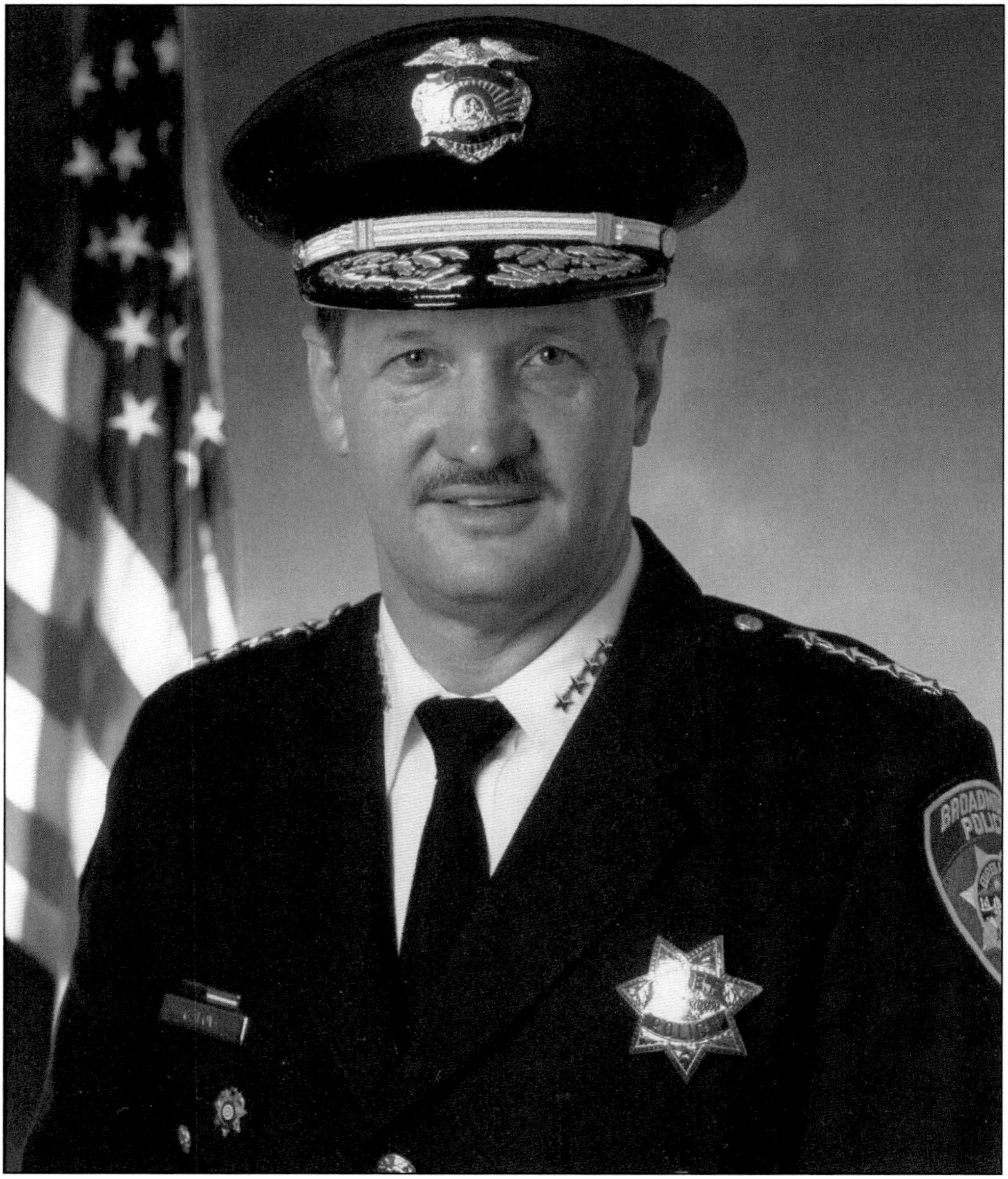

Broadmoor police chief Greg Love is pictured here. Chief Love took over the helm in 2002, and it has been under his guidance, along with the police commissioners and the Broadmoor Property Owners, that wounds caused from annexations have healed. It is through the efforts of Chief Love and the citizens that Broadmoor Village continues in 2010 to survive on its own independent and separate of Daly City. Losing 80 percent of its tax revenues due to annexations by Daly City, loss of insurance in the 1970s, and police protection districts being done away with by the state has not stopped this little community from remaining independent. Independence is, after all, what the United States of America is all about. So, for Chief Love and all of those who served before, chiefs and officers alike, thank you. It has also been Chief Love and his department who have been so helpful with the accuracy and information contained in this book. It could not have happened without him and the gang at Broadmoor Police Department. (Courtesy Chief Love, Broadmoor Police Department.)

Five

"UNINCORPORATED COLMA"

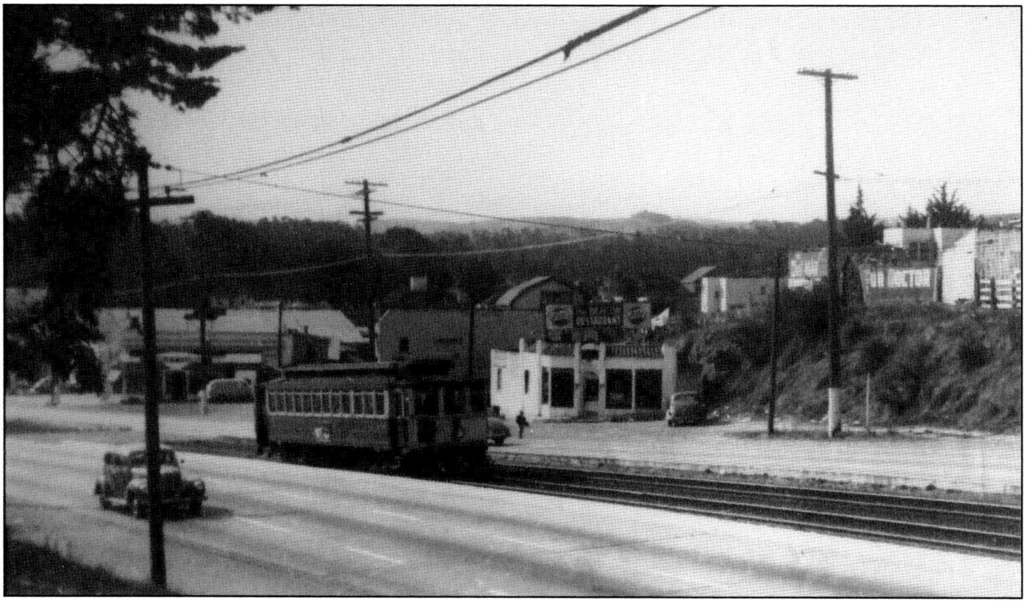

In 1941, the U.S. Postal Department informed Lawndale to change its name because there was another Lawndale in Southern California. The northern Lawndale then changed its name to Colma, and now there are two Colmas: the incorporated town and the other area being unincorporated. As irony would have it, the Lawndale in Southern California did not incorporate until 1959. (Courtesy Chief Love, Broadmoor Police Department.)

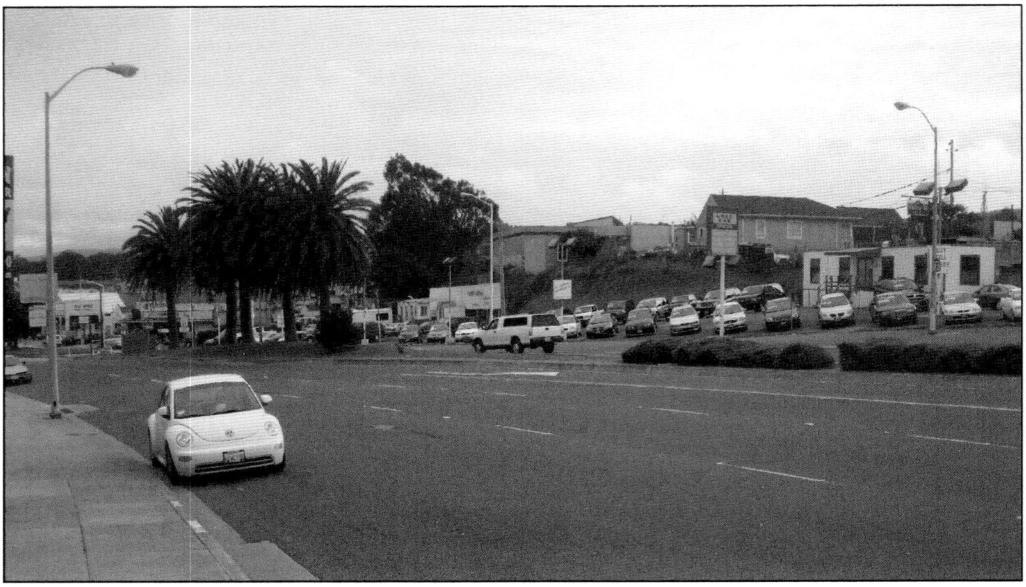

The trolley car or streetcar on the previous page was part of the San Francisco Municipal Railway and operated in San Mateo County from 1903 to 1949. It ran through Daly City and Colma down Mission Street. Here is Mission Street in 2010, close to where the picture on the previous page was taken. This portion of Mission Street is still Unincorporated Colma.

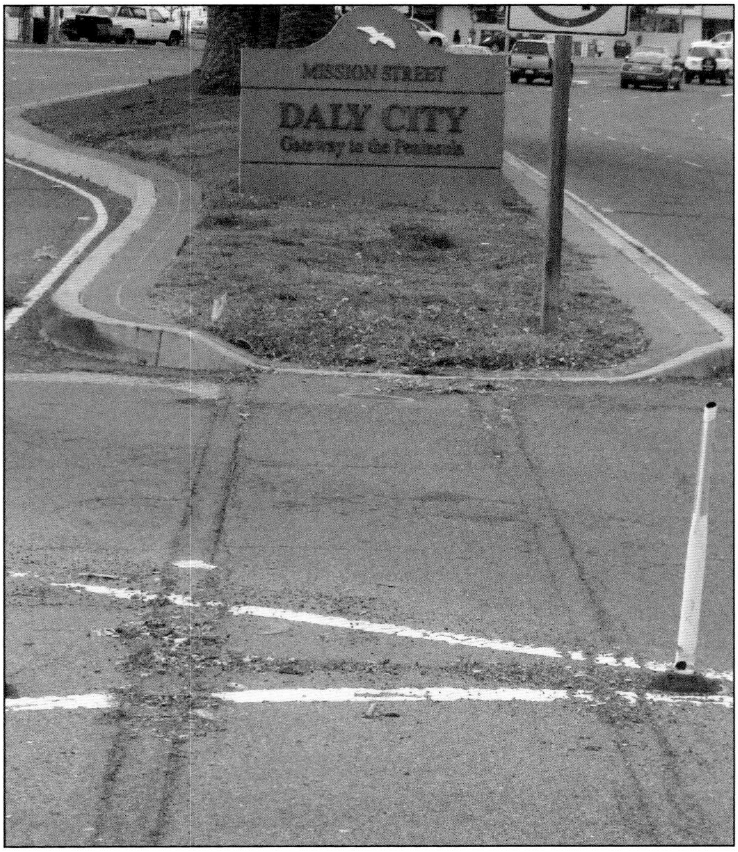

Here is evidence of the tracks once used by the streetcars. Daly City and Colma have done their best to wipe out this memory with street improvements. These tracks can be found on Mission Street, south of San Pedro Avenue, at the Daly City welcome sign, and north of A Street at the Colma welcome sign. In other words, these tracks in 2010 are in Unincorporated Colma.

Here is a local newspaper from the early 1950s that was distributed to many of the unincorporated communities. Listed at the top are Broadmoor Village, Winston Manor (which eventually was annexed by the city of South San Francisco), Garden Village, and Sterling Park. Broadmoor got the headlines in local newspapers, even though all of these communities will be mentioned as separate well into the 1980s. (Courtesy Colma Historical Association.)

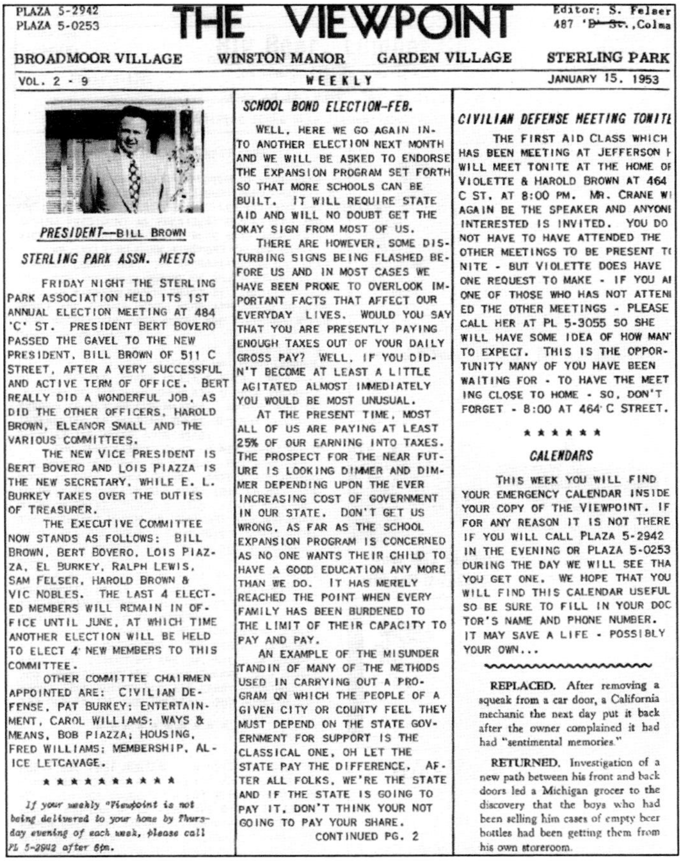

PLAZA 5-2942
PLAZA 5-0253

THE VIEWPOINT

Editor: S. Felser
487 'B' St., Colma

BROADMOOR VILLAGE WINSTON MANOR GARDEN VILLAGE STERLING PARK

VOL. 2 - 9 WEEKLY JANUARY 15. 1953

PRESIDENT—BILL BROWN

STERLING PARK ASSN. MEETS

FRIDAY NIGHT THE STERLING PARK ASSOCIATION HELD ITS 1ST ANNUAL ELECTION MEETING AT 484 'C' ST. PRESIDENT BERT BOVERO PASSED THE GAVEL TO THE NEW PRESIDENT, BILL BROWN OF 511 C STREET, AFTER A VERY SUCCESSFUL AND ACTIVE TERM OF OFFICE. BERT REALLY DID A WONDERFUL JOB, AS DID THE OTHER OFFICERS, HAROLD BROWN, ELEANOR SMALL AND THE VARIOUS COMMITTEES.

THE NEW VICE PRESIDENT IS BERT BOVERO AND LOIS PIAZZA IS THE NEW SECRETARY, WHILE E. L. BURKEY TAKES OVER THE DUTIES OF TREASURER.

THE EXECUTIVE COMMITTEE NOW STANDS AS FOLLOWS: BILL BROWN, BERT BOVERO, LOIS PIAZZA, EL BURKEY, RALPH LEWIS, SAM FELSER, HAROLD BROWN & VIC NOBLES. THE LAST 4 ELECTED MEMBERS WILL REMAIN IN OFFICE UNTIL JUNE, AT WHICH TIME ANOTHER ELECTION WILL BE HELD TO ELECT 4 NEW MEMBERS TO THIS COMMITTEE.

OTHER COMMITTEE CHAIRMEN APPOINTED ARE: CIVILIAN DEFENSE, PAT BURKEY; ENTERTAINMENT, CAROL WILLIAMS; WAYS & MEANS, BOB PIAZZA; HOUSING, FRED WILLIAMS; MEMBERSHIP, ALICE LETCAVAGE.

★ ★ ★ ★ ★ ★ ★ ★ ★ ★

If your weekly "Viewpoint is not being delivered to your home by Thursday evening of each week, please call PL 5-2942 after 6pm.

SCHOOL BOND ELECTION-FEB.

WELL, HERE WE GO AGAIN INTO ANOTHER ELECTION NEXT MONTH AND WE WILL BE ASKED TO ENDORSE THE EXPANSION PROGRAM SET FORTH SO THAT MORE SCHOOLS CAN BE BUILT. IT WILL REQUIRE STATE AID AND WILL NO DOUBT GET THE OKAY SIGN FROM MOST OF US.

THERE ARE HOWEVER, SOME DISTURBING SIGNS BEING FLASHED BEFORE US AND IN MOST CASES WE HAVE BEEN PRONE TO OVERLOOK IMPORTANT FACTS THAT AFFECT OUR EVERYDAY LIVES. WOULD YOU SAY THAT YOU ARE PRESENTLY PAYING ENOUGH TAXES OUT OF YOUR DAILY GROSS PAY? WELL, IF YOU DIDN'T BECOME AT LEAST A LITTLE AGITATED ALMOST IMMEDIATELY YOU WOULD BE MOST UNUSUAL.

AT THE PRESENT TIME, MOST ALL OF US ARE PAYING AT LEAST 25% OF OUR EARNING INTO TAXES. THE PROSPECT FOR THE NEAR FUTURE IS LOOKING DIMMER AND DIMMER DEPENDING UPON THE EVER INCREASING COST OF GOVERNMENT IN OUR STATE. DON'T GET US WRONG, AS FAR AS THE SCHOOL EXPANSION PROGRAM IS CONCERNED AS NO ONE WANTS THEIR CHILD TO HAVE A GOOD EDUCATION ANY MORE THAN WE DO. IT HAS MERELY REACHED THE POINT WHEN EVERY FAMILY HAS BEEN BURDENED TO THE LIMIT OF THEIR CAPACITY TO PAY AND PAY.

AN EXAMPLE OF THE MISUNDERSTANDIN OF MANY OF THE METHODS USED IN CARRYING OUT A PROGRAM ON WHICH THE PEOPLE OF A GIVEN CITY OR COUNTY FEEL THEY MUST DEPEND ON THE STATE GOVERNMENT FOR SUPPORT IS THE CLASSICAL ONE, OH LET THE STATE PAY THE DIFFERENCE. AFTER ALL FOLKS, WE'RE THE STATE AND IF THE STATE IS GOING TO PAY IT, DON'T THINK YOUR NOT GOING TO PAY YOUR SHARE.

CONTINUED PG. 2

CIVILIAN DEFENSE MEETING TONITE

THE FIRST AID CLASS WHICH HAS BEEN MEETING AT JEFFERSON H WILL MEET TONITE AT THE HOME OF VIOLETTE & HAROLD BROWN AT 464 C ST. AT 8:00 PM. MR. CRANE WI AGAIN BE THE SPEAKER AND ANYONE INTERESTED IS INVITED. YOU DO NOT HAVE TO HAVE ATTENDED THE OTHER MEETINGS TO BE PRESENT TONITE - BUT VIOLETTE DOES HAVE ONE REQUEST TO MAKE - IF YOU A ONE OF THOSE WHO HAS NOT ATTENDED THE OTHER MEETINGS - PLEASE CALL HER AT PL 5-3055 SO SHE WILL HAVE SOME IDEA OF HOW MAN TO EXPECT. THIS IS THE OPPORTUNITY MANY OF YOU HAVE BEEN WAITING FOR - TO HAVE THE MEETING CLOSE TO HOME - SO, DON'T FORGET - 8:00 AT 464 C STREET.

★ ★ ★ ★ ★ ★

CALENDARS

THIS WEEK YOU WILL FIND YOUR EMERGENCY CALENDAR INSIDE YOUR COPY OF THE VIEWPOINT. IF FOR ANY REASON IT IS NOT THERE IF YOU WILL CALL PLAZA 5-2942 IN THE EVENING OR PLAZA 5-0253 DURING THE DAY WE WILL SEE THA YOU GET ONE. WE HOPE THAT YOU WILL FIND THIS CALENDAR USEFUL SO BE SURE TO FILL IN YOUR DOCTOR'S NAME AND PHONE NUMBER. IT MAY SAVE A LIFE - POSSIBLY YOUR OWN...

REPLACED. After removing a squeak from a car door, a California mechanic the next day put it back after the owner complained it had had "sentimental memories."

RETURNED. Investigation of a new path between his front and back doors led a Michigan grocer to the discovery that the boys who had been selling him cases of empty beer bottles had been getting them from his own storeroom.

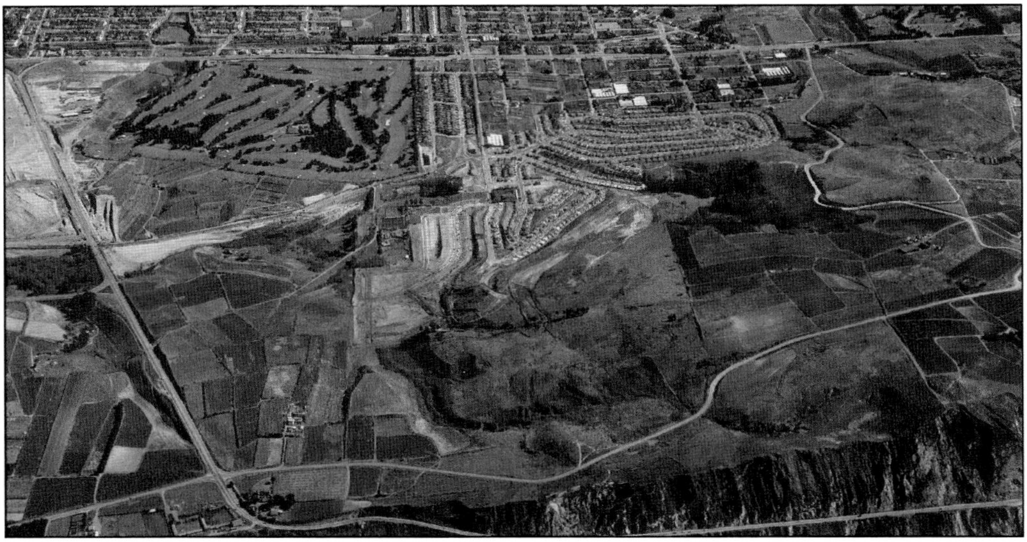

This 1947 aerial photograph shows Broadmoor Village still being built. Junipero Serra Boulevard and the farms of Unincorporated Colma are east, at the top of the picture with Alemany Boulevard running down the left side of the photograph. To the north, west, and south of Broadmoor is only farmland that land developers and Daly City wanted to get at. (Courtesy HJW Geospatial Inc. and Pacific Aerial Surveys. Oakland, California.)

PLAZA 5-2942
PLAZA 5-0253

TH

BROADMOOR VILLAGE W

VOL. 2 - 8

ANNEXATION???

SPECULATIONS AS TO THE FUTURE OF THE PEOPLE IN THE BROADMOOR AREA WERE EXTREMELY VARIED THIS WEEK AFTER THE ORIGINAL ANNOUNCEMENT MADE BY SUPERVISORS IN SAN FRANCISCO ON THE SUBJECT OF ANNEXATION.

WE MADE A SURVEY OF OUR OWN THROUGH OUT THE AREA AND CAME UP WITH SO MANY DIFFERENT IDEAS ON THE SUBJECT THAT WE ARE UNABLE AT THIS TIME TO GIVE AN ACCURATE COUNT AS TO THE PRO AND CONS. AT THIS MOMENT, THE SUBJECT SEEMS TO HAVE BEEN DROPPED BY THE MAJORITY OF PEOPLE IN THE INTERESTED AREAS AND WILL BE DISCUSSED ONLY AT THE GENERAL MEETINGS SCHEDULED FOR THE 8TH OF JANUARY. SAY THATS TONIGHT FOR THE BROADMOOR VILLAGE ASSN. SO IF YOUR INTERESTED WHY NOT ATTEND AT THE NEWLY DECORATED CENTER. IT OUGHT TO BE INTERESTING.

★ ★ ★ ★ ★ ★ ★ ★

Here is an article from the *Viewpoint*, a local newspaper, that reports on January 8, 1953, that there are plans by, not Daly City, but San Francisco to annex Broadmoor Village. This kind of subject matter can be found in newspaper articles with an even earlier date than the one posted here. (Courtesy Colma Historical Association; 55/10,046)

COUNTY ANNEXATION.

To The San Francisco Examiner:

I am writing this letter regarding the lack of interest that the San Francisco Board of Supervisors has taken to the annexation of Westlake and Broadmoor. They are studying plans to keep the downtown area intact but have not taken any action for a greater San Francisco.

Remember that the life blood of San Francisco will have to come from San Mateo and if the board won't do something about it San Francisco will soon be a ghost town. The people of Westlake, Broadmoor, Sharp Park, Bayshore, Brisbane and a lot of people from South San Francisco and Daly City want to join the city but the politicians are the ones who won't talk, including the gentlemen on the San Francisco Board of Supervisors. . . .

JOHN BROOKS,
Westlake, Calif.

JUL 13 1953

The entire area described in this letter to the *San Francisco Examiner* was indeed at one time part of San Francisco. This letter was printed in 1953; perhaps the writer of the letter was unaware of the separation 100 years prior to his suggestion. (Courtesy San Francisco Public Library.)

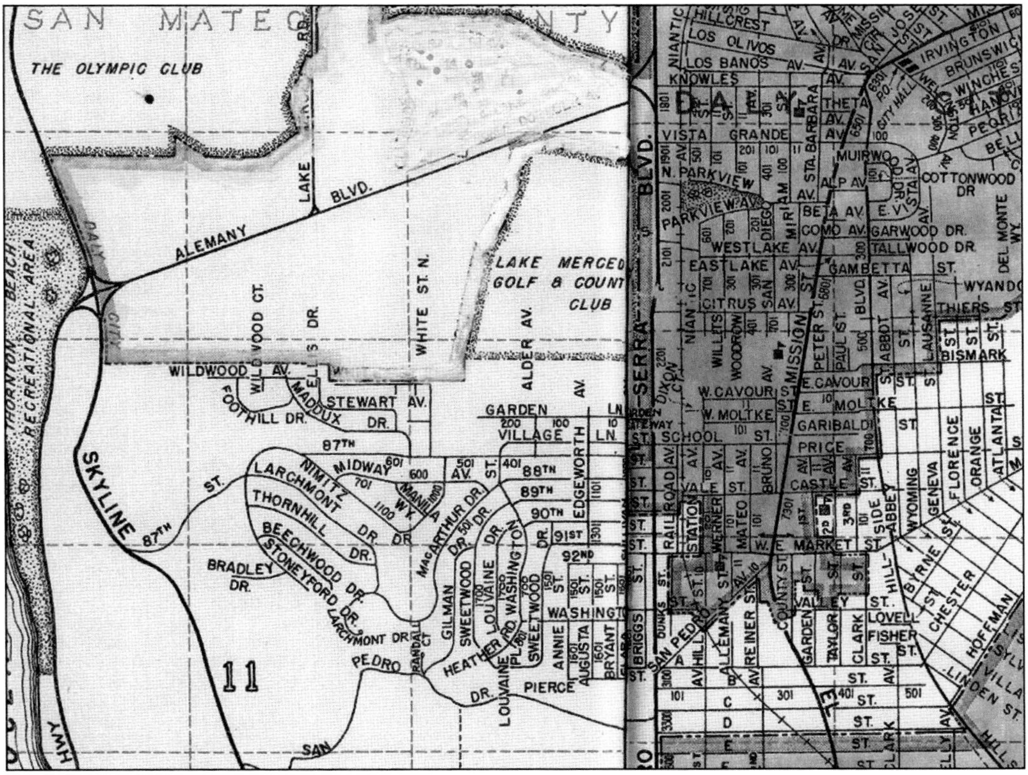

This map from 1949 has been slightly modified to prove a point. In 1947, the shaded area in the upper right corner is Daly City. The shaded area in the lower right is Incorporated Colma. The white in between is Unincorporated Colma; the white area to the left is also Unincorporated Colma including Broadmoor Village. (Courtesy San Francisco Public Library.)

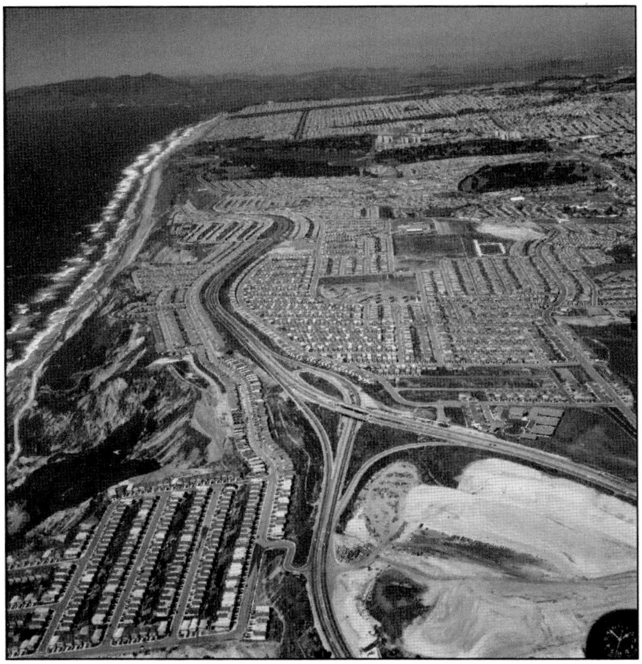

This aerial photograph, taken on April 20, 1962, shows Daly City almost completely surrounding Broadmoor Village. Even the Lake Merced Country Club will eventually be annexed in October 1976. In all, there were some 52 annexations of Unincorporated Colma and Broadmoor Village by Daly City. (Courtesy HJW Geospatial Inc. and Pacific Aerial Surveys. Oakland, California.)

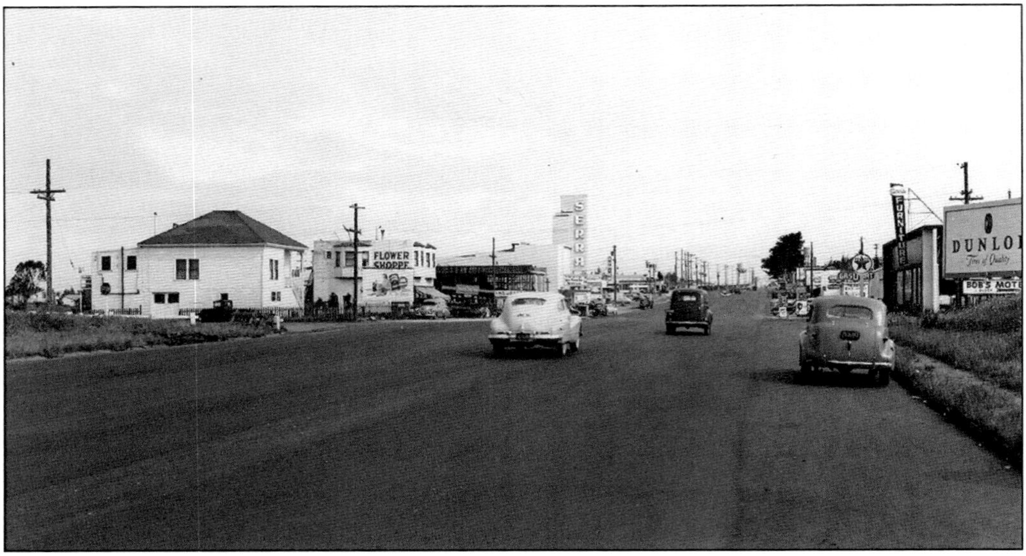

This is Junipero Serra Boulevard facing north in the early 1950s. On the left (west) side is, at this time, Unincorporated Colma. The house on the left belongs to Marie and Mario Feno on the corner of Ninety-second Street and Junipero Serra Boulevard. This area will fall under attack by expanding the cities' borders. To the right are businesses in, at this time, Unincorporated Colma. (Courtesy Mrs. Alvina Wegscheider.)

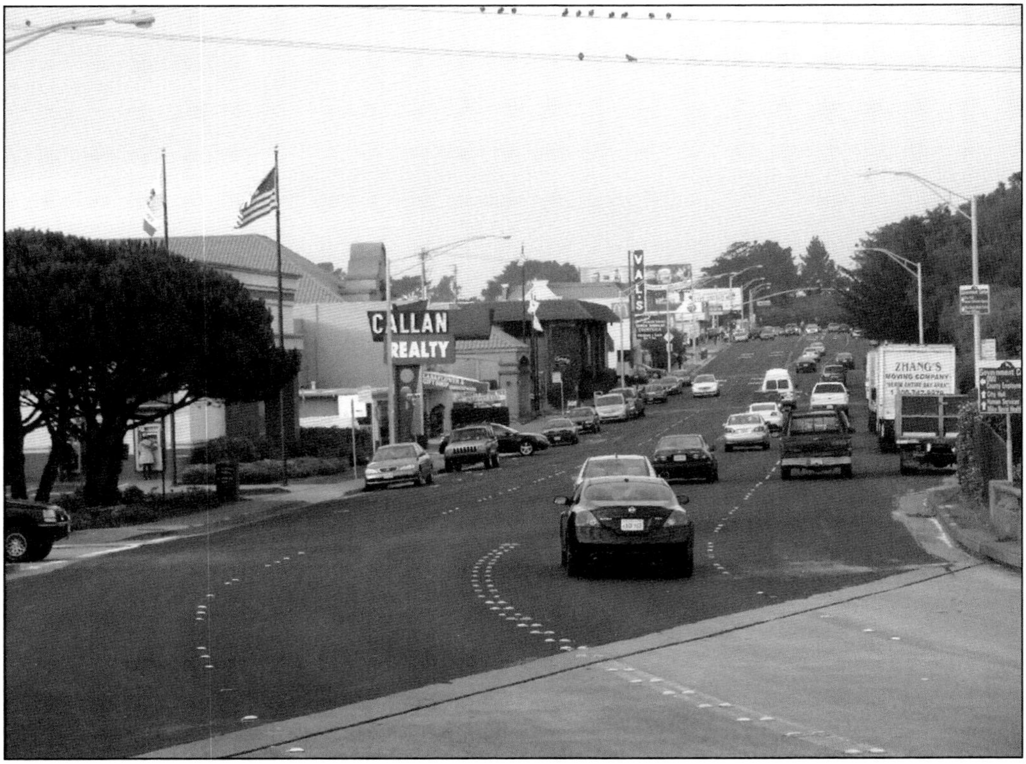

Here is Junipero Serra Boulevard facing north in 2010. The trees to the left are at the corner of Ninety-second Street where the Feno house once was and are part of the parking lot for the Chase Bank. This whole area is now part of Daly City after decades of annexations.

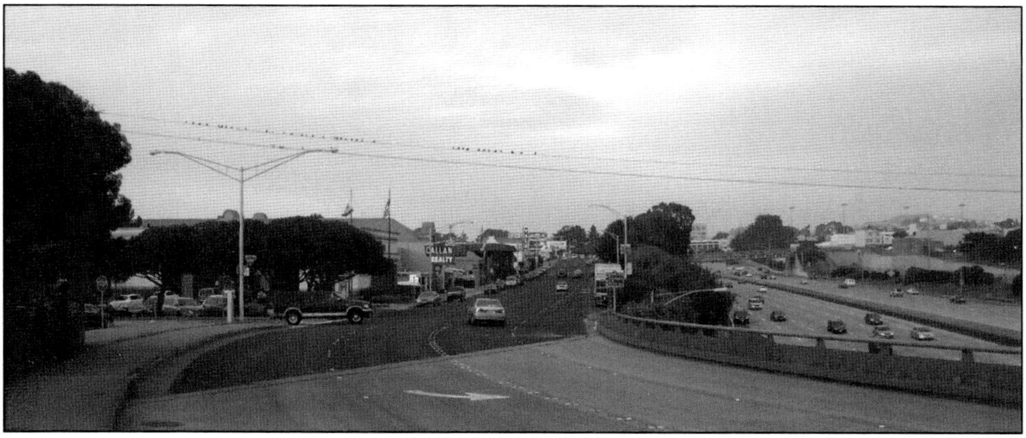

Still looking north on Junipero Serra Boulevard at Ninety-second Street, there are no longer businesses on the right (east) side of the street. The businesses, Railroad Avenue, Dunks Street, and a lot of land that was Unincorporated Colma was eliminated to make way for U.S. Interstate 280. For that matter, the original Southern Pacific Railroad tracks, just to the east of U.S. Interstate 280 have given way to the new tracks of Bay Area Rapid Transit (BART).

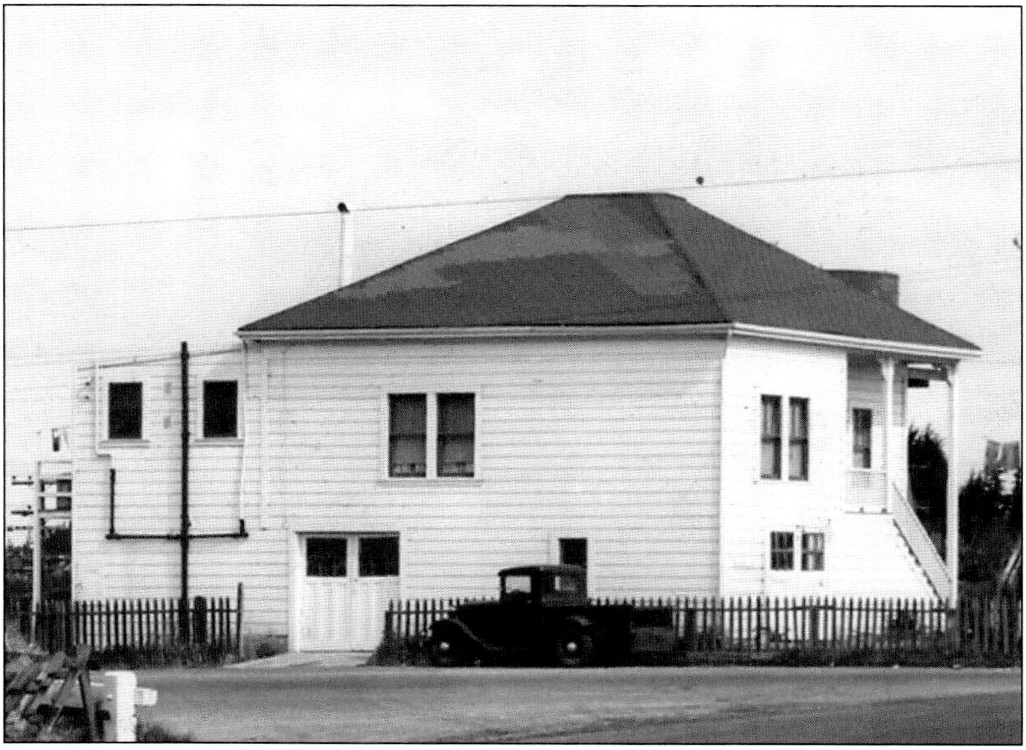

This is the home of Marie and Mario Feno at the corner of Junipero Serra and Ninety-second Street. Mario was one of many farmers who worked the lands in Unincorporated Colma that stretched west from Junipero Serra Boulevard to Broadmoor Village. Some of the crops grown were lettuce, potatoes, Swiss chard, carrots, beats, and various flowers. Their children, Alma, Frank, and Alvina, grew up in this house. (Courtesy Mrs. Alvina Wegscheider.)

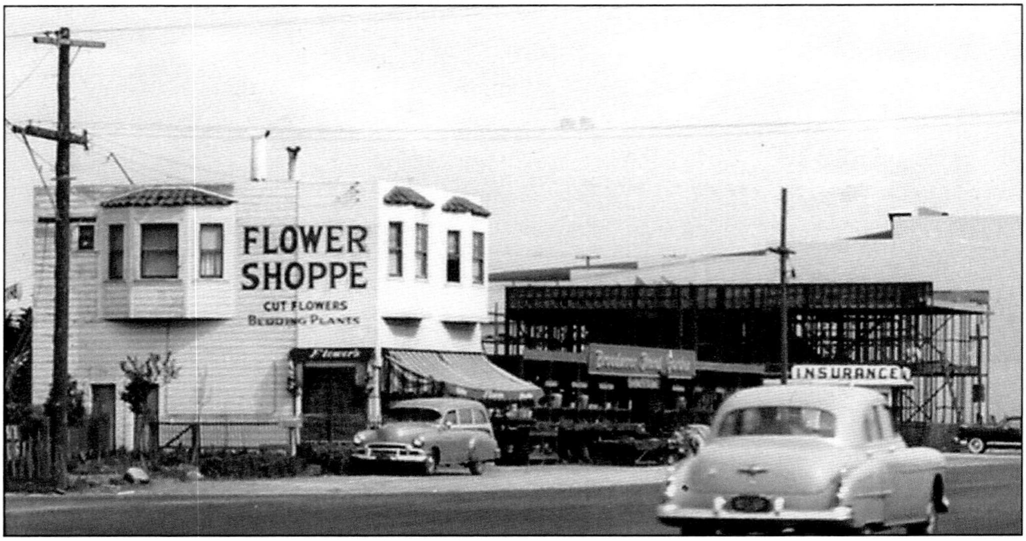

Pictured here is Mario's Flower Shoppe at the corner of Junipero Serra at Ninety-first Street. This parcel of land was also Unincorporated Colma and was very successful for years. Eldest daughter Alma married Frank Stangelini, and the couple then moved in upstairs from the flower shop. Behind the shop to the north is the Serra Theater. (Courtesy Mrs. Alvina Wegscheider.)

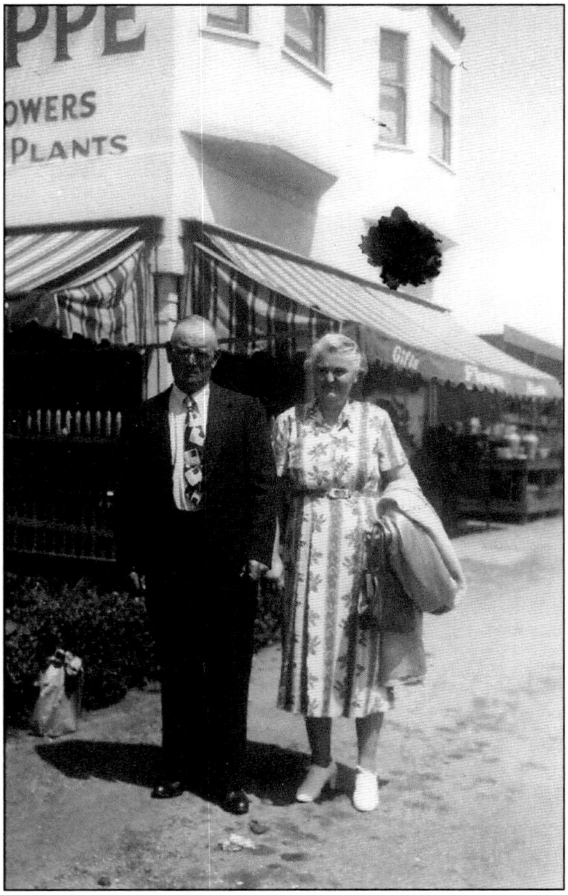

This photograph shows the two proud business owners in Unincorporated Colma, Mario and Marie Feno. The address, not the flower shop, of their house was 196 Ninety-second Street, and the house was moved here from a location in San Francisco. It was actually less expensive to move a house at that time than to build a new one. The Chase Bank now occupies this land. (Courtesy Mrs. Alvina Wegscheider.)

One block north of Mario's Flower Shoppe on the corner of Junipero Serra Boulevard at Ninetieth Street is the Serra Theater. This marks the border with Daly City. In the far background, the King's market in the Broadmoor Shopping Center can be seen. The Broadmoor Shopping Center, located in Daly City, not Broadmoor, is at the corner of Junipero Serra at Eighty-seventh Street. (Courtesy Mrs. Alvina Wegscheider.)

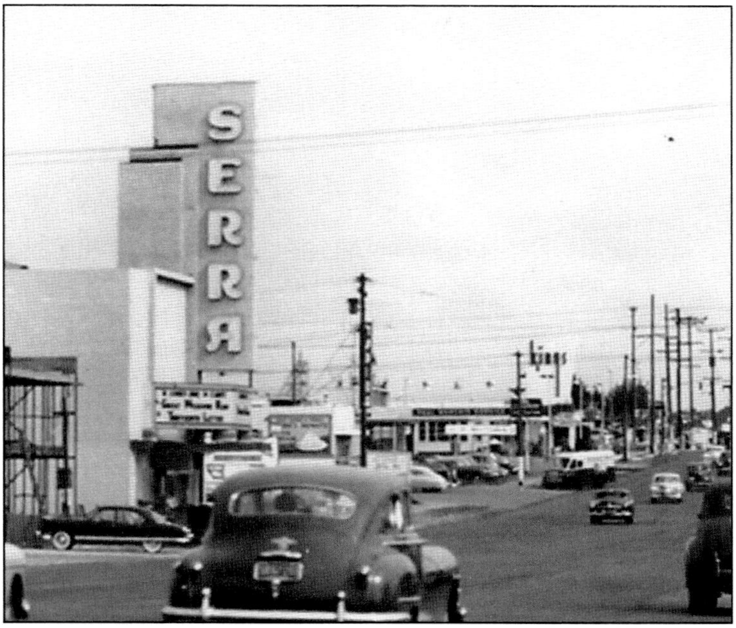

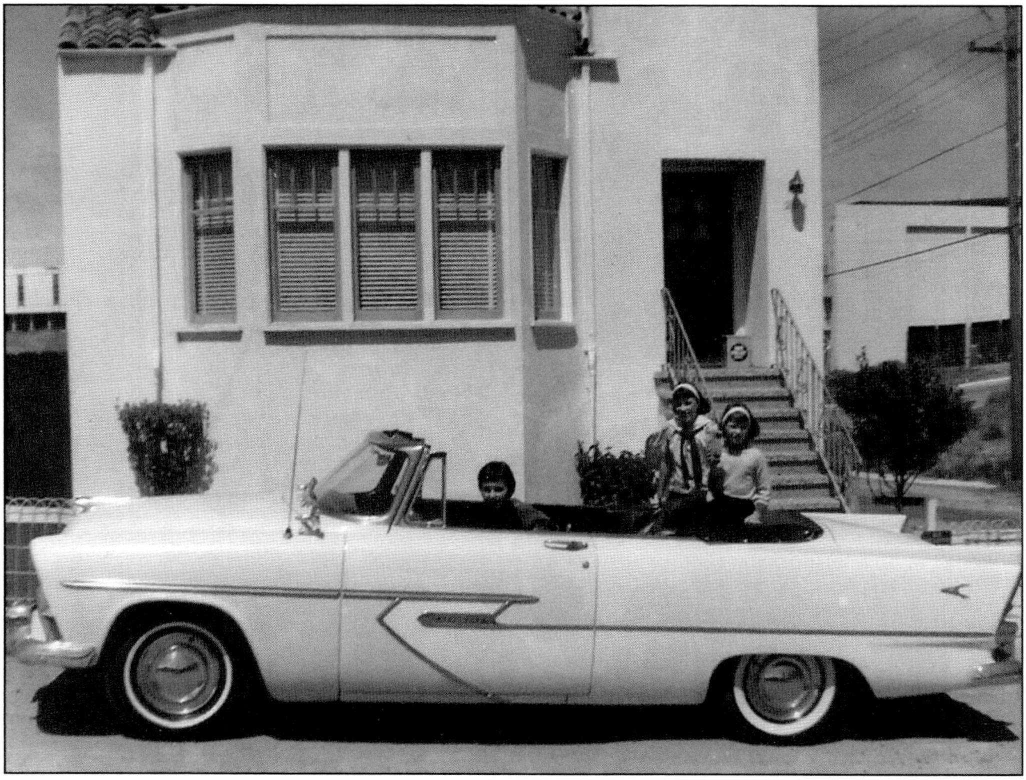

Mr. Feno's youngest daughter, Alvina, married and had a family of her own. Another house was moved in 1955, located on Portola Drive in San Francisco and moved due to widening of streets. The final address is 204 Ninety-second Street at Sullivan Avenue. In the car with Alvina are her two daughters, Debbie and Vicki. A Sun Valley Dairy can is on the porch. (Courtesy Mrs. Alvina Wegscheider.)

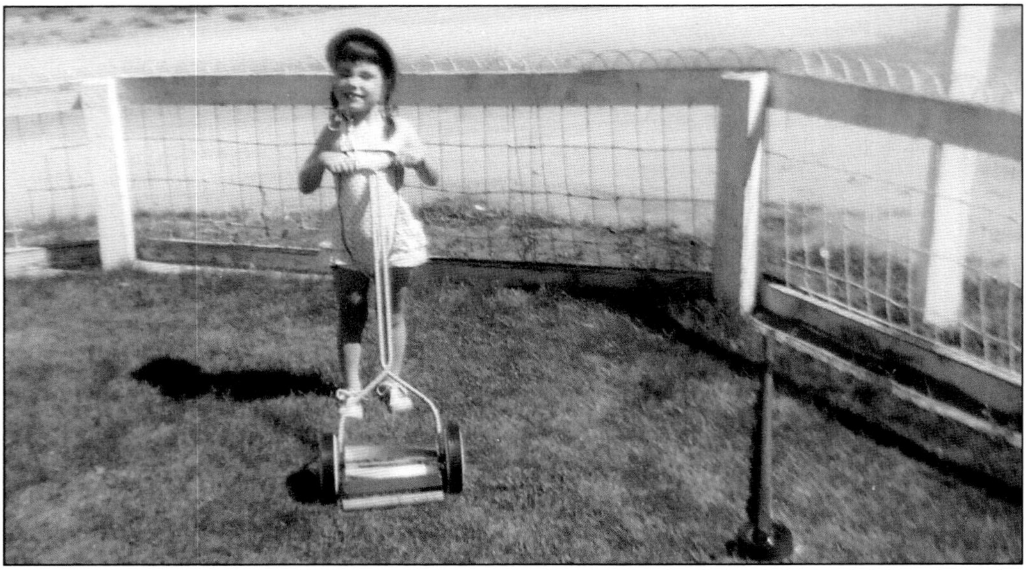

In the front yard, young Debbie Wegscheider is at play. She is the first of three children from the marriage of Allan "Wick" Wegscheider and Alvina Feno. Grandma and Grandpa Feno are one block behind her to the east. The intersection of Sullivan Avenue and Ninety-second Street has no sidewalks at this time. (Courtesy Mrs. Alvina Wegscheider.)

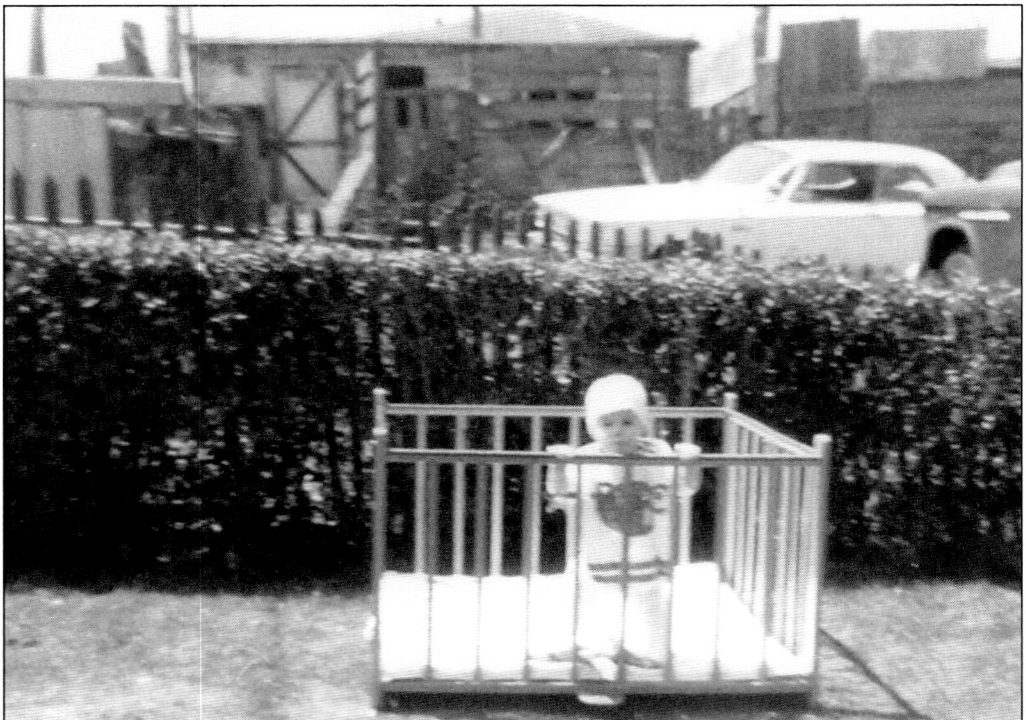

Also in the front yard, a few years later, younger brother Allan Wegscheider Jr. is working on his tan. Behind little Allan, to the south of the Wegscheider House, are old barns and horse stables that will be torn down and replaced with the Department of Motor Vehicles building. (Courtesy Mrs. Alvina Wegscheider.)

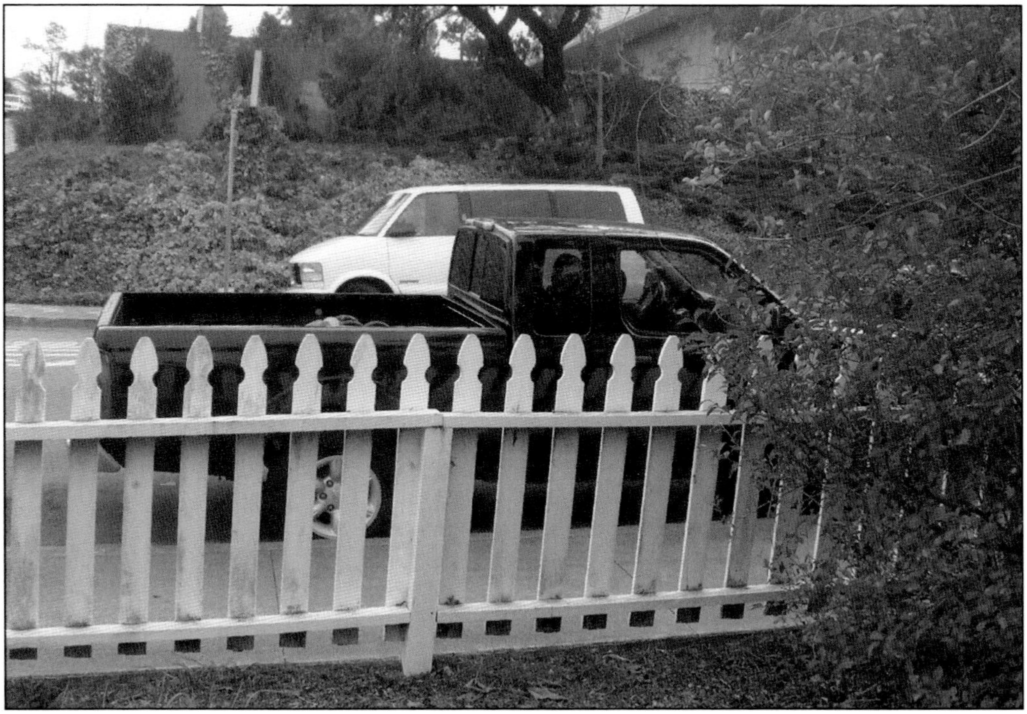

Here is the same view from the same yard in 2010. Gone are the barns, gone are the stables, the hedge is missing, and little Allan grew up and now works on his tan in San Jose. The fence is still there, and the building for the DMV completes the view.

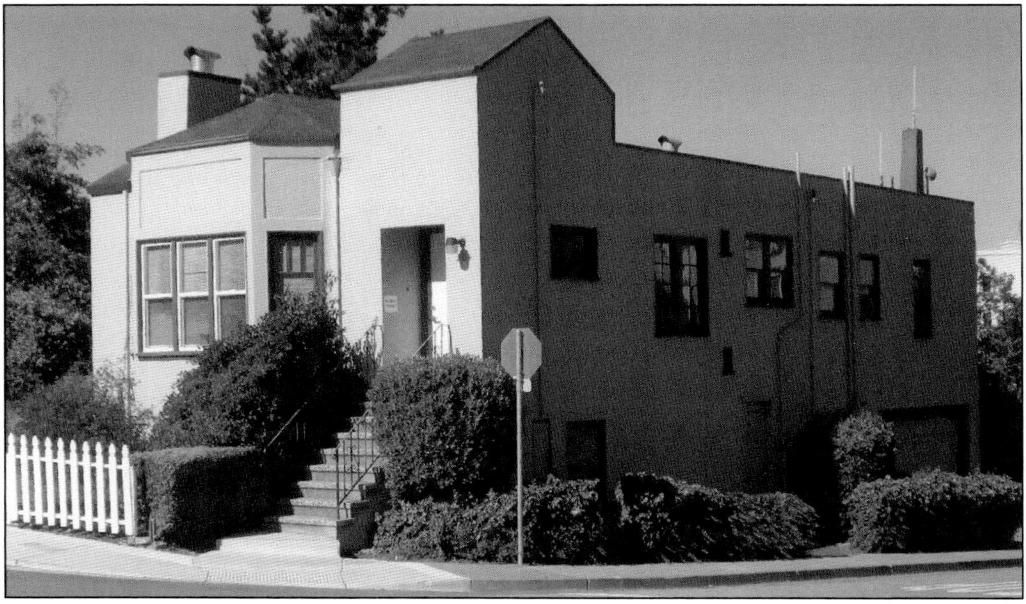

Here is the former Wegscheider house in 2010. The land was annexed by Daly City in 1971. The city then claimed eminent domain and forced the family to move, while Mr. Wegscheider was in the hospital with blood poisoning and facing possible amputation of his hand. This left Mrs. Wegscheider to raise three children, shop for a new house, and fend off harassing phone calls from city officials that came almost "daly."

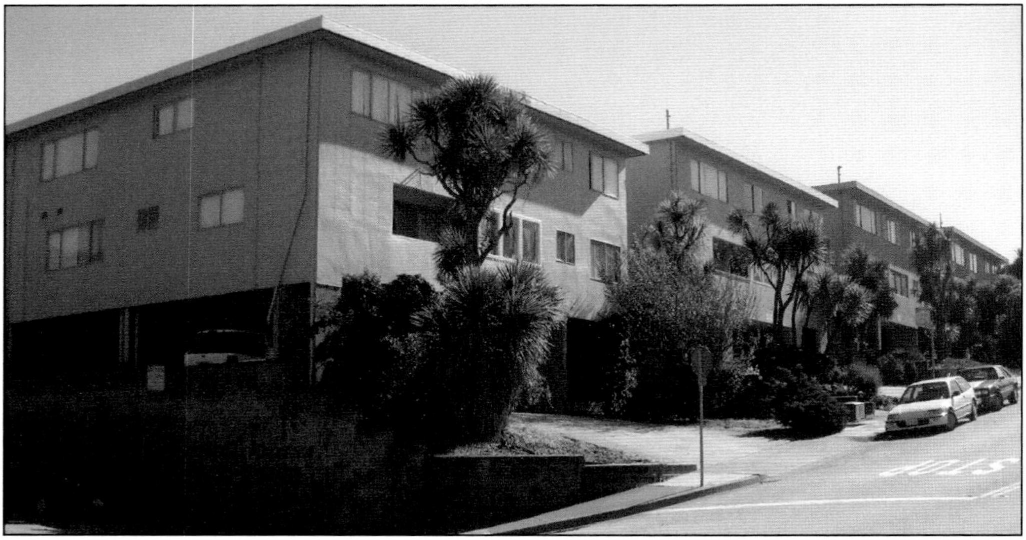

The former Wegscheider house is on the northwest corner of Ninety-second Street and Sullivan Avenue. On the southeast corner are several buildings of apartments. Because there were more than 12 people living in these buildings, Daly City could not declare eminent domain and was forced to allow the residents and owners to vote on whether they wanted to be annexed or not. The choice was to stay unincorporated.

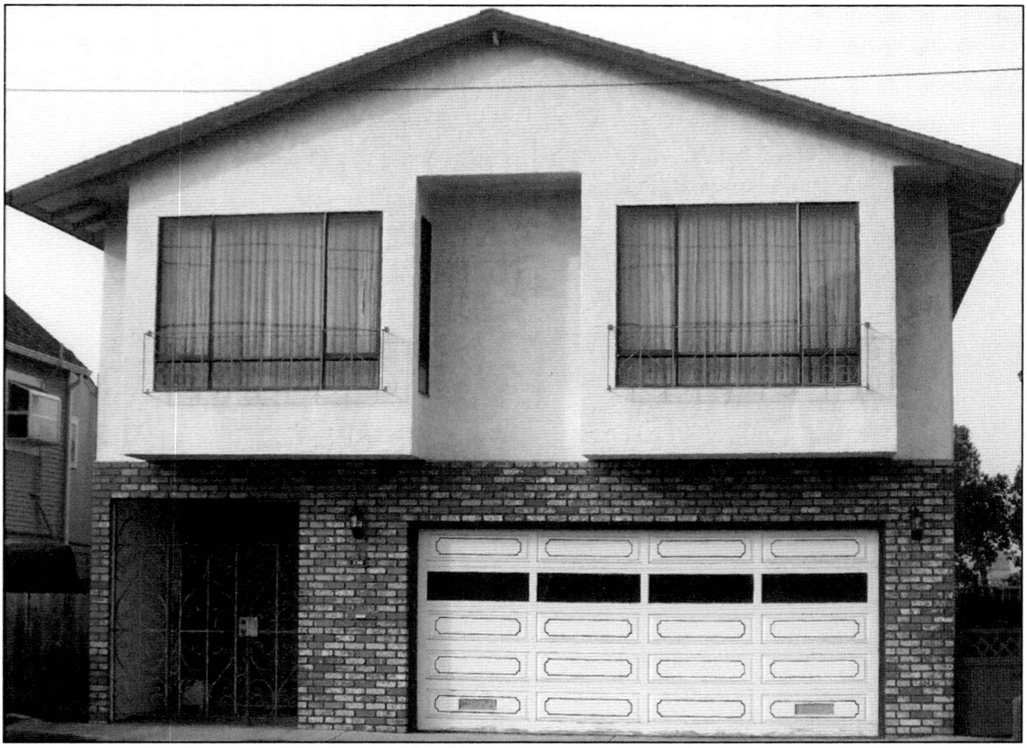

Daly City used this loophole in the laws to allow the city to take what it wanted without any recourse. The Wegscheider family did move to this house at 250 Station Avenue. The new house was in Unincorporated Colma when it was built. Like the ghost of Christmas past, Daly City's expansion plans caught up with them, and again Daly City implemented an annexation in June 1972.

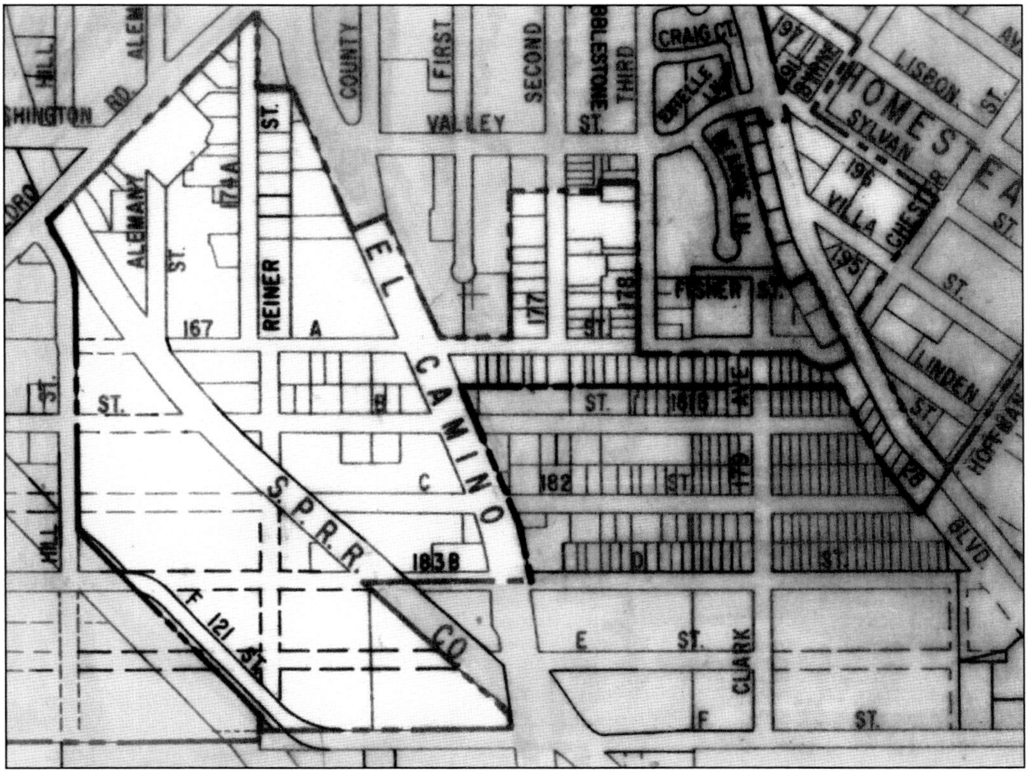

This is what is left of Unincorporated Colma, shown in white. This area is east of U.S. Interstate 280 and shares the zip code 94014 with the town of Colma and Daly City that is also east of the freeway. Some of this is the original Sterling Park community. The incorporated town of Colma is to the south, and north is Daly City. (Courtesy San Mateo County Public Works Department)

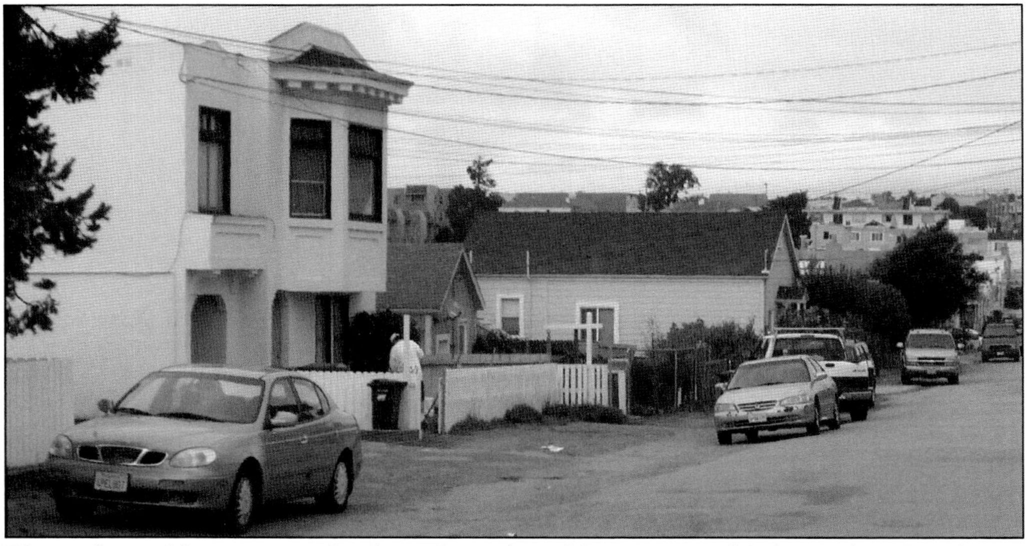

The residents of this area consider themselves to be in Unincorporated Colma and not Broadmoor, even though they are protected by the Broadmoor Police Department. Some of these residents have asked to be annexed by the incorporated Town of Colma, to no avail. They have been told, off the record, that the Town of Colma does not want to pay for street upgrades like sidewalks.

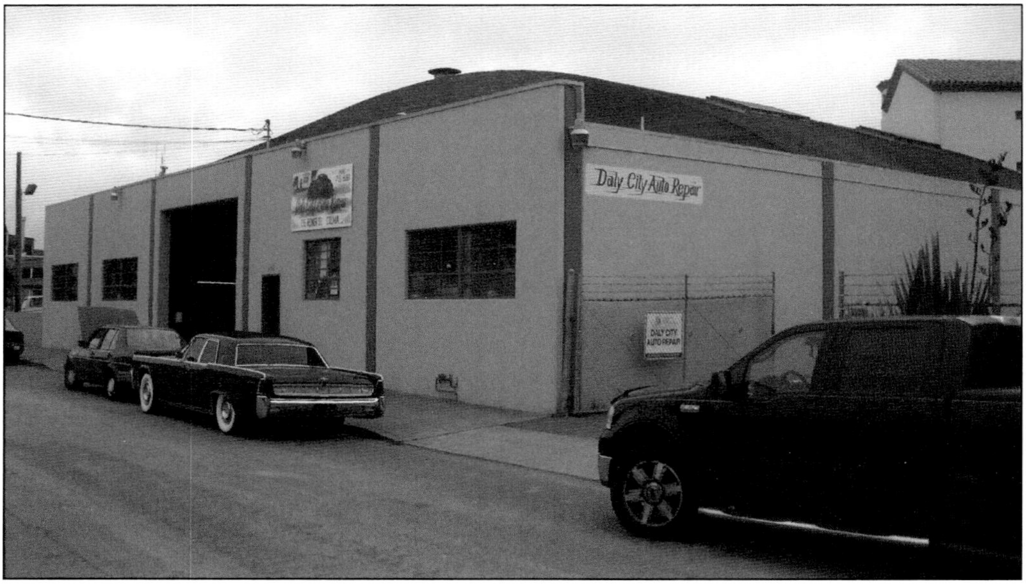

One of the businesses that have been in Unincorporated Colma for years is Daly City Auto Repair on Reiner Street. The street is located at an angle to San Pedro Road, which puts the shop to the back of Holy Angel's Church, seen to the right of this picture. Holy Angel's Church on San Pedro is also still in Unincorporated Colma.

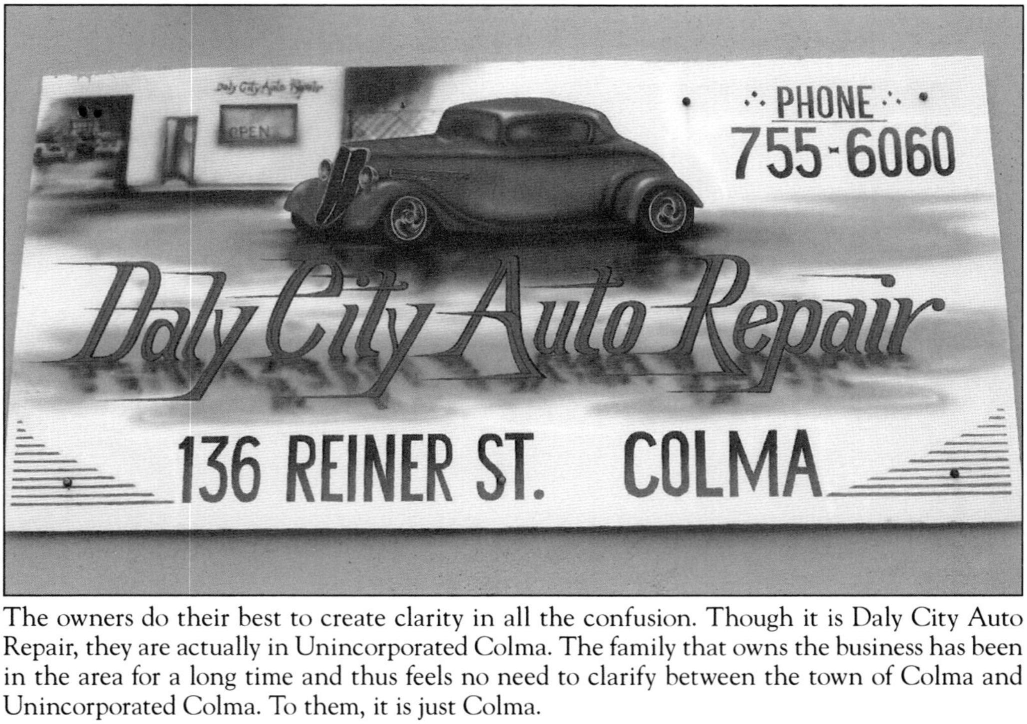

The owners do their best to create clarity in all the confusion. Though it is Daly City Auto Repair, they are actually in Unincorporated Colma. The family that owns the business has been in the area for a long time and thus feels no need to clarify between the town of Colma and Unincorporated Colma. To them, it is just Colma.

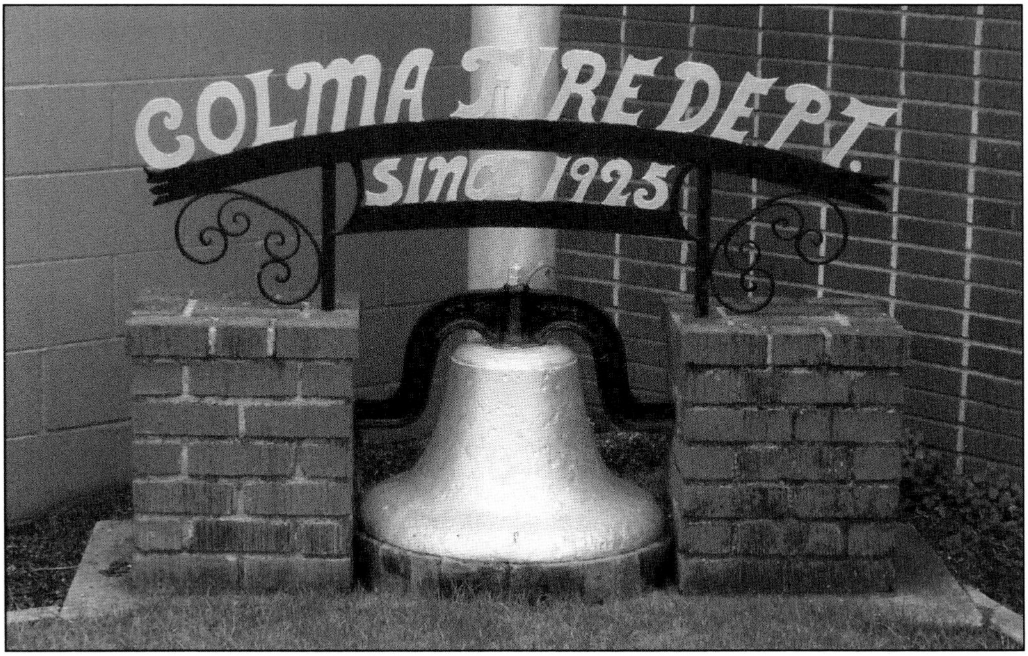

Established in 1925 and named after the original community it served then and now, is the Colma Fire Protection District or simply the Colma Fire Department. The district serves Broadmoor Village as well and for years was an all-volunteer fire department. As an all-volunteer fire department, Colma had a better response time than some of the incorporated and full-time departments like San Francisco.

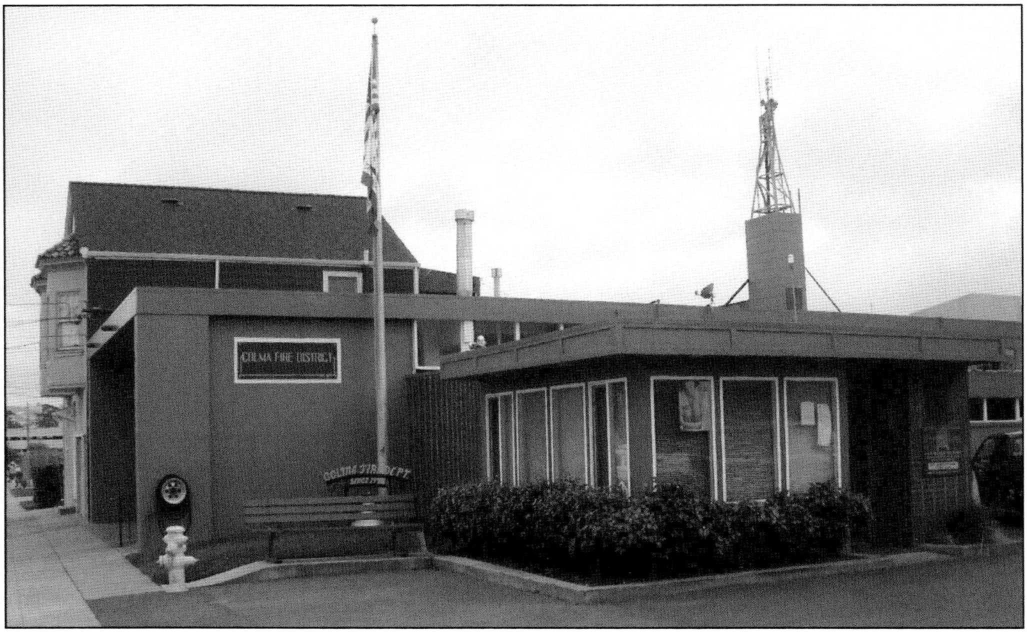

The fire department is right next door to Daly City Auto Repair Shop on Reiner Street, just on the south side. The Colma Fire Department creates something very simple just when one needed a little simplicity; in other words, the Colma Fire Department is in Colma Unincorporated, not the town of Colma.

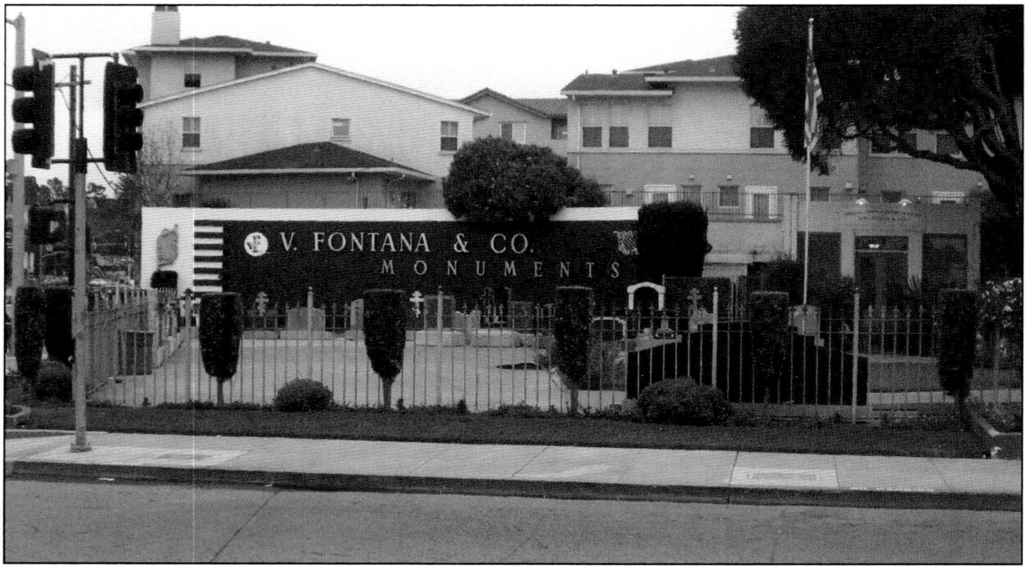

Another business that has been in Colma Unincorporated since the "dawn of time" is V. Fontana and Company Monuments. Located at the corner of El Camino Real and A Street, Mark Fontana now runs the company. He is the son of Elio, who named Westmoor High School in the day when he was on the school board.

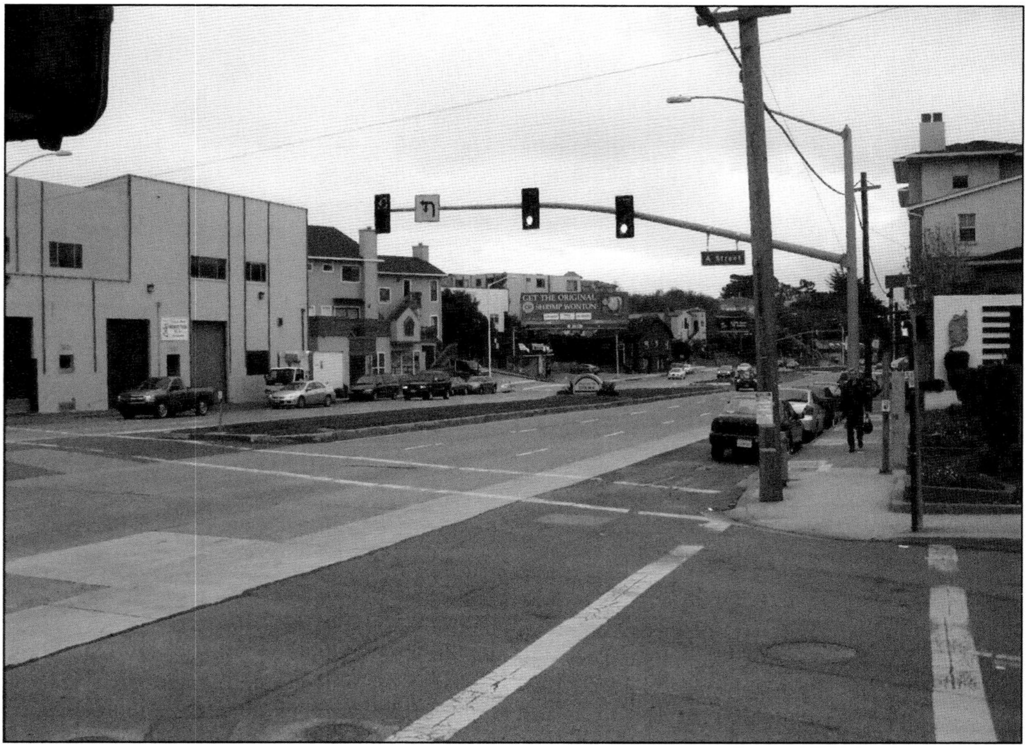

This photograph looks south down El Camino toward the new bridge used by BART trains. The right side of the street in this picture (in other words, the west side of the street) is Unincorporated Colma. Across the street are businesses in the town of Colma. Behind the photographer, a block to the north, El Camino Real becomes Mission Street at the Daly City limits.

Now east of U.S. Interstate 280, how does one know where Unincorporated Colma or the town of Colma begins and ends? Like on the west side discerning the difference in Broadmoor and Daly City can be seen in the street signs that are used. Unincorporated Colma like Broadmoor has kelly green signs with white writing.

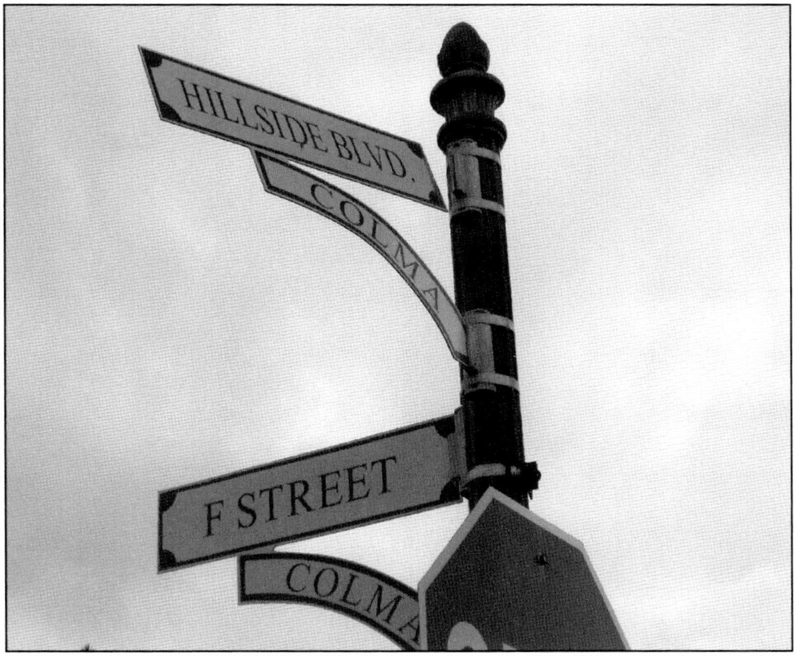

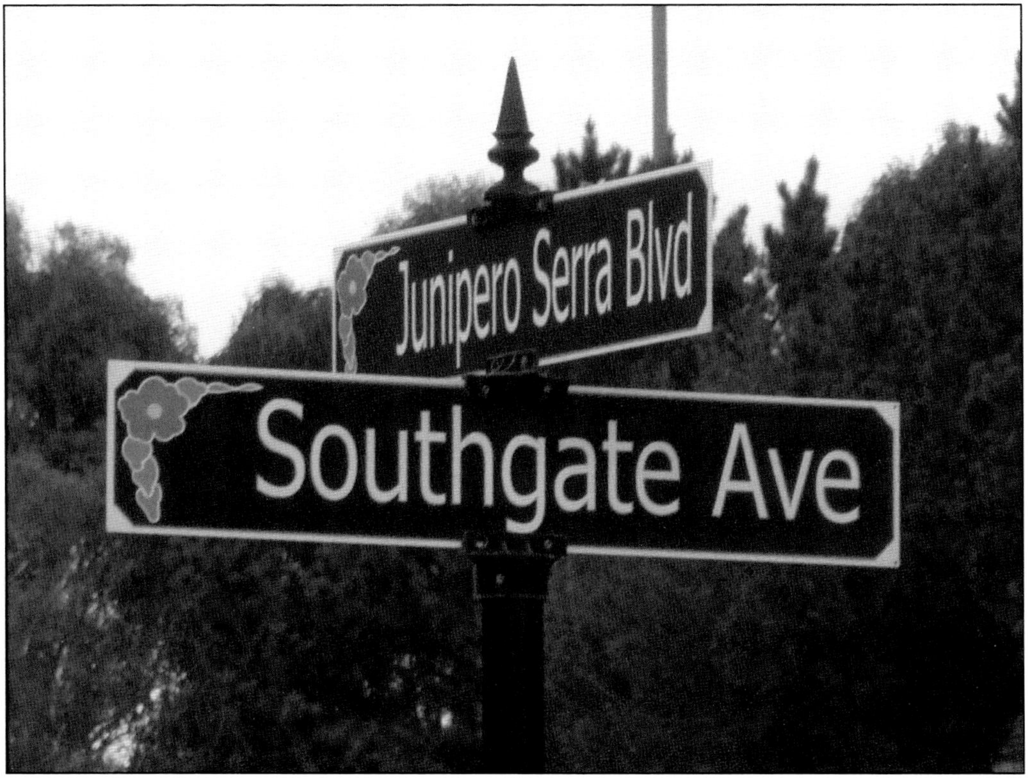

The town of Colma has white signs with dark green writing. As if to make a point, some areas have a Colma sign as well. Dark green signs with white letters and a blue flower in the town of Colma are also found in Colma. Daly City, again, has blue street signs with white writing and a seagull for a logo.

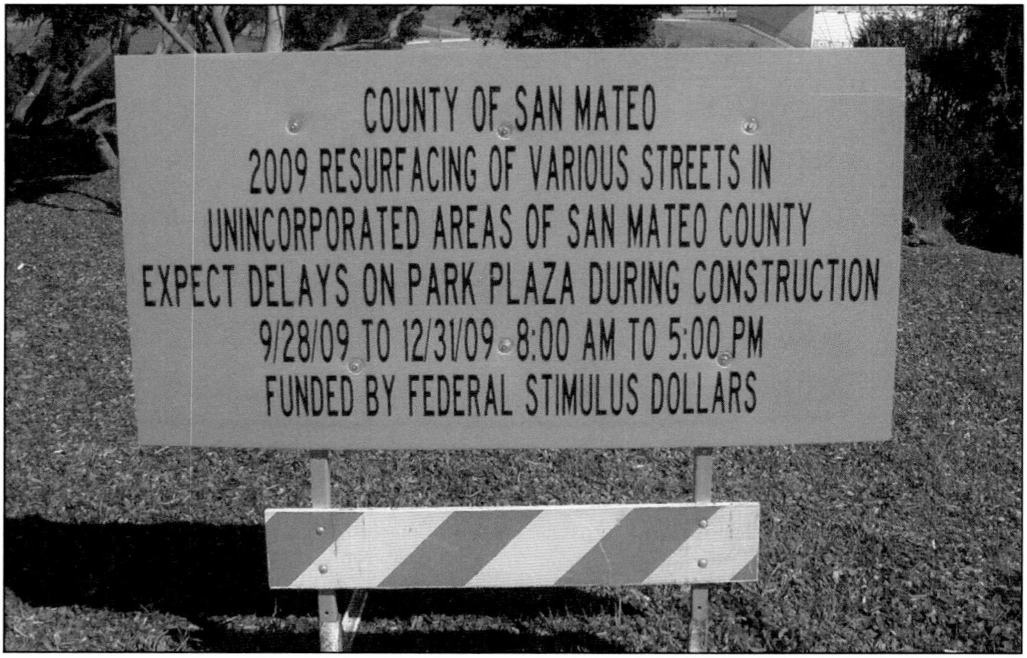

As if to prove another point, here is a sign informing residents of street improvements in Broadmoor on Park Plaza Drive, note that Garden Village School is in the background. On this county sign the phrase "Unincorporated areas of San Mateo County" is used. Nowhere on the sign are the terms Broadmoor, Broadmoor Village, or Unincorporated Colma.

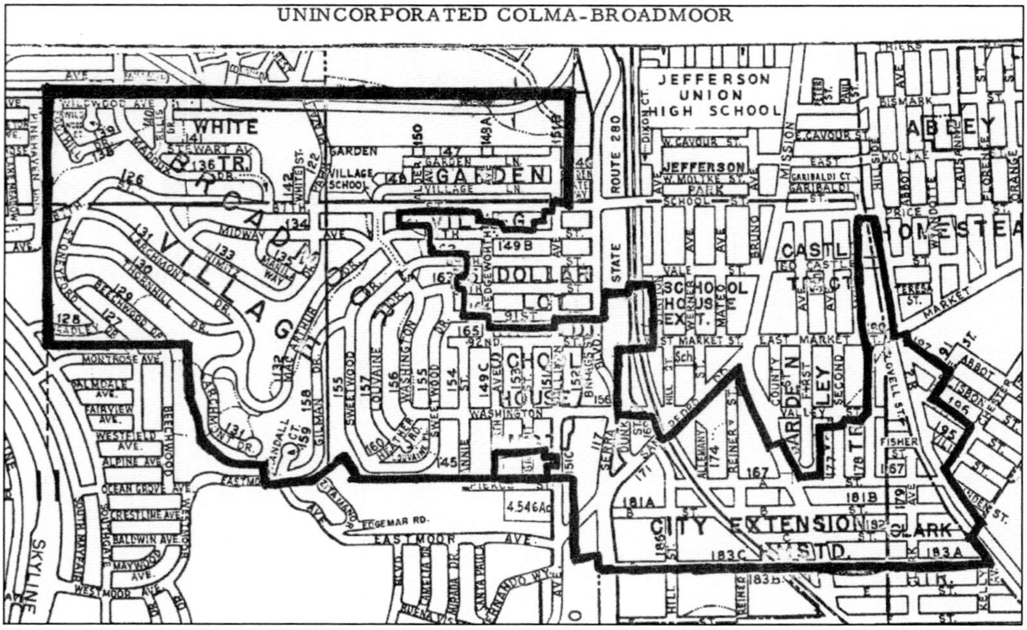

In July 1967, the Broadmoor Property Owners Association again took the lead and paid for a study to look into the possibility of becoming an incorporated city to put an end to annexations once and for all. This is a map of what the proposed city would have looked like. It would have included Broadmoor Village, Garden Village, Sterling Park, and the connecting lands. (Courtesy Chief Love, Broadmoor Police Department.)

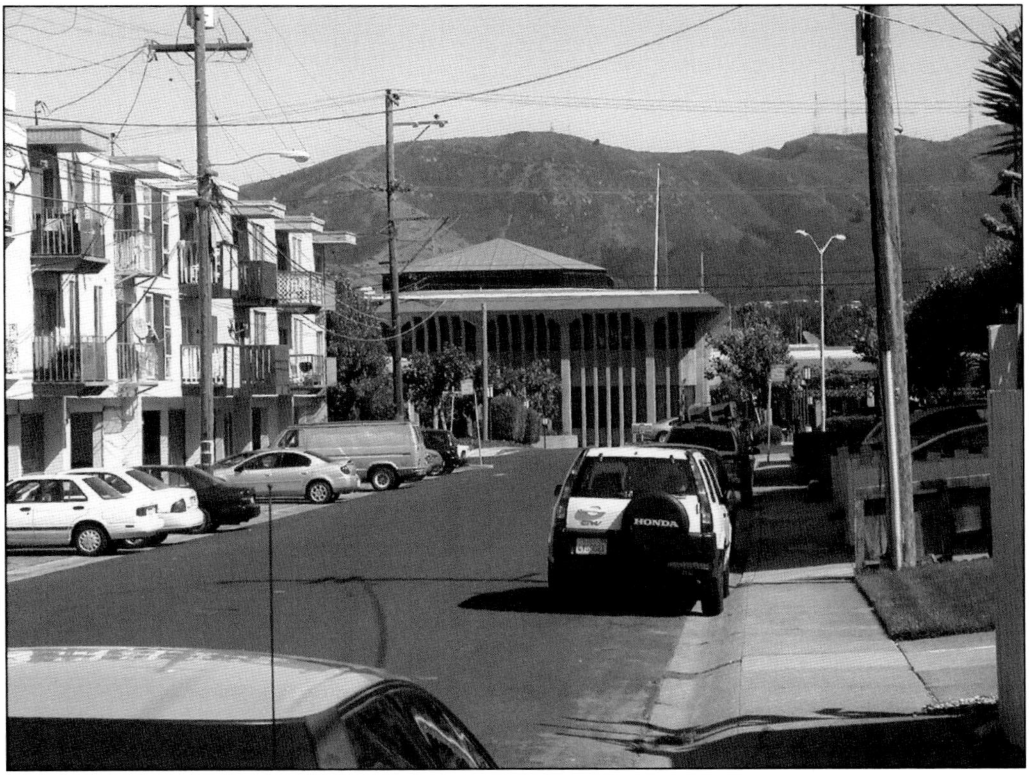

The 1967 survey concluded that there were not enough businesses to support the budget needed for an incorporated city of Broadmoor. It was suggested that Broadmoor stay unincorporated, leaving the door open for more annexations cutting off Broadmoor from Unincorporated Colma. Daly City then picked the businesses making way for a new city hall. The city hall is on lands annexed in January 1954, February 1965, and April 1971.

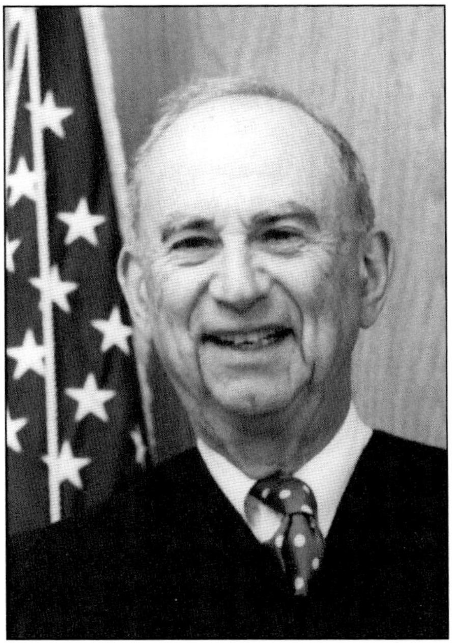

All was not lost for Broadmoor. Again due to the political activism of its citizens, the aid of state senator Quentin Kopp was enlisted. It was Senator Kopp who introduced legislation that, once it finally passed, put an effective end to piecemeal annexations by Daly City. In the bill, it states that future annexation of Broadmoor would be put to a vote of all its residents.

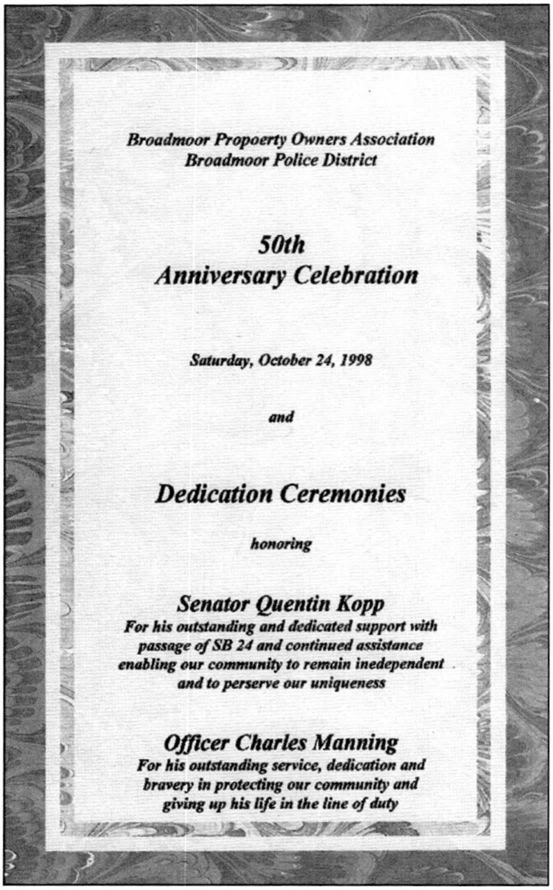

Broadmoor Propoerty Owners Association
Broadmoor Police District

50th
Anniversary Celebration

Saturday, October 24, 1998

and

Dedication Ceremonies

honoring

Senator Quentin Kopp
For his outstanding and dedicated support with passage of SB 24 and continued assistance enabling our community to remain inedependent and to perserve our uniqueness

Officer Charles Manning
For his outstanding service, dedication and bravery in protecting our community and giving up his life in the line of duty

The upside of all of this is that Broadmoor, its property owners association, and its police force remain intact and independent as ever in 2010. The challenge for Broadmoor, because it is still unincorporated, is the confusion as to what and where Broadmoor is and what, and where, it is not.

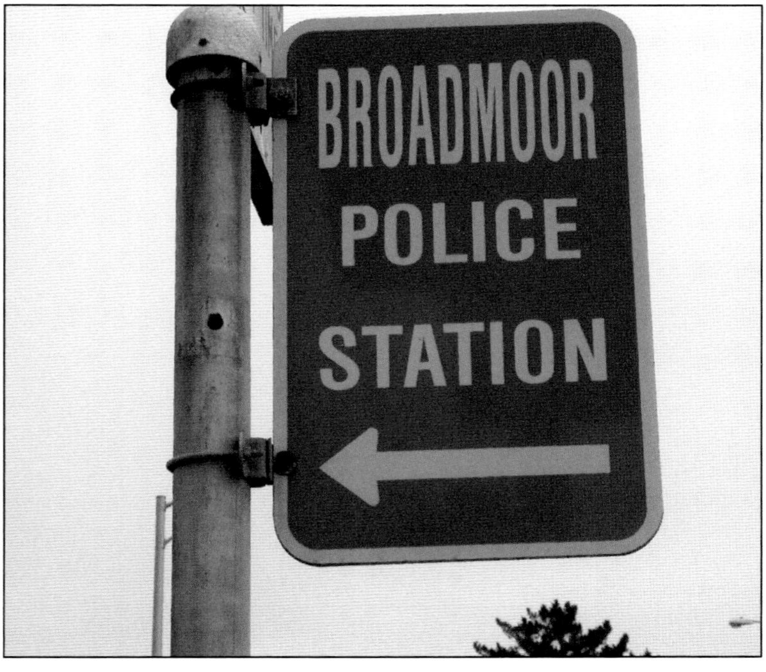

If one does a Mapquest search for the Broadmoor Community Center at 501 Eighty-seventh Street in Broadmoor, the answer is that very address in Daly City, California, 94015. This is due to the fact that the post office has much influence over G. P. S. systems and prefers that unincorporated areas be lumped into the closest, incorporated town and or city.

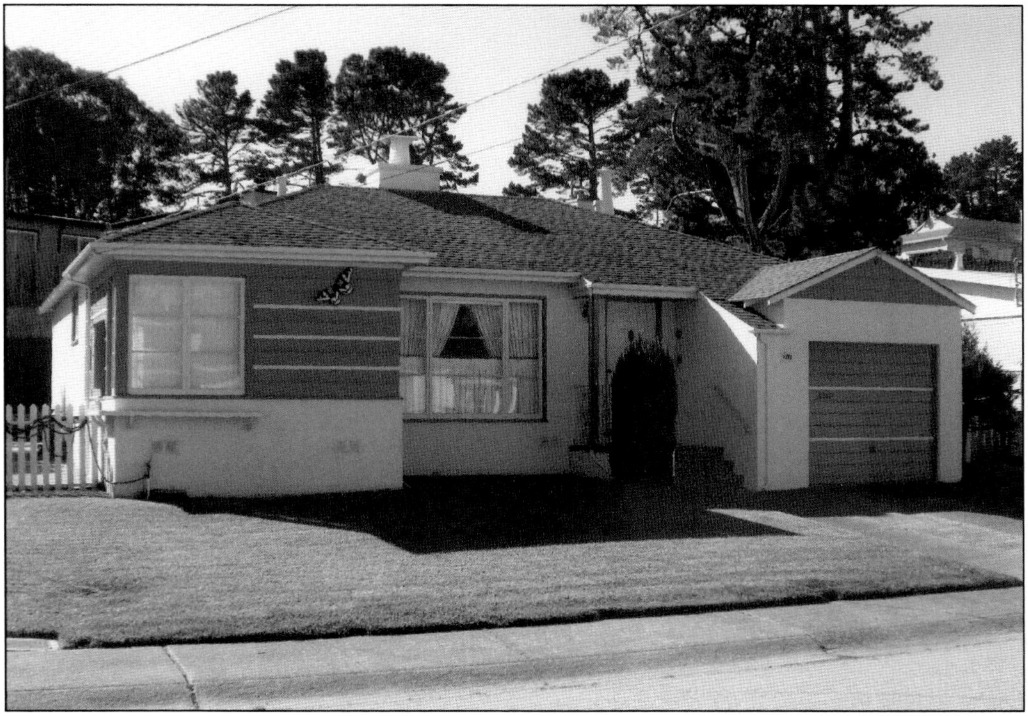

Burlingame and Hillsborough share the same zip code, 94010, yet one will get Burlingame as the town when one does a search for a Burlingame street and the same with a Hillsborough one. Both are incorporated. So, to find Broadmoor, a more old-fashioned search needs to be made. Look for the green street signs, the round curbs, and the best bet—the Stoneson built houses.

The Broadmoor Police Department
Invites you to join us in
Celebrating the Grand Opening of our
New Police Station

388-88th Street
Friday, April 30, 2004
At 1 P.M.

The Master of Ceremony
Supervisor Mike Nevin

Tours of the facility will follow
Through 4 P.M.
(refreshments will be served)

R.S.V.P. (650) 755-3840

Even after hostile annexations by its neighbors, budget cuts and all, Broadmoor Village remains independent. Here is an invitation to yet another celebration—the opening of the new police station in April 2004, proof that the community is well and moving into the future. (Courtesy Chief Love, Broadmoor Police Department.)

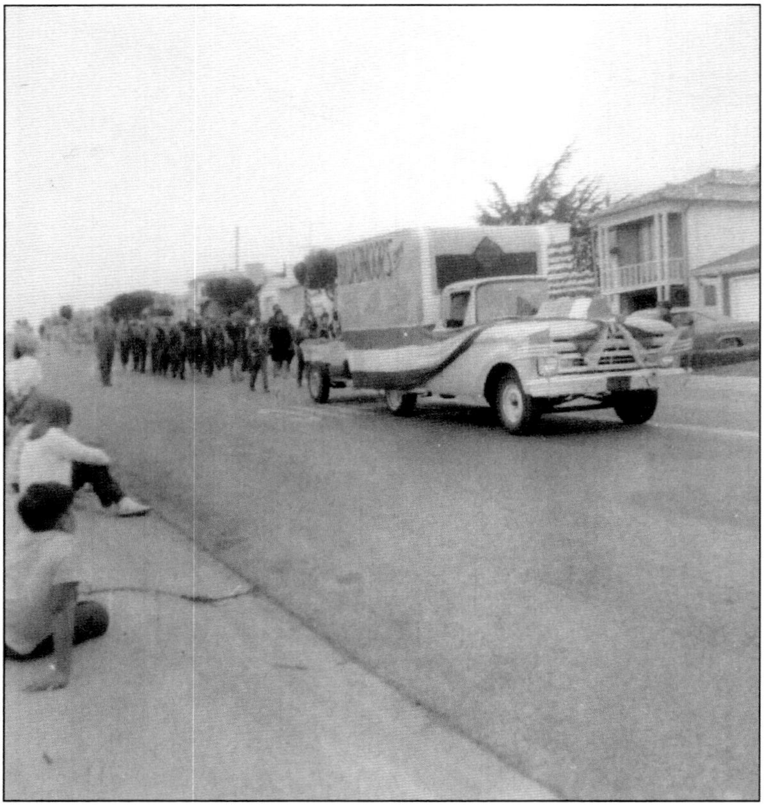

The Broadmoor Halloween parade involved much of the community. Beginning at the intersection of Stoneyford Drive and Eighty-seventh Street, the route would then follow a path down the hill on Eighty-seventh Street, turn right (south) on Washington Street, and end at Sweetwood Drive. The Carlson family got a great view from their home on 511 Eighty-seventh Street. (Courtesy Leif and Lauri Carlson.)

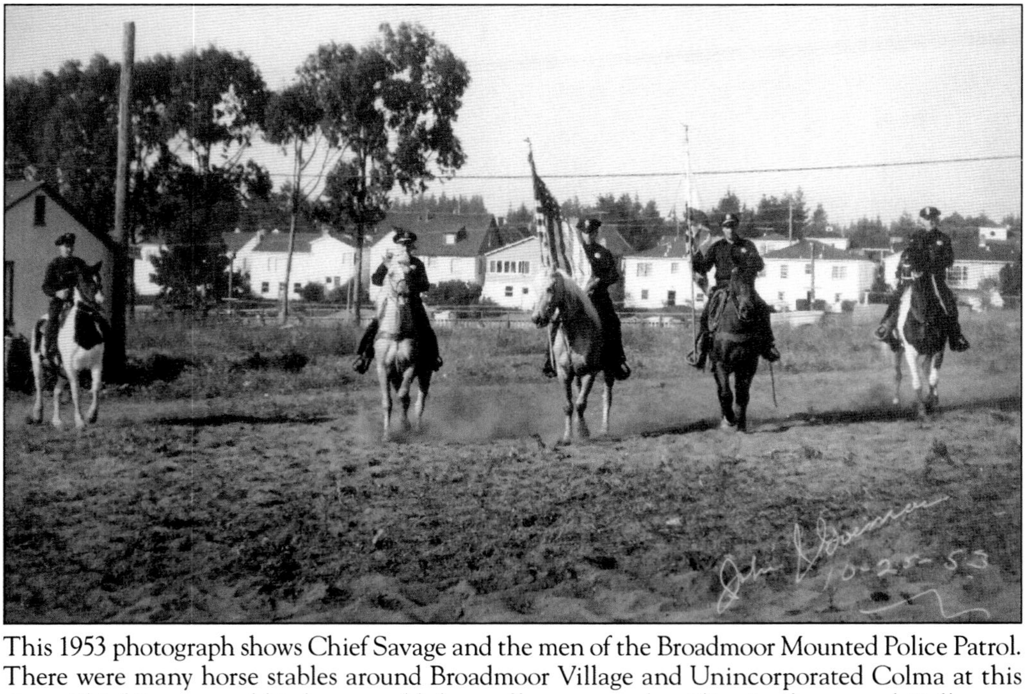

This 1953 photograph shows Chief Savage and the men of the Broadmoor Mounted Police Patrol. There were many horse stables around Broadmoor Village and Unincorporated Colma at this time. Chief Savage and his boys would show off every year by riding in the annual Halloween parade. (Courtesy Chief Love, Broadmoor Police Department.)

Six

Here and There

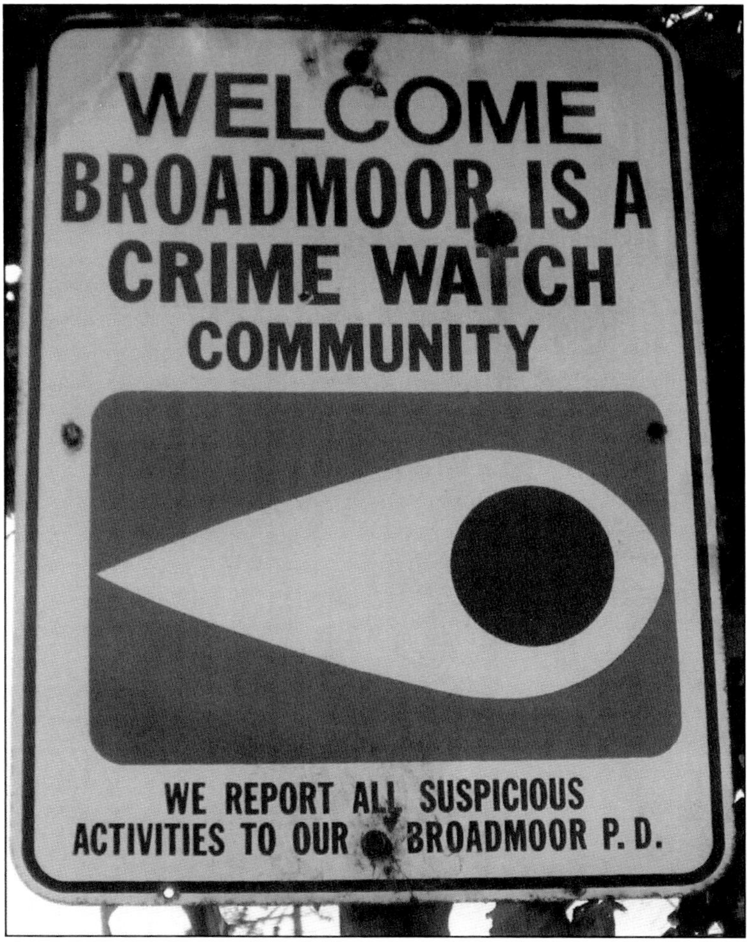

Currently the only sign that lets one know that they are in Broadmoor and is accurate is this Crime Watch sign put up by Chief Bill Noonan and the Broadmoor Police Department. It is barely visible because of the ivy growing over it, but it is located on Eighty-ninth Street right where the apartments in Daly City stop and the Stoneson houses in Broadmoor start.

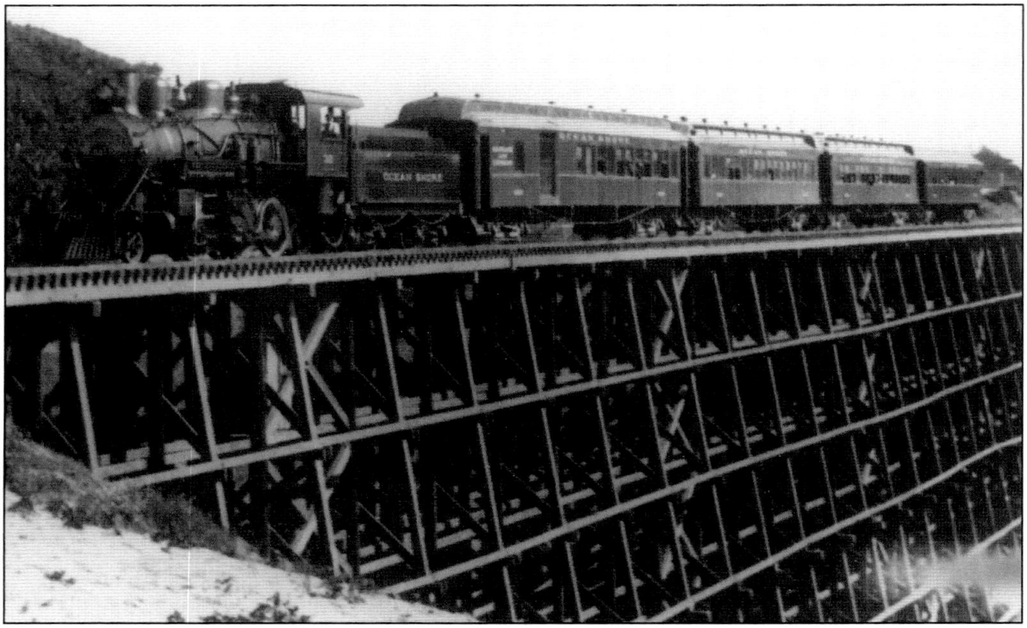

The Ocean Shore Railway, which ran through Daly City-Westlake area in 1905 and went under in 1920. Here is a train headed for San Francisco crossing a deep ravine in Daly City. The Ocean Shore Railroad called this trestle "Spring Valley Trestle Number One." It was parallel to Junipero Serra Boulevard. There were three trestles in the Spring Valley (Westlake) area. (Courtesy John Schmale.)

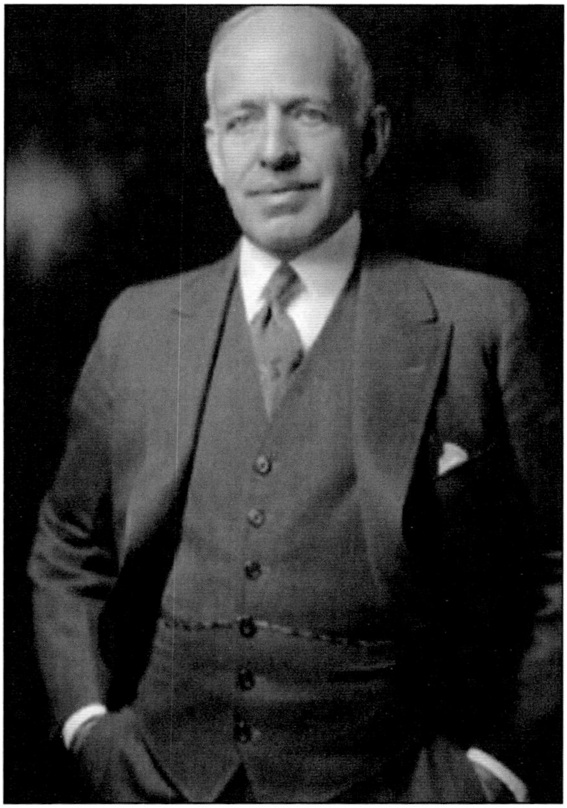

Born in 1866, Mortimer Fleishhacker was a banker who invested in lands all over California, including what would become known as Garden Village. The county subdivided this area of land in 1938 and houses on Garden Lane, and parts of Village Lane were built from 1939 to 1941 before the Stonesons came and built Broadmoor Village. (Courtesy David Fleishhacker family.)

Shown here is Mortimer's younger brother Herbert Fleishhacker, born in 1872. The San Francisco Zoo was originally named after him. The famous Olympic-size pool that was next to the zoo, now the parking lot, was also named after Herbert. (Courtesy David Fleishhacker family)

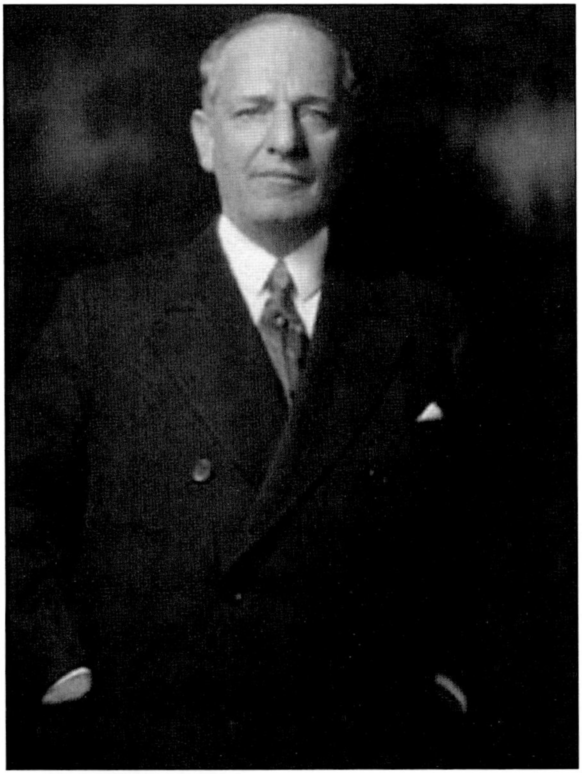

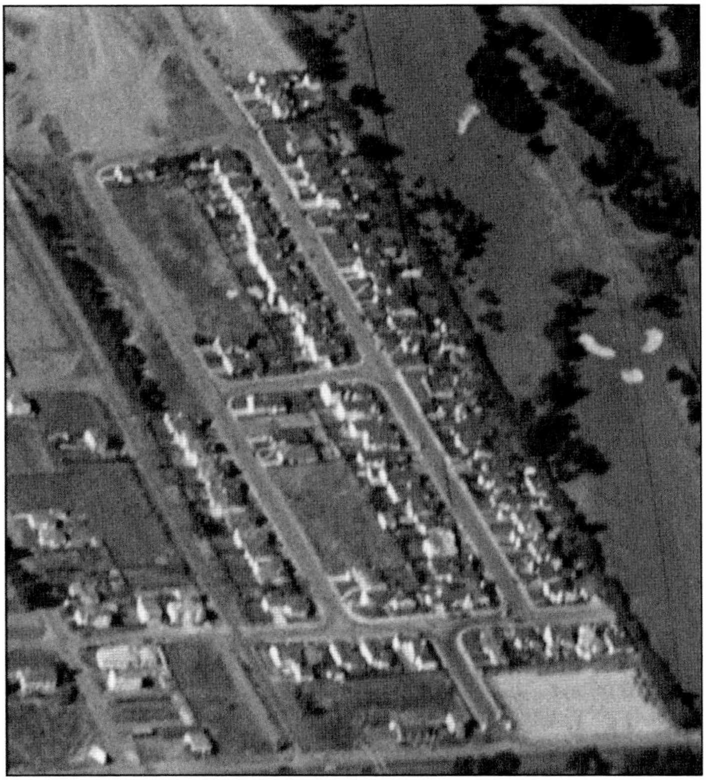

At the bottom of this photograph (east) is Junipero Serra Boulevard, which Garden Gateway intersects with. On the right, parallel to the Lake Merced Country Club, Garden Lane is full of houses, and Village Lane is only partially inhabited. Sullivan Avenue crosses the two at the bottom and Alder Lane crosses in the middle of this photograph. This was taken November 2, 1946. (Courtesy HJW Geospatial Inc. and Pacific Aerial Surveys. Oakland, California.)

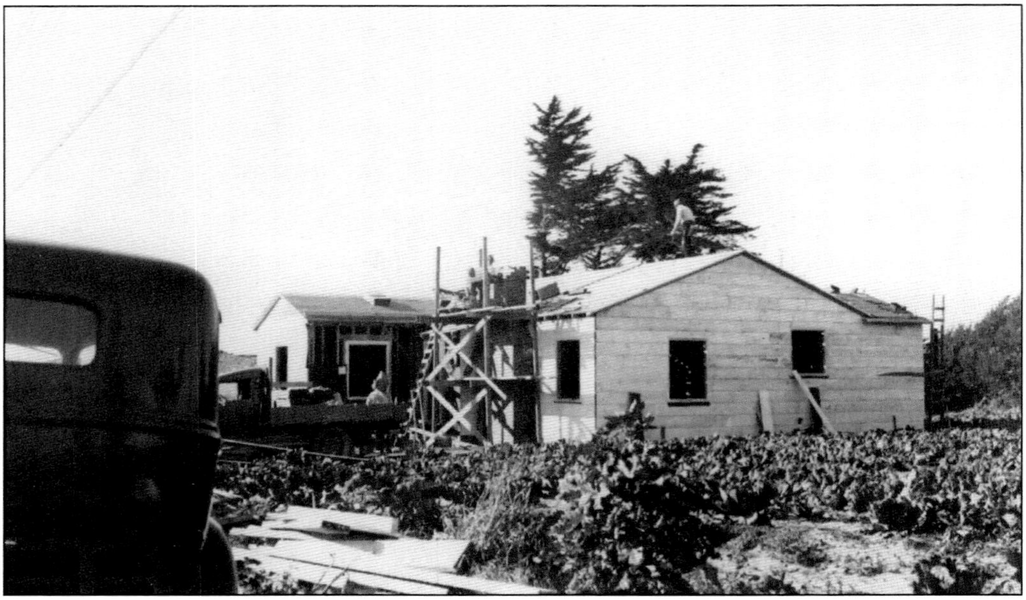

Pictured here is 19 Garden Lane being built in 1938. It is interesting to note that the house is being built in the middle of what was then a lettuce patch. These houses were a few years before the Stoneson Company built Broadmoor Village. According to locals Ray Geribaldi and Tom Callan, the Paul Waters Company built Garden Village. (Courtesy Janette Rasor.)

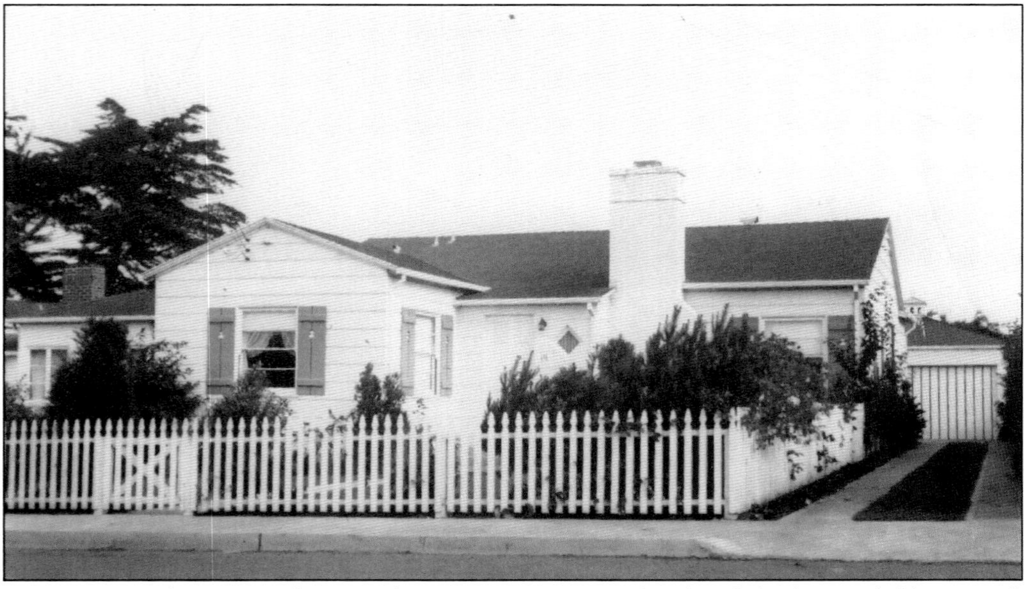

Here is 19 Garden Lane a few years later, once it was completed and the lettuce field removed. This photograph, provided by Janette Rasor, shows the home of her future husband and his family. Garden Village was, until the 1980s, always mentioned as a community separate from Broadmoor Village. To this day the owners of the Paul Waters built houses are not members of the Broadmoor Property Owners Association. (Courtesy Janette Rasor.)

On February 23, 1948, when this picture was taken, houses are being built to fill out Village Lane. These are Stoneson houses. In both photographs, Broadmoor Shopping Center along Junipero Serra Boulevard is missing. (Courtesy HJW Geospatial Inc. and Pacific Aerial Surveys. Oakland, California.)

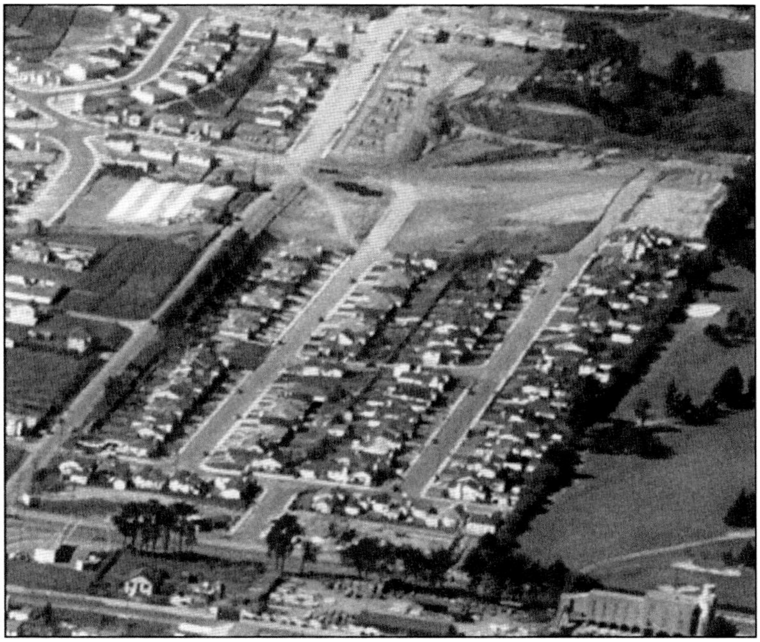

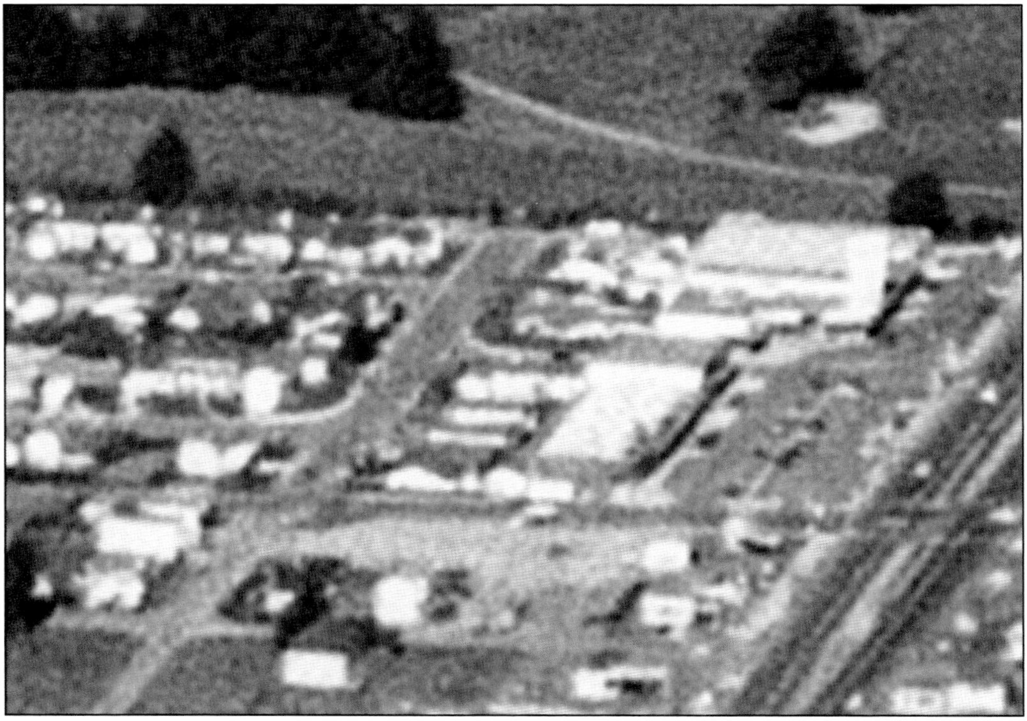

This photograph, taken February 19, 1955, shows Broadmoor Shopping Center. Stoneson has completed houses on the empty lots of Village Lane, not pictured. Only the residents in the Stoneson Houses on the west part of Village Lane are, to this day, part of the Broadmoor Property Owners Association. (Courtesy HJW Geospatial Inc. and Pacific Aerial Surveys. Oakland, California.)

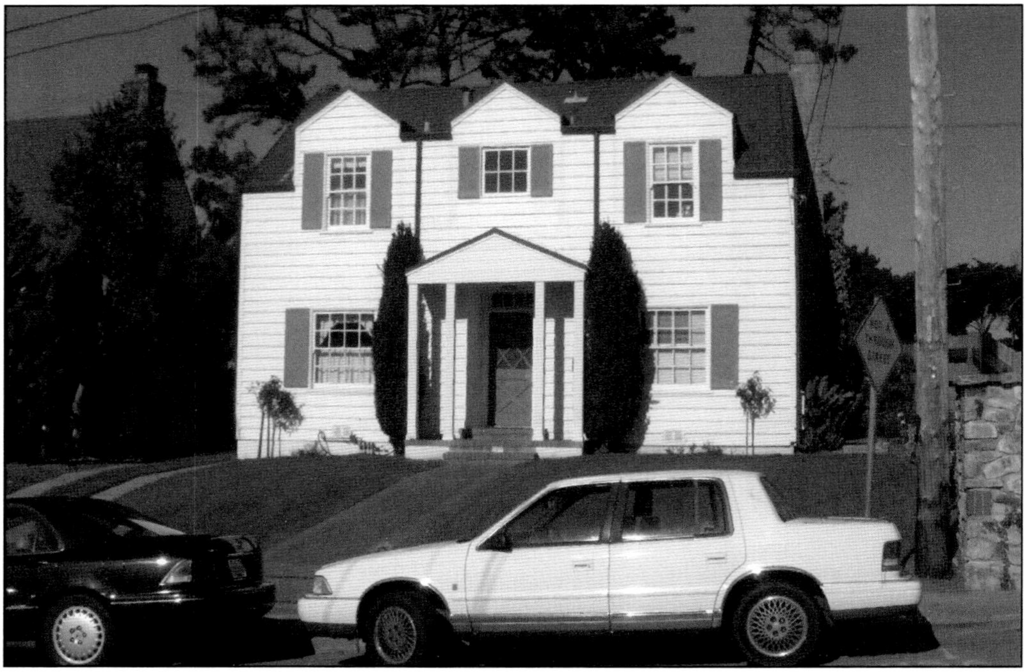

This is a typical example of a house on Garden Lane. In newspaper articles, while Broadmoor always got the headlines, Garden Village and Sterling Park are mentioned as separate communities in Unincorporated Colma. In 2010, because it is part of a contiguous unincorporated land mass that included Broadmoor, the county now labels these lands of Garden Village as Broadmoor.

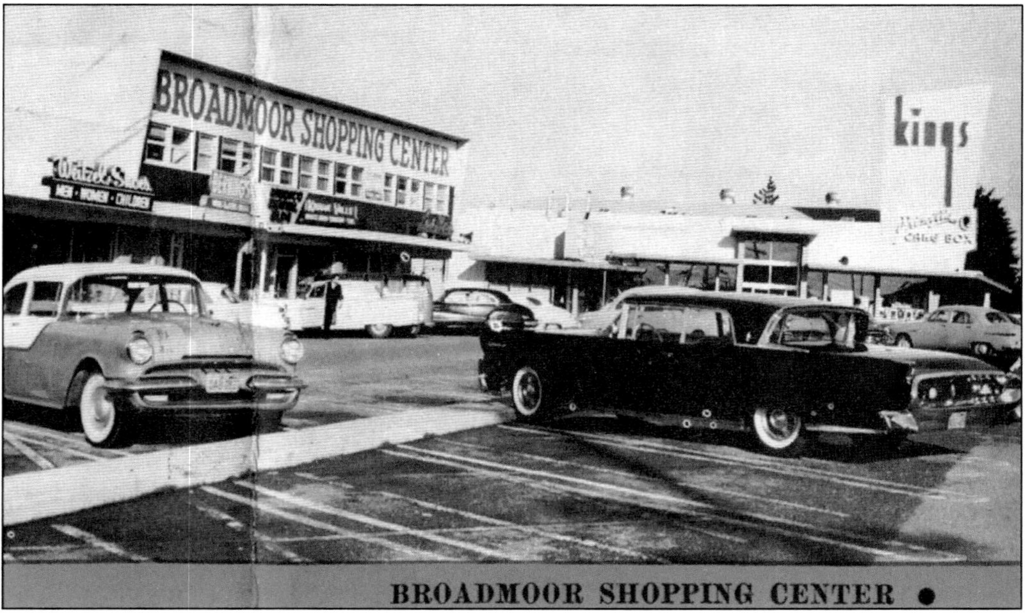

The confusion over where Broadmoor Village is located is not helped by the fact that many things are declared to be in Broadmoor but are not. The Broadmoor Police Department was in Unincorporated Colma and now is actually in Daly City. An advertisement from the Daly City Chamber shows the Broadmoor Shopping Center, built in 1948 on land that was annexed by Daly City in 1931. (Courtesy San Francisco Public Library.)

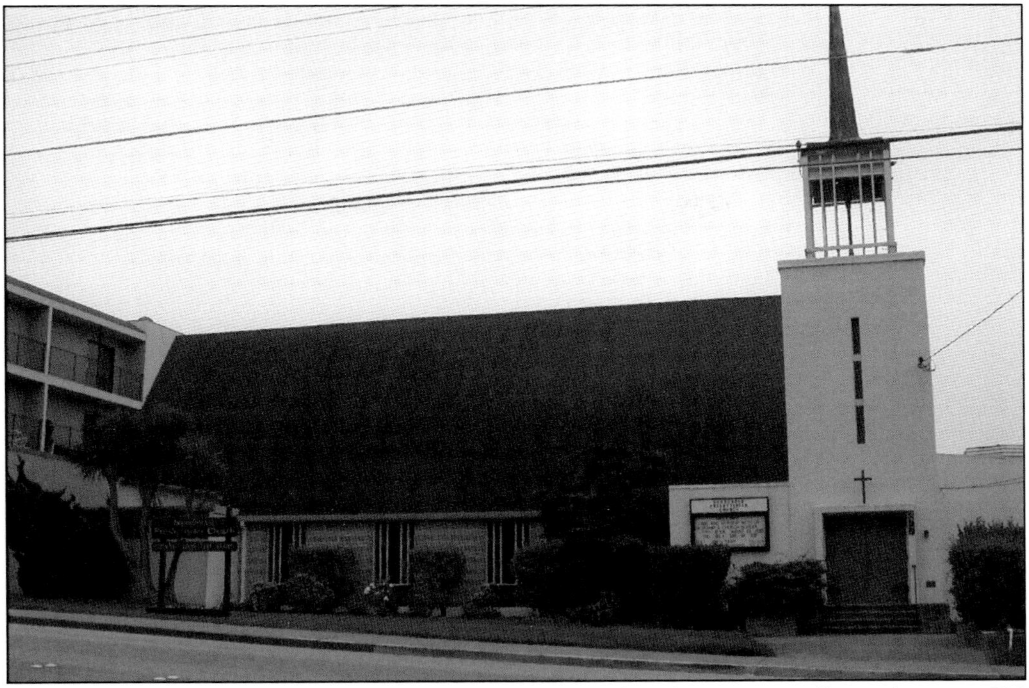

When the congregation of the Broadmoor Presbyterian Church met originally in a house at 820 Larchmont Drive, they were in Broadmoor Village. When the church was finally built and opened at its current address on Eighty-seventh Street, they were in Unincorporated Colma, which has since been annexed by Daly City.

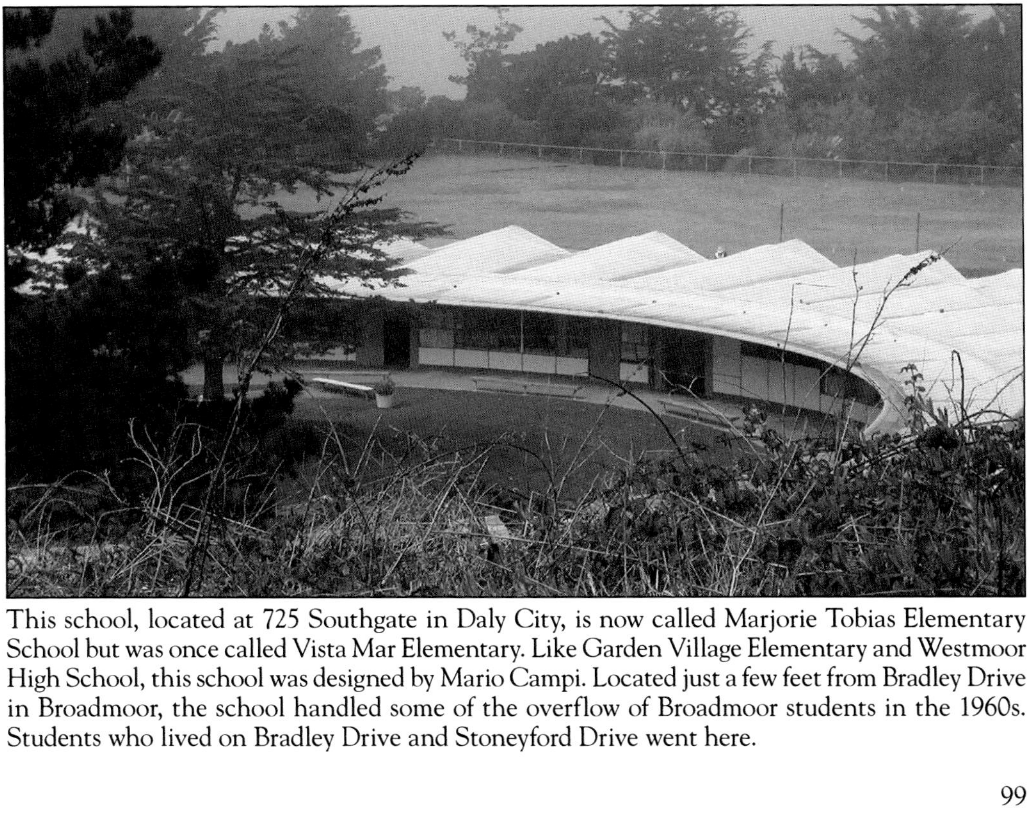

This school, located at 725 Southgate in Daly City, is now called Marjorie Tobias Elementary School but was once called Vista Mar Elementary. Like Garden Village Elementary and Westmoor High School, this school was designed by Mario Campi. Located just a few feet from Bradley Drive in Broadmoor, the school handled some of the overflow of Broadmoor students in the 1960s. Students who lived on Bradley Drive and Stoneyford Drive went here.

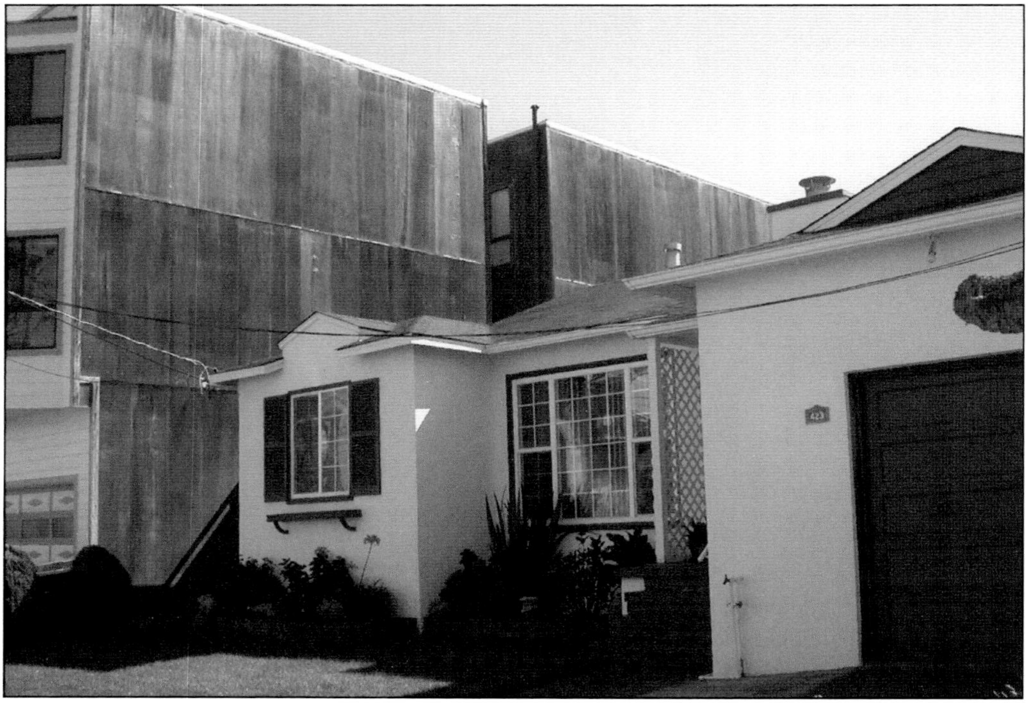

On the east side of Broadmoor Village midway through the blocks of Eighty-eighth, Eighty-ninth, Ninetieth, and Ninety-first Streets, the Stoneson houses stop and apartments begin. This is also where Broadmoor Village stops and Daly City begins. There are no clear markings or signs, even if one uses the street signs, whether green or blue.

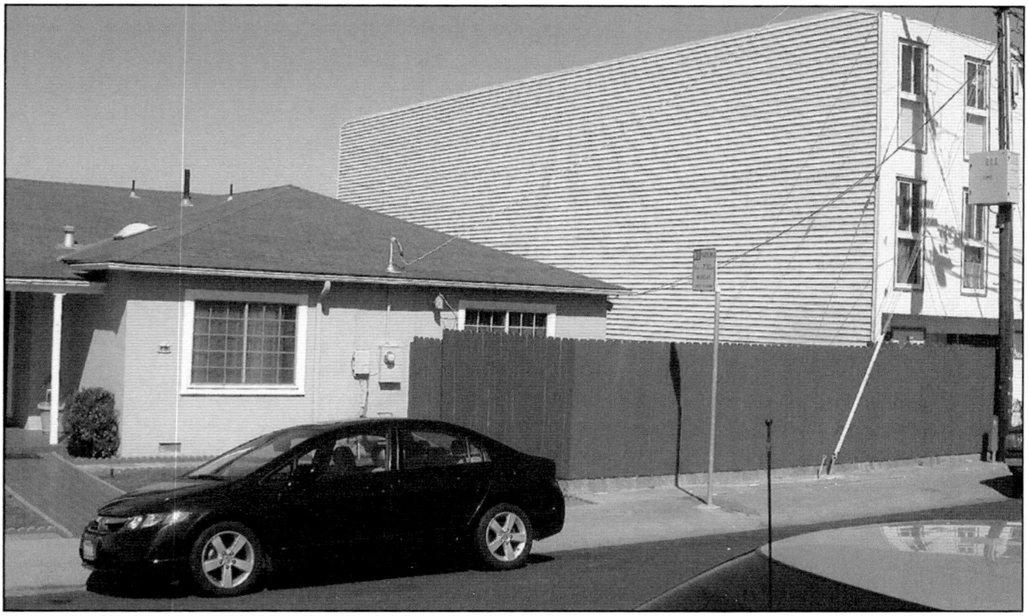

Here is another block and another set of apartments that are the result of yet another annexation. All of these streets look the same midway though the blocks. The houses are the only real marker of the east boundary line of Broadmoor Village from what is now Daly City, what was once Unincorporated Colma.

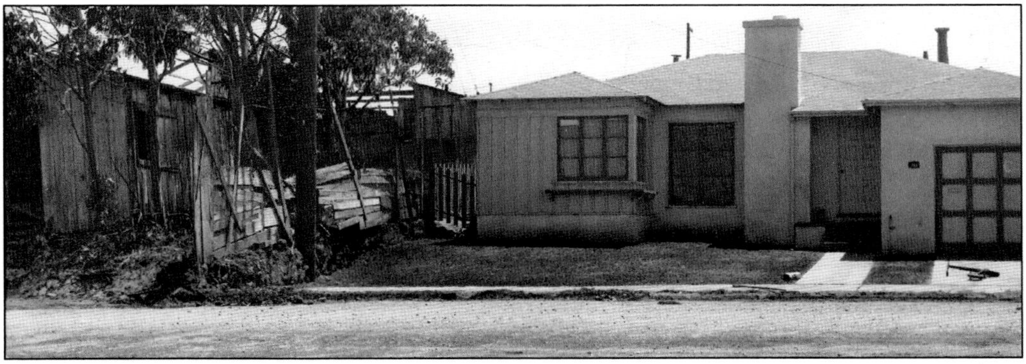

Broadmoor Village was, and is, a subdivision in Unincorporated Colma. Back in 1948 on these very same blocks of Eighty-eighth, Eighty-ninth, Ninetieth, and Ninety-first Streets, it was not apartments that met the house midway in the block, but old decaying barns from hog farms long abandoned. (Courtesy San Francisco Public Library and the *San Francisco News-Call Bulletin.*)

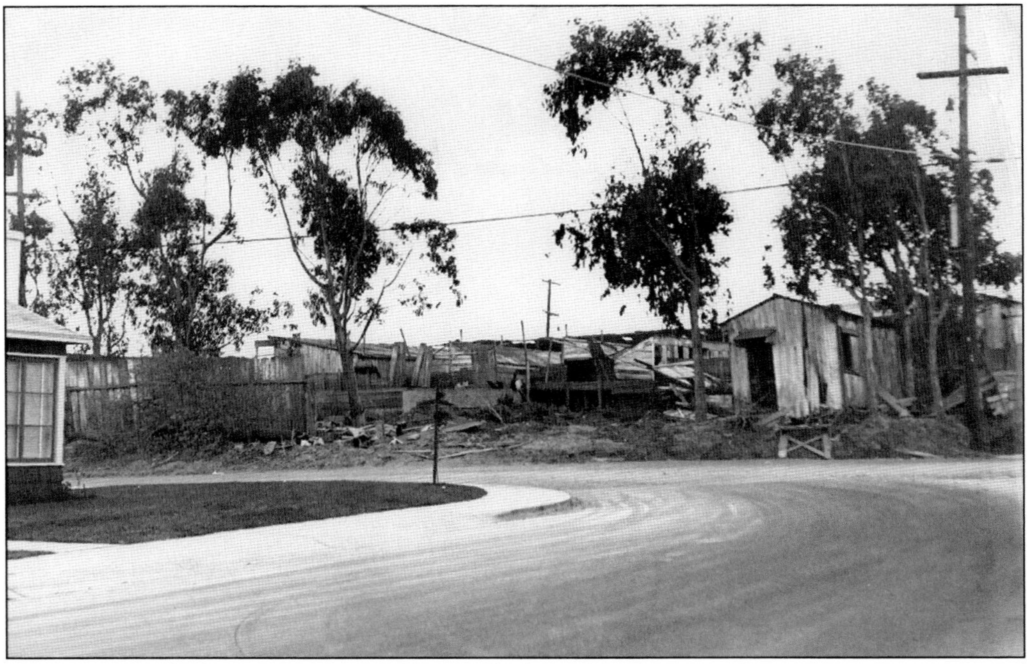

Here is a better look at the dilapidated barns, sheds, and feeding pens from 1948. Unincorporated Colma was farmland well into the 1960s. Yet these pictures show Broadmoor as a state-of-the-art community for its time. These early photographs also show that Unincorporated Colma, the farmland, is not Broadmoor Village. (Courtesy San Francisco Public Library and the *San Francisco News-Call Bulletin.*)

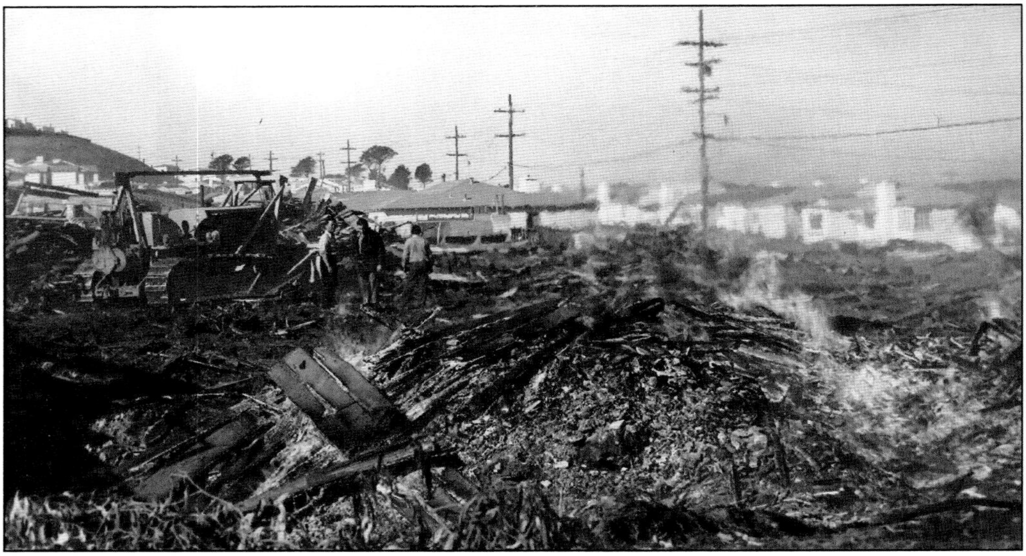

In 1948 and 1949, the neighbors banded together to burn and bulldoze the old obsolete farm buildings as they were deteriorating; the wood was rotting and roofs were caving in. These old barns were also rat infested causing great concern for the health and safety of properties and children. (Courtesy San Francisco Public Library and the *San Francisco News-Call Bulletin.*)

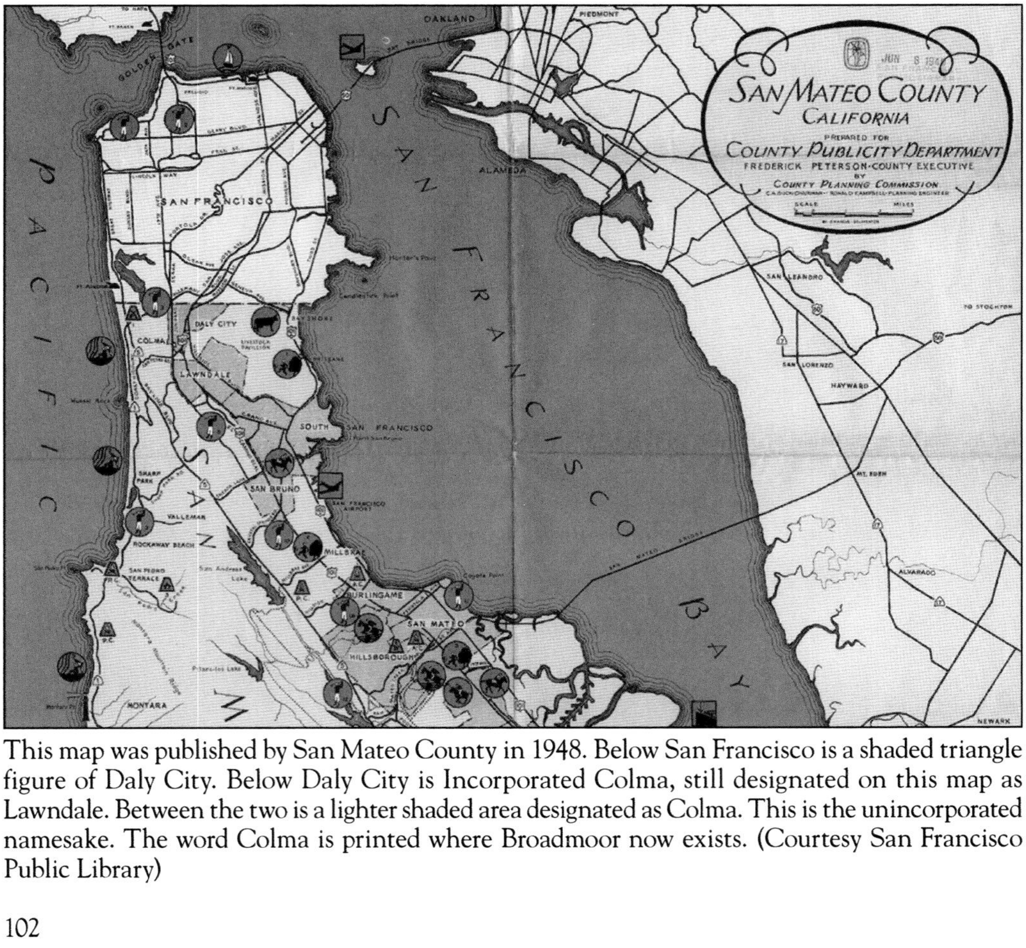

This map was published by San Mateo County in 1948. Below San Francisco is a shaded triangle figure of Daly City. Below Daly City is Incorporated Colma, still designated on this map as Lawndale. Between the two is a lighter shaded area designated as Colma. This is the unincorporated namesake. The word Colma is printed where Broadmoor now exists. (Courtesy San Francisco Public Library)

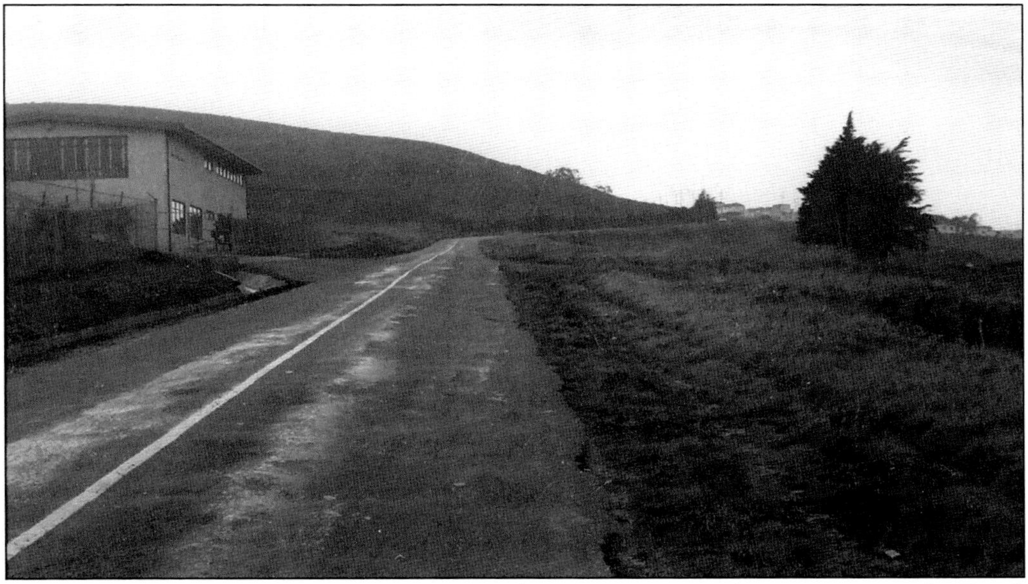

This photograph was taken in October 1957. This street was once known as San Pedro Road, renamed Edgemar Road. Today it is known as Eastmoor Avenue. This photograph is looking west, up the hill where the road will intersect with Gilman Drive and Randall Court in Broadmoor. At the top is farmland that was Unincorporated Colma annexed by Daly City in January 1956. Now it is Westmoor High School. (Courtesy Eloisa Avendano-Johnsen.)

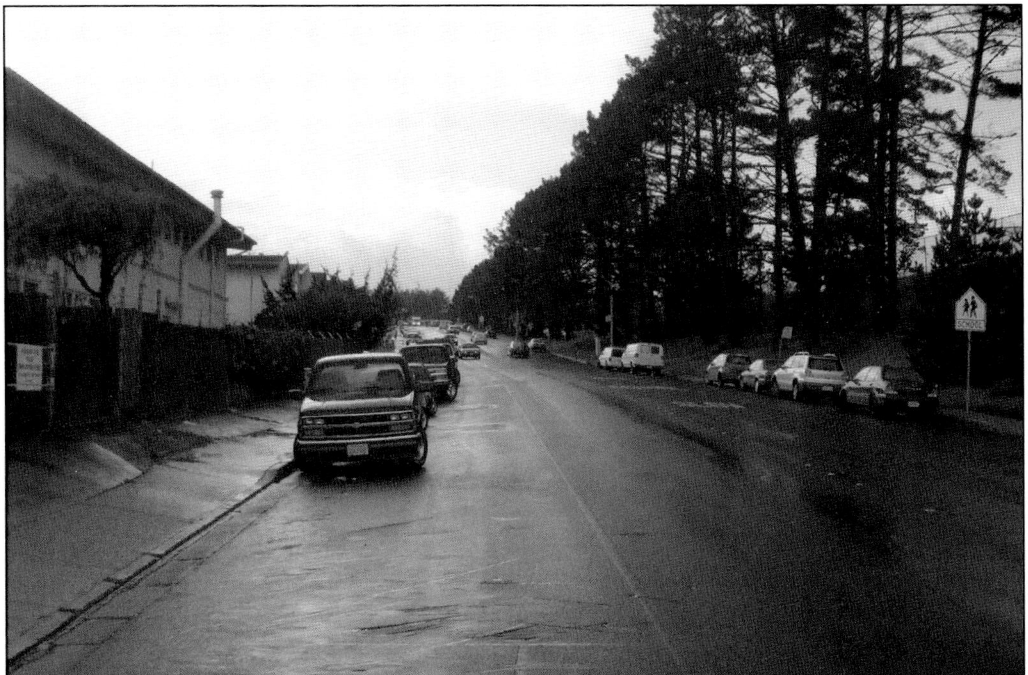

Here is Eastmoor Avenue in 2010. The Pacific, Gas, and Electric Power station is still there on the left. Though the station is designated as the Colma Service Center, the actual address is 450 Eastmoor Avenue, Daly City. Across the street and up the hill a little ways is M. Pauline Brown Elementary School.

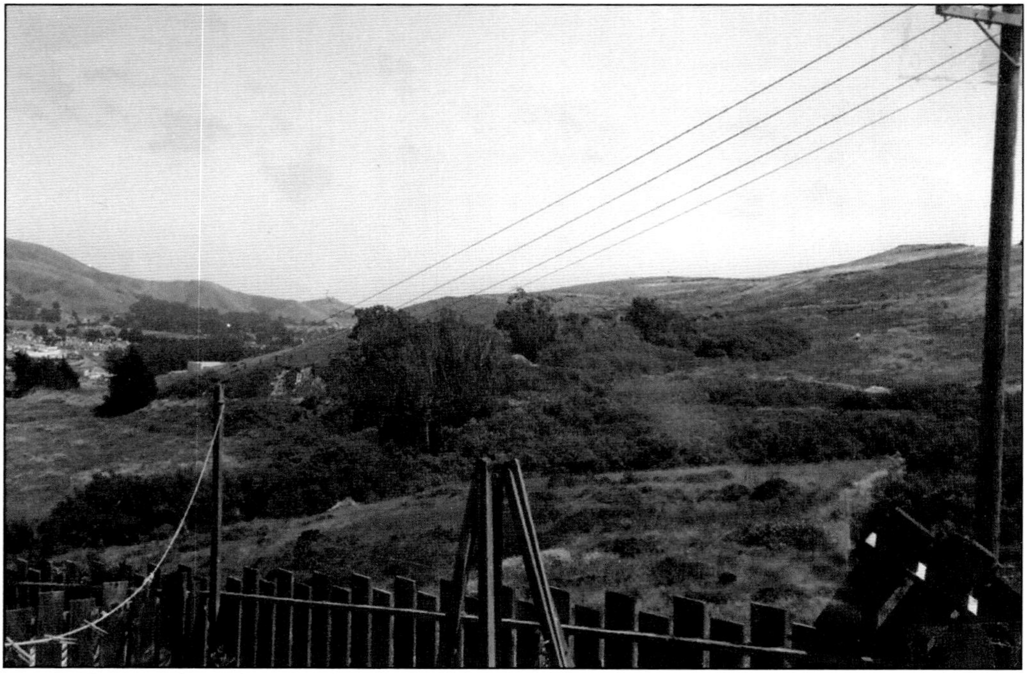

Here is the view from the Avendano house at 1069 Gilman Drive in October 1957. Colma is visible in the distance; the rest is just countryside left in its natural state. This view was typical at the north, west, and south edges of Broadmoor. At the time, the Avendanos also lived next door to future Daly City historians Ken and Bunny Gillespie. (Courtesy Eloisa Avendano-Johnsen.)

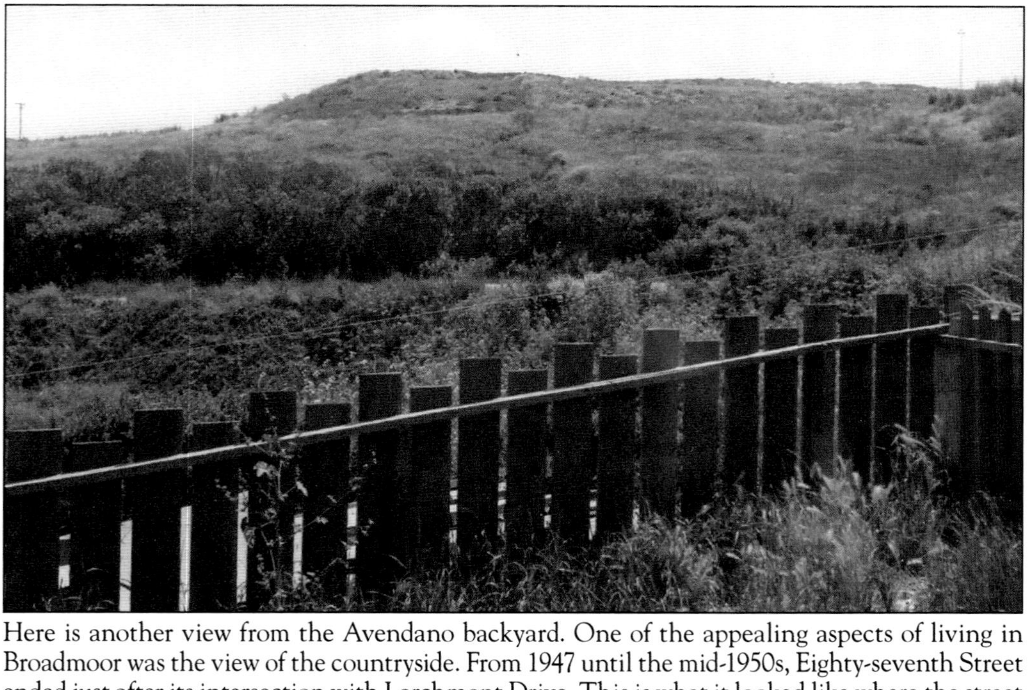

Here is another view from the Avendano backyard. One of the appealing aspects of living in Broadmoor was the view of the countryside. From 1947 until the mid-1950s, Eighty-seventh Street ended just after its intersection with Larchmont Drive. This is what it looked like where the street stopped. The ends of Beechwood Drive, Stoneyford Drive, Bradley Drive, and Wildwood Avenue all looked the same. (Courtesy Eloisa Avendano-Johnsen.)

Here is a copy of a Herb Caen column, published January 4, 1994, that outraged many of the independence-thinking citizens of Broadmoor. In it, Herb Caen refers to Broadmoor Village as "Little Daly City." While most Broadmoor Village and Daly City residents prefer to live in a spirit of cooperation and be peaceful neighbors, no one wants to live in the shadow of someone or something else. (Courtesy Terrie Powers.)

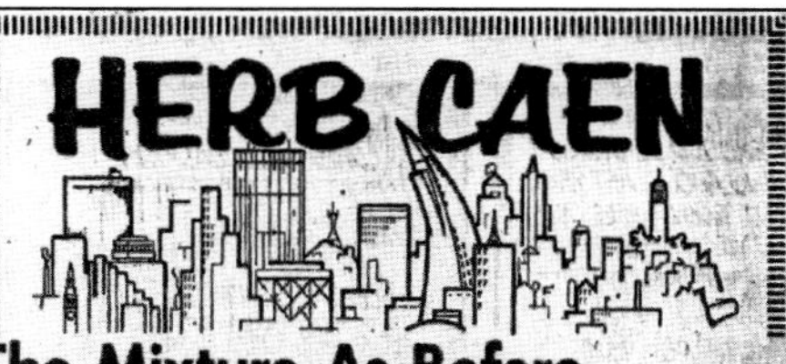

The Mixture As Before

HERE IT is 1994, or thereabouts, and what's the population of San Francisco? If you don't care, you betta off: on the Golden Gate Bridge, heading south, the sign reads 711,407; at the intersection of 280 and San Jose Ave., it's 719,200; on the county line at Junipero Serra, we have 728,700, and on the Bay Bridge, coming thisaway, the count is exactly 715,674, and you know what? I'll bet they're all wrong . . . Add Sanfranciscana, this from Jim Toland, resident historian: Ever wondered why little Daly City has streets with such big and unlikely numbers as 87th, 88th, 89th and 90th? Because early S.F. planners mapped out numbered streets all the way to South S.F., figuring the areas in between would be incorporated into the city and county of S.F. That should have happened but didn't, and so we have San Mateo . . . I noted recently that if you want to get the cross street for an address on downtown Market and Mission, you subtract four — example: The Chron, at 901 Mission is at Fifth — and you know why? Because after the '06 quakefire, four blocks of bay fill were added to downtown . . . Jimmy Barnes of Smith River, up in Del Norte, poses a mystery: Minna, Tehama, Clara and Louisa are historic South o' Market alleys, are they not? They is. So he forwards a map of Brooklyn and, near Ft. Hamilton, there they are again, all in a row: Minna, Tehama, Clara and Louisa. Howcum, especially when Tehama is an Indian name? All solutions gracefully received, on tippy-toes.

* * *

Feb. 5th 1994

Dear Mr. Caen,

As a resident of Broadmoor Village, I must correct your reference to 87th, 88th, 89th, and 90th streets in what you and Jim Toland claim to be in "little Daly City". I called your office the day the column appeared (Jan. 4th 1994) to make mention of this error and was told we weren't on the map!

The afore mentioned streets are part of Broadmoor Village, an unincorporated community. I'm enclosing a map so you can clear up this misunderstanding. Please make the necessary corrections.

Herb, we are not still fighting the Indians (oh! Excuse indigenous people) here in Broadmoor Village. We have a wonderful little community and would like to keep our identity alive.

Thank You,

Mrs. Terrie A. Powers

Here is a letter sent to Herb Caen by one such outraged citizen. Terrie Powers decided to be proactive and vent her concerns about the oversight. Ms. Powers lives on Eighty-ninth Street in the house she grew up in and is a graduate of Westmoor High School class of 1969. (Courtesy Terrie Powers.)

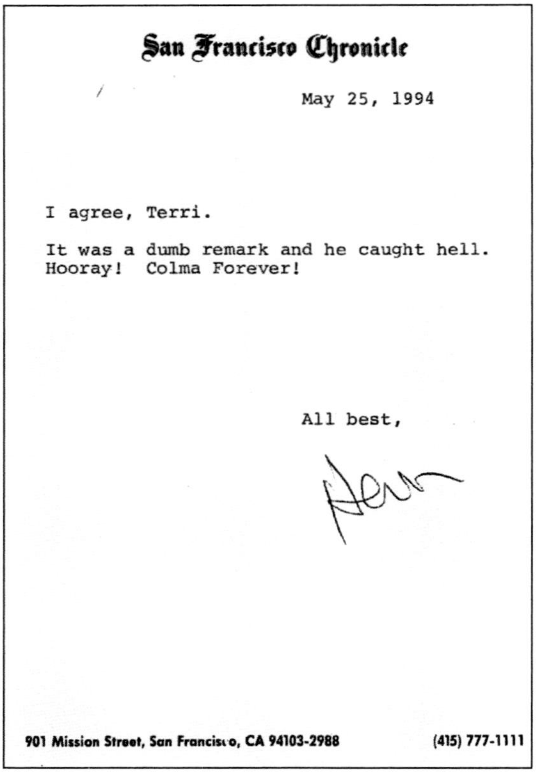

San Francisco Chronicle

May 25, 1994

I agree, Terri.

It was a dumb remark and he caught hell.
Hooray! Colma Forever!

All best,

Herb

901 Mission Street, San Francisco, CA 94103-2988 (415) 777-1111

Here is a copy of the letter of apology to Ms. Powers from Herb Caen himself. It would appear, however, that even after the complaint, Mr. Caen did not take the time to do his homework, as he fails to mention Broadmoor Village in his letter. It cannot be discerned from his phrase if "Colma forever" refers to the town or the unincorporated namesake. (Courtesy Terrie Powers.)

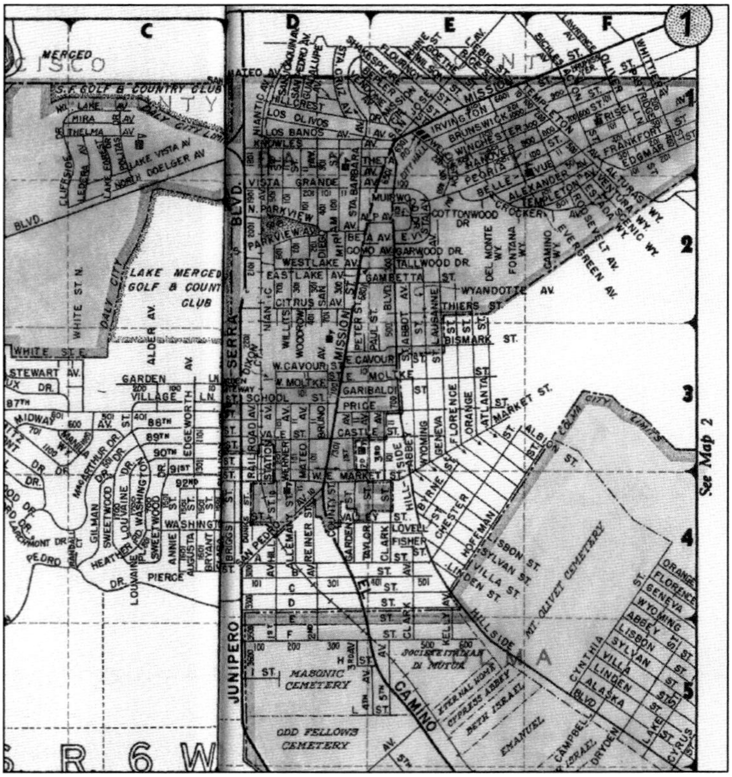

In this 1949 Thomas Brothers map, the shaded area to the southeast, bottom right corner, is incorporated Colma, formerly Lawndale. The shaded corner to the northeast, upper right corner is Daly City. The white area in the middle is Unincorporated Colma with Broadmoor on the left. The shaded area directly north of Broadmoor is newly annexed land where Westlake will be built. (Courtesy San Francisco Public Library.)

Seven

AROUND TOWN

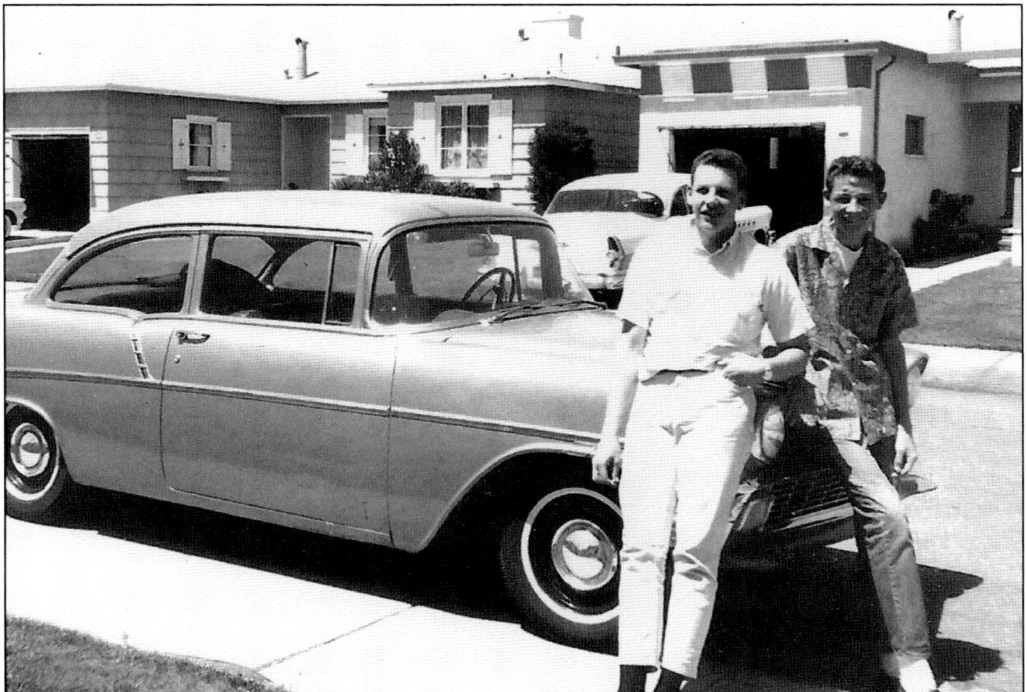

Though Broadmoor Village is not an incorporated town or city, it has its citizens and areas of interest. Here is a picture from Linda Borge, who lived on Thornhill Drive. These are newer houses in the subdivision, and the design of these Stoneson houses is slightly different. Note the garages. (Courtesy Linda and Tony Borge.)

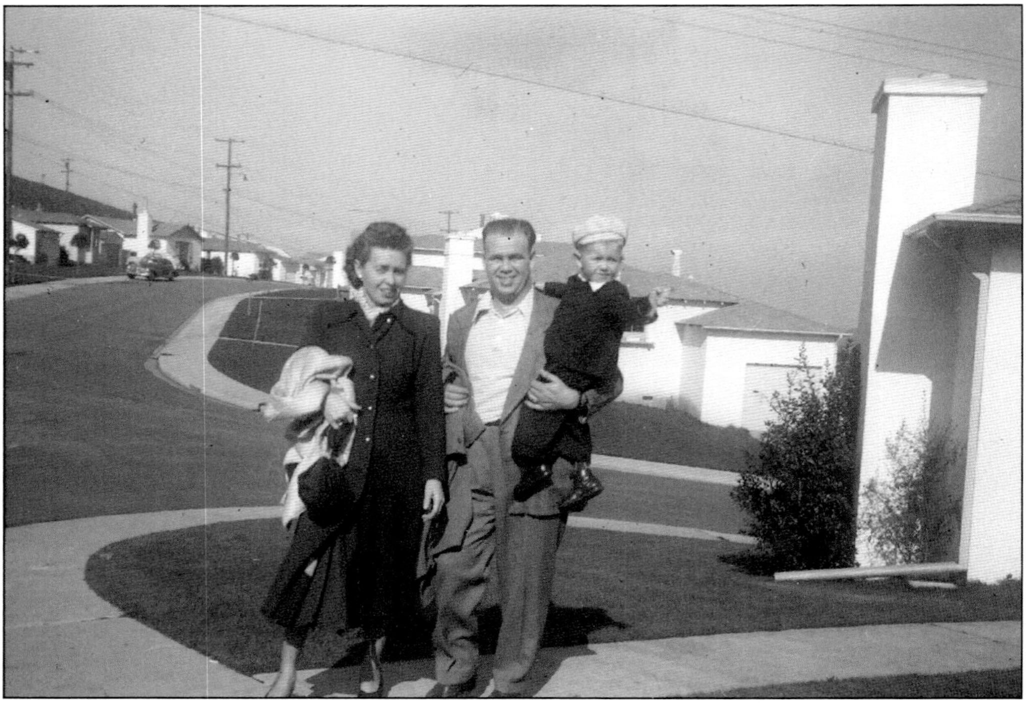

Pictured here are Ted and Pauline Christopherson with their eldest son, Rob, in 1946. This picture was taken outside their then new home at 1660 Sweetwood Drive in Broadmoor Village. They are the typical family who moved into Broadmoor Village; young parents, mostly veterans of the U.S. forces, with young children. (Courtesy Roy Christopherson.)

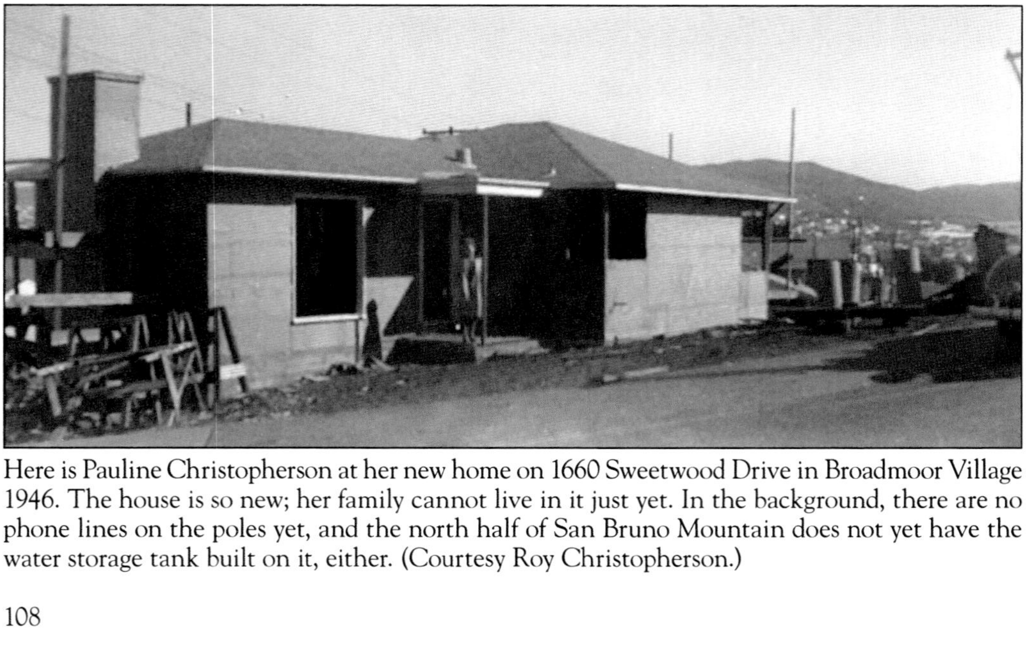

Here is Pauline Christopherson at her new home on 1660 Sweetwood Drive in Broadmoor Village 1946. The house is so new; her family cannot live in it just yet. In the background, there are no phone lines on the poles yet, and the north half of San Bruno Mountain does not yet have the water storage tank built on it, either. (Courtesy Roy Christopherson.)

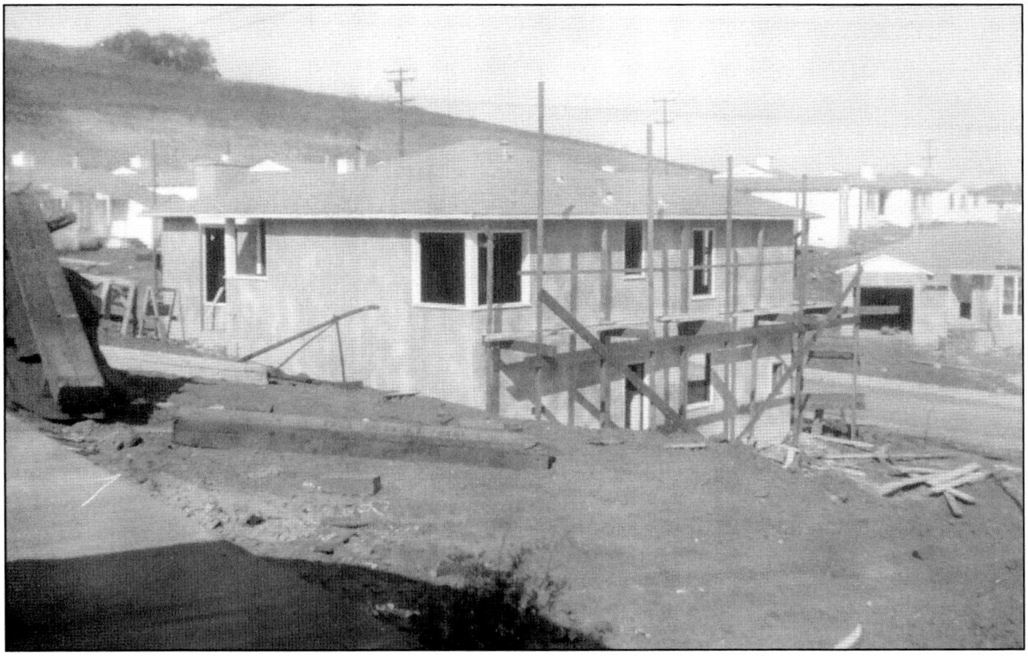

Here is 1660 Sweetwood Drive facing north. The road and house on the right side with garage door open is on Heather Road. The houses in the background to the left and then to the right, above the Heather Road house are all on Sweetwood Drive. The hill of grass and shrubs to the upper left will eventually be Gilman Drive. (Courtesy Roy Christopherson.)

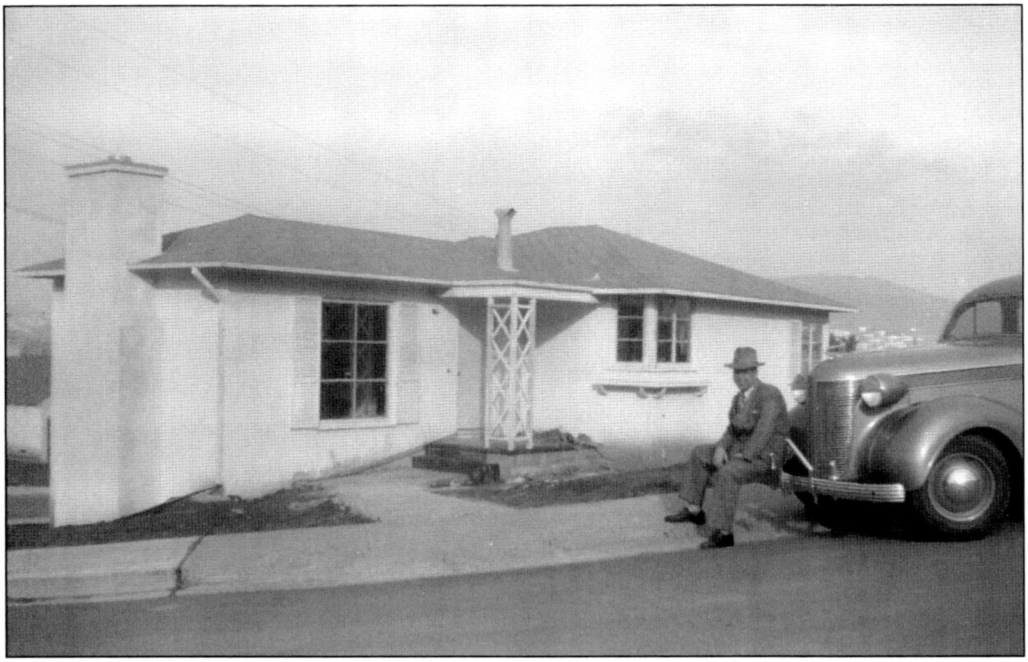

Here is Ted Christopherson in front of the almost completed house. Christopherson was in the Army Air Corps during World War II and served in the Asia-Pacific theater. He was another veteran wanting to make a better life for himself and his family. It also helped that he was the nephew of Harry and Ellis Stoneson. (Courtesy Roy Christopherson.)

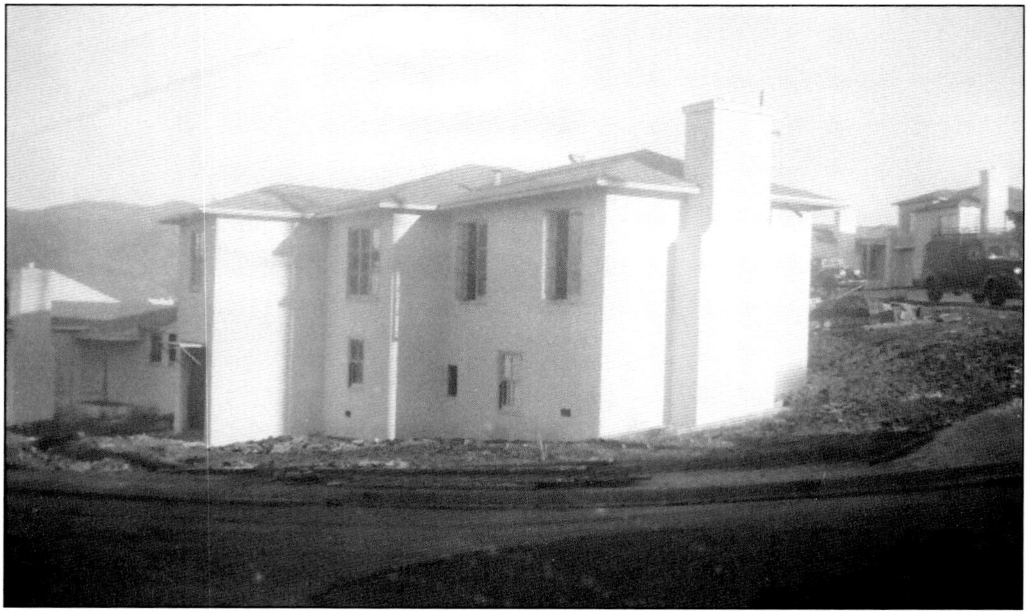

The Christopherson house was at the corner of Sweetwood Drive and Heather Road. It is not an exact 90 degree intersection; it more or less wraps around the house giving the illusion that the house has two front sides. Here is the actual backside on Heather Road. There are, as yet, no sidewalks and no transmission towers yet built on San Bruno Mountain. (Courtesy Roy Christopherson.)

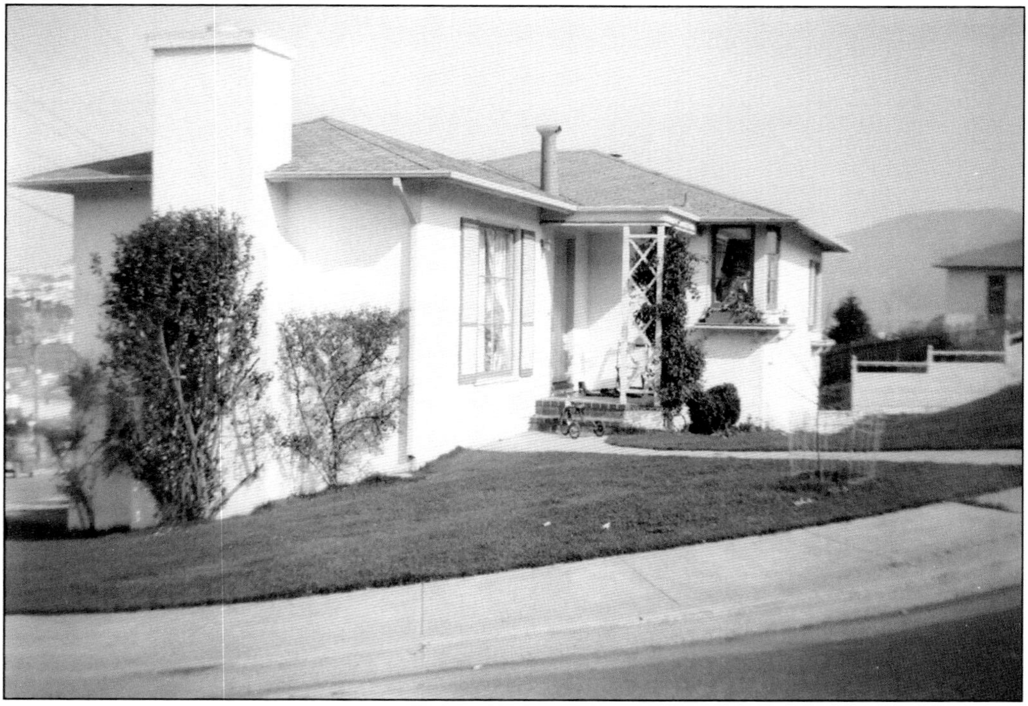

Here is 1660 Sweetwood Drive looking east. The house is completed, the lawn is in, the sidewalks and streets are paved, and the fences are up. Most of the Stoneson houses were one-story ranchers with an occasional bedroom above the garage. This is one of the very few two-story houses originally built by the Stonesons in Broadmoor. (Courtesy Roy Christopherson.)

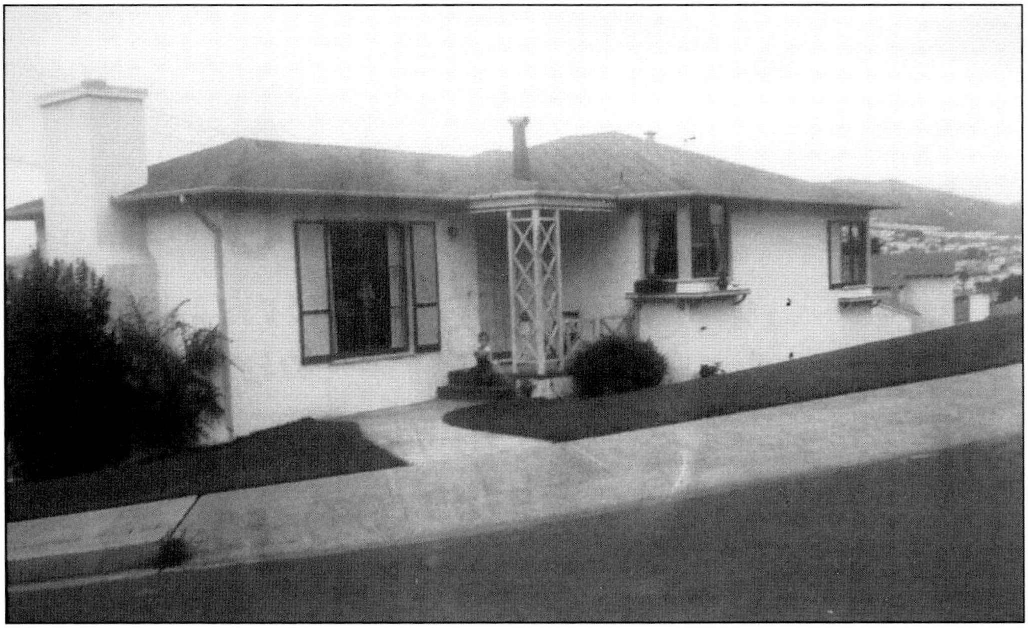

Here is another photograph of the finished house with young Robert on the porch. The fog must be in, a very common occurrence, because there are not many shadows. The wrap-around effect of the intersection the Christopherson house is at is not uncommon in Broadmoor Village. Similar are the intersections of Nimitz Drive and Eighty-seventh Streets (the west intersection) and Larchmont Drive at MacArthur Drive. (Courtesy Roy Christopherson.)

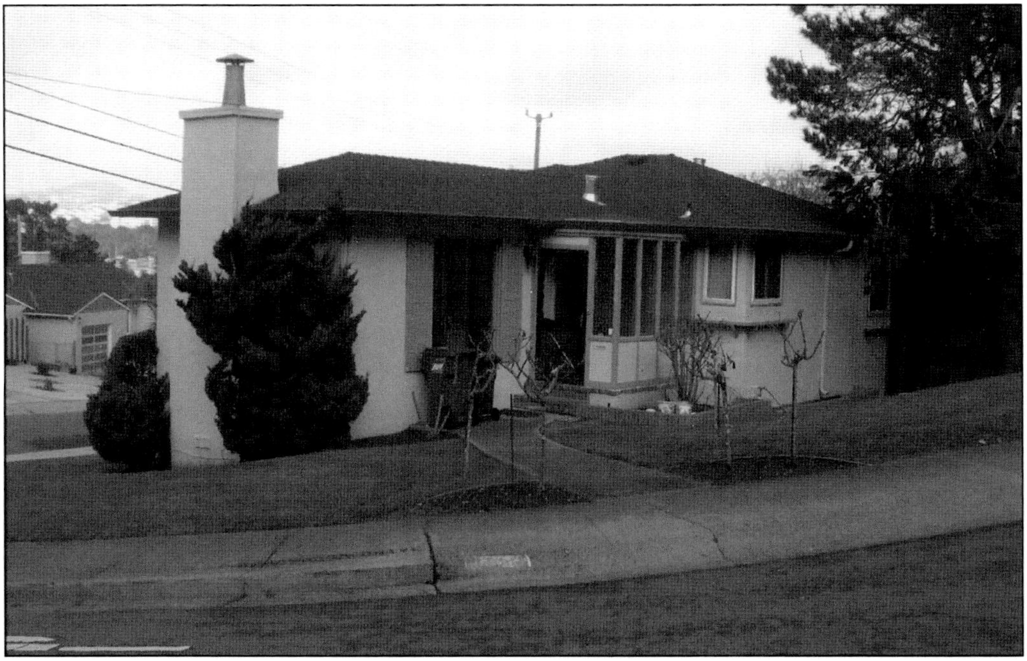

This is a photograph of 1660 Sweetwood Drive in 2010. The trees are a little bigger, and there has been an addition to the porch to keep the wind out. The house has been kept up in remarkable good shape. Most houses in Broadmoor Village have been tended to over the years to varying degrees of success.

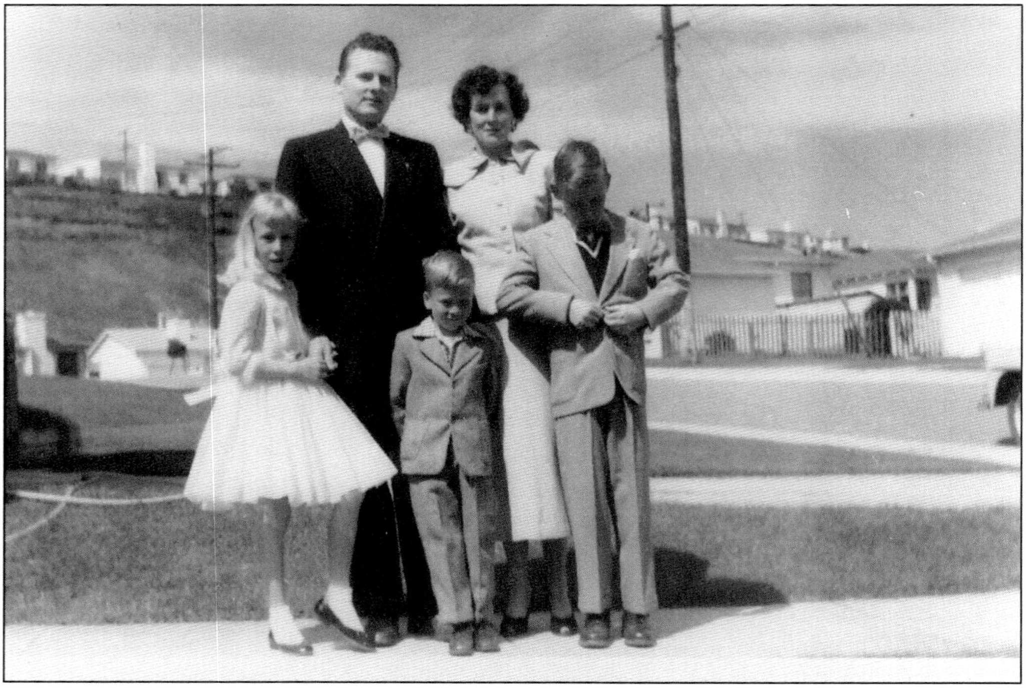

This family picture was taken in 1955 and is of John and Alice Travinsky with their children, (from left to right) Cynthia, Terry and John. They lived on the 700 block of Midway Avenue. Behind them is Nimitz Drive, and on the hill is Larchmont Drive. To the left, below Larchmont Drive, is a retaining wall that was put in because of landslides and flooding that would be common throughout the years. (Courtesy John Travinsky.)

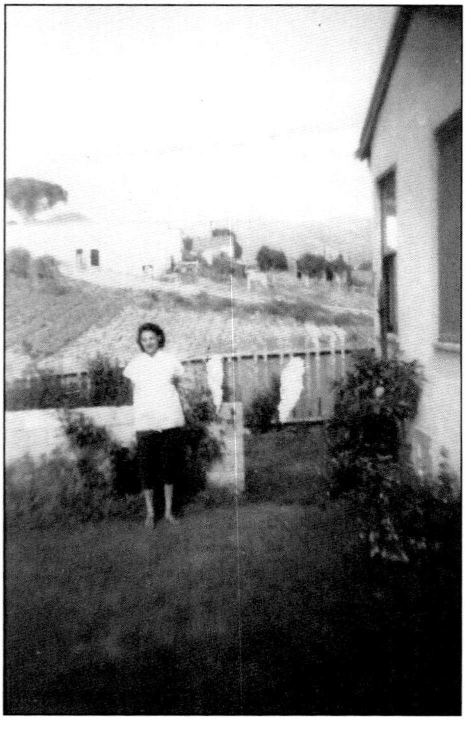

This is the home of Bill and Yolanda Stevenson at Eighty-nineth Street in Broadmoor in 1950. Behind Mrs. Stevenson, looking east is farmland, horse stables, and San Bruno Mountain. Also behind her is the Stoneson built fence, the wood one, and a brick barrier that the Stevensons had put in. (Courtesy Terri Powers.)

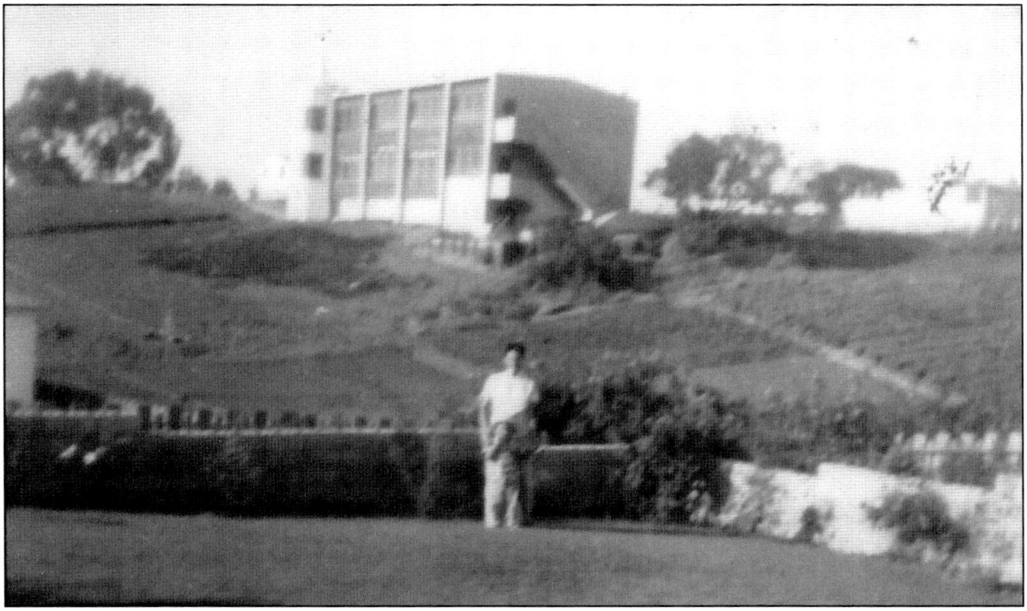

Here is Mr. Stevenson in the backyard. In the far background, to the northeast, is the Broadmoor Presbyterian Church. Between the fence and the church is more farmland that is Unincorporated Colma. This house and other Stoneson built houses, on Eighty-eighth Street, Eighty-nineth Street, and others, represent the east border of Broadmoor Village. (Courtesy Terri Powers.)

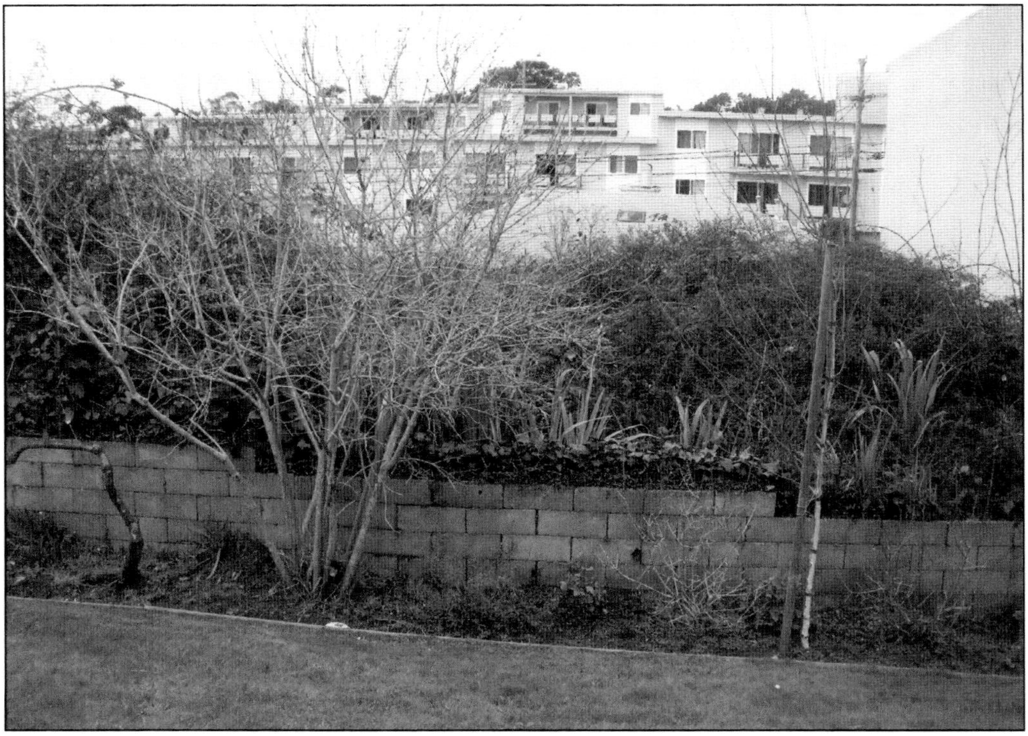

Here is the same backyard looking northeast in 2010. The view of the church is totally blocked by apartments built on lands annexed by Daly City in 1963. The view to the south is also lost on the same apartment building complex. The brick barrier remains keeping a silent vigil.

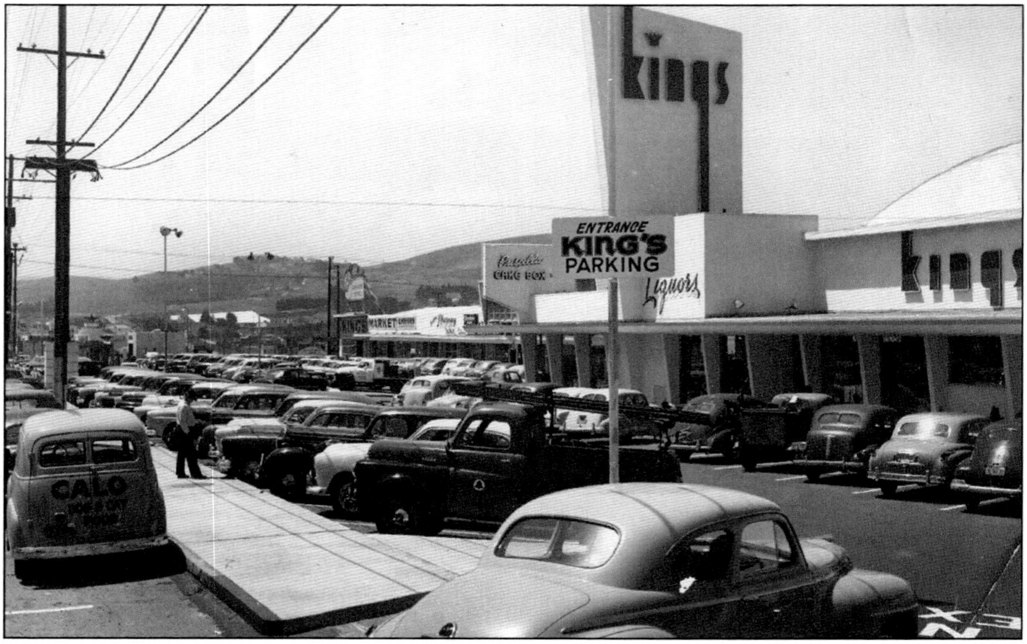

The Broadmoor Shopping Center at the corner of Junipero Serra Boulevard and Eighty-seventh Street is featured in this south-facing view from the early 1950s. The shopping center was built by the Stoneson Company and opened in fall 1948. Just a few blocks east of the Broadmoor Portals on Eighty-seventh Street, the center was never in Broadmoor. (Courtesy San Francisco Public Library and the *San Francisco News-Call Bulletin*.)

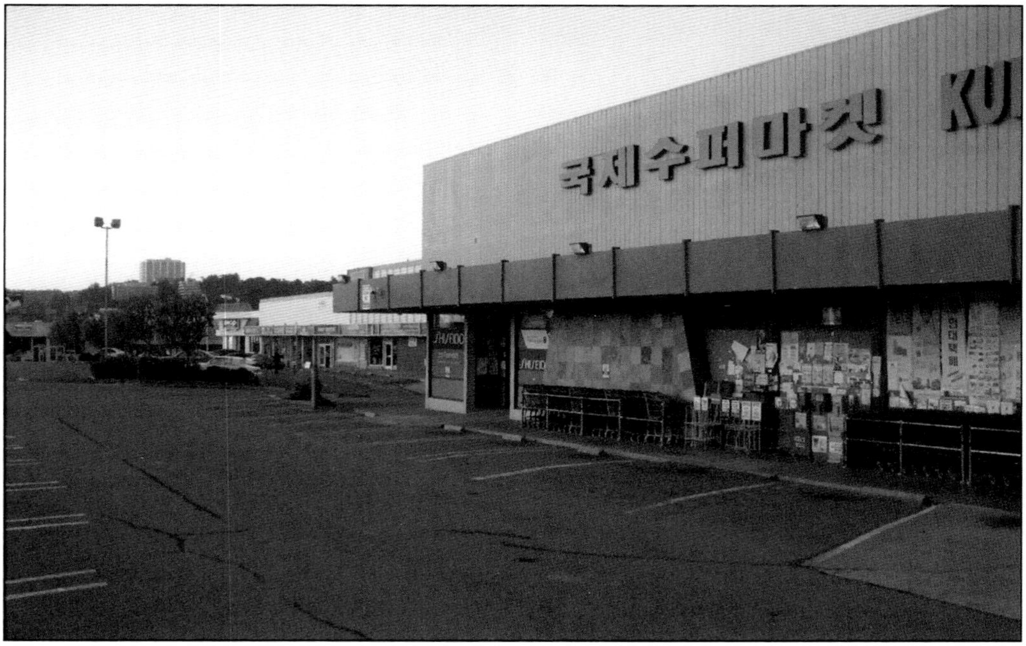

This is the shopping center as it looks in 2010. The building just north of Garden Gateway has always been a market of some kind, though it has changed tenants over the years. After it was a Kings Market, it became a Mayfair Market and then an Asian market. The building was vacant in 2010. Note the changes in the background. On the left in the background is Seaton Hospital.

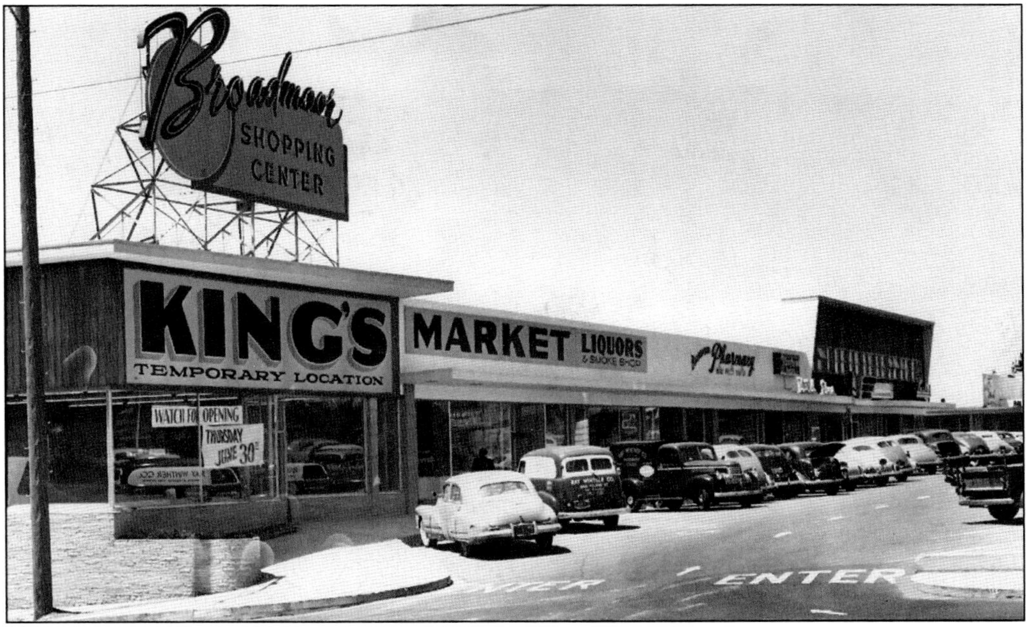

The southern building makes up the center, when looking north. This photograph was also taken in the early 1950s. Note that the Kings Market is also at this end of the center. This was a temporary location after a fire burned down the northern building. (Courtesy San Francisco Public Library and the *San Francisco News-Call Bulletin*.)

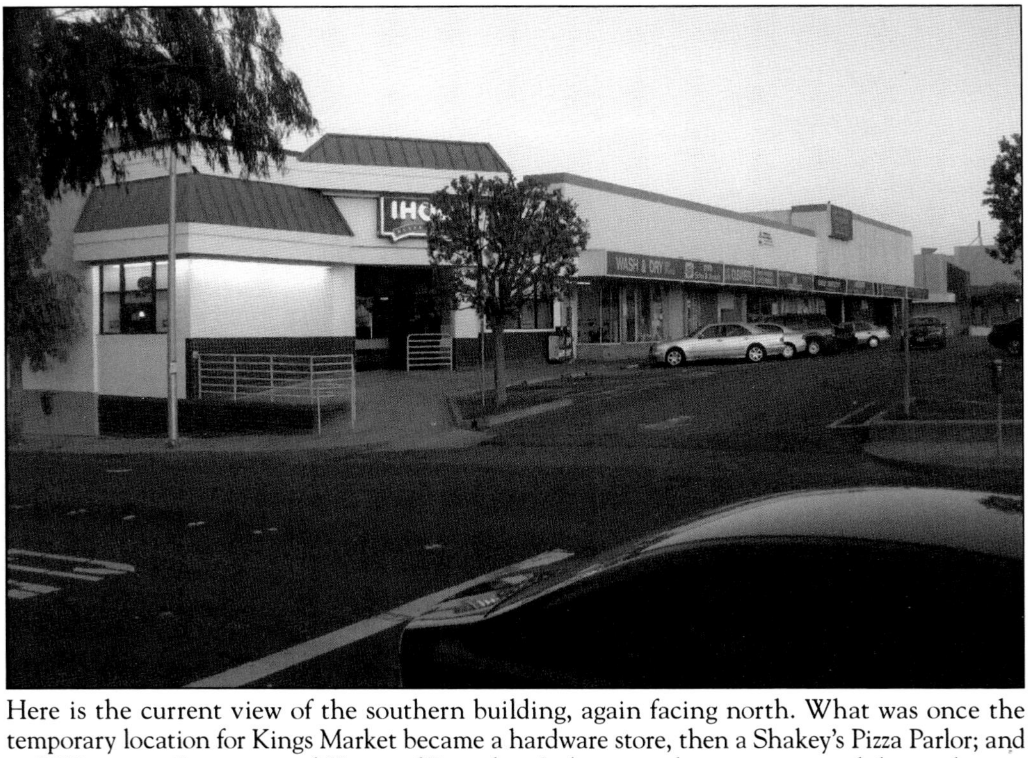

Here is the current view of the southern building, again facing north. What was once the temporary location for Kings Market became a hardware store, then a Shakey's Pizza Parlor; and in 2010, it is an International House of Pancakes. In between the restaurant and the market are a laundromat and various shops.

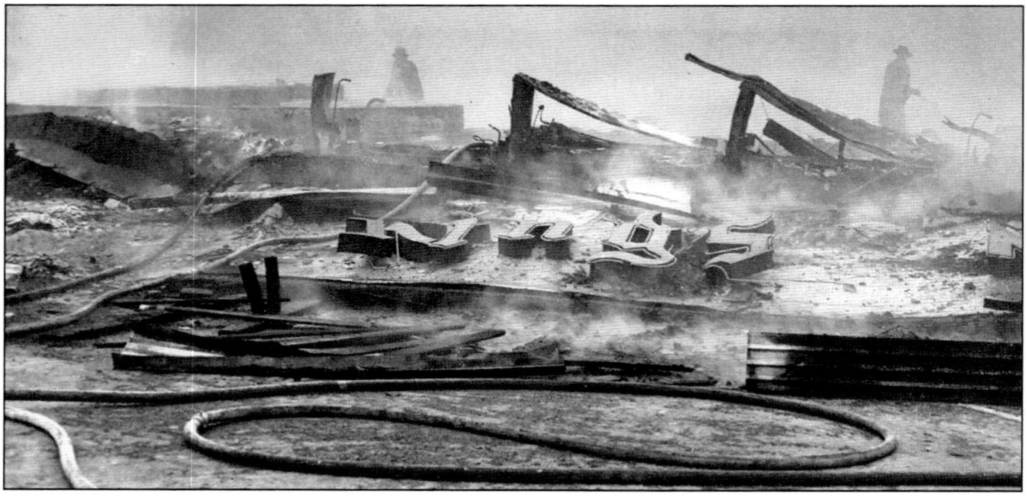

On May 25, 1949, seven months after opening, the Kings Market burned to the ground during a devastating fire. It was proven that an arsonist started the fire, and the sign for the market was all that was left. (Courtesy San Francisco Public Library and the *San Francisco News-Call Bulletin.*)

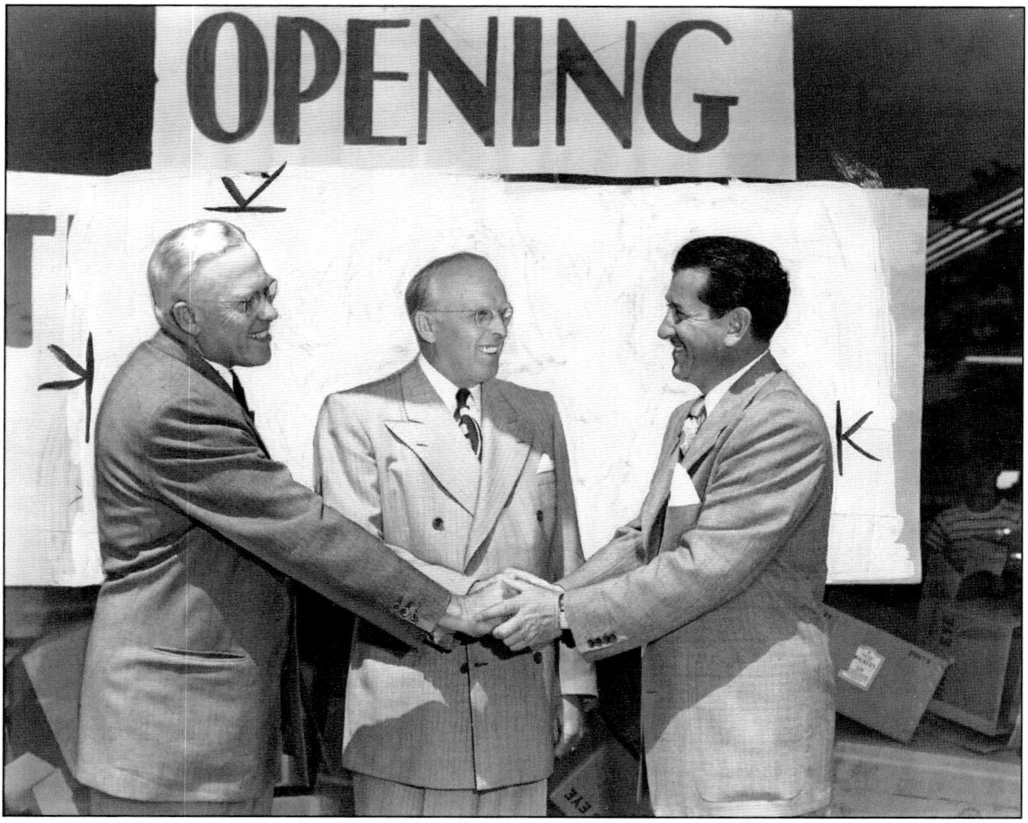

This retouched picture with crop marks for the original newspaper pasteup shows the opening for the temporary location of the Kings Market, one month after the fire. Pictured from left to right are Ellis and Henry Stoneson, who built the shopping center originally; and Mike Jacobs, co-owner of the market. The Stoneson Company eventually rebuilt the market. (Courtesy San Francisco Public Library and the *San Francisco News-Call Bulletin.*)

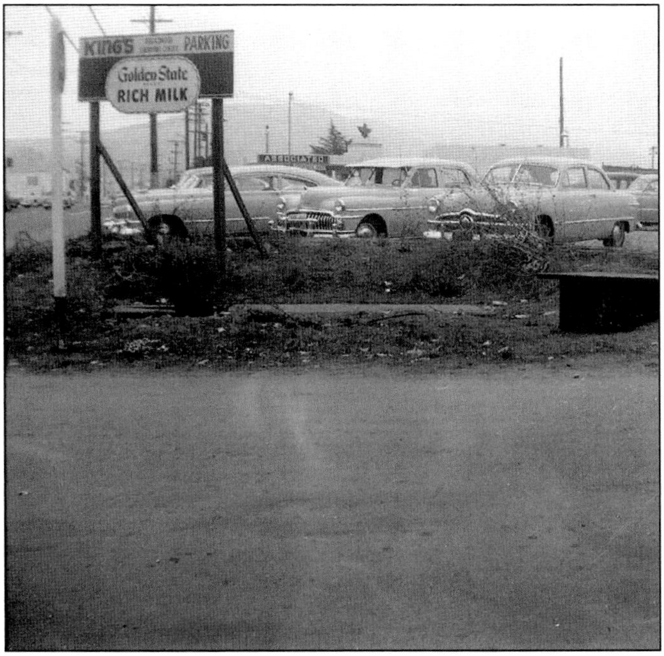

Pictured here is the corner of Sullivan Avenue and Eighty-seventh Street in Unincorporated Colma. This was a parking lot for the Broadmoor Shopping Center located in Daly City. Above the windshield of the car in the middle is the logo for the Flying A Gas Station located a block to the east on Eighty-seventh Street and Junipero Serra Boulevard in Daly City. (Courtesy Roy Christopherson.)

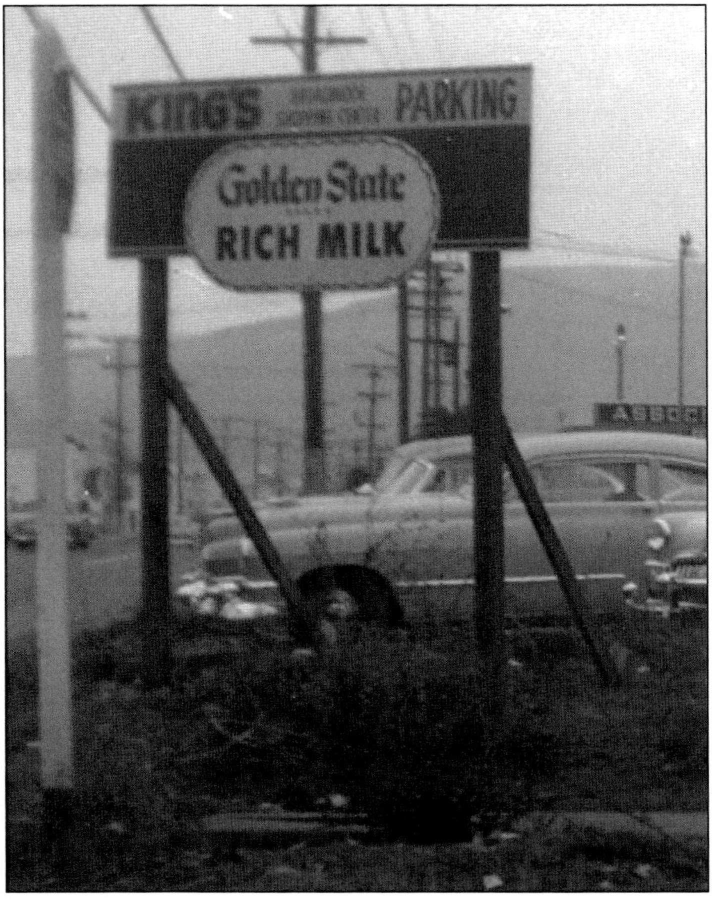

As Eighty-seventh Street crosses Junipero Serra Boulevard, it turns into School Street. This photograph is looking east with San Bruno Mountain in the background; notice the Silver Moon Saloon on the left on School Street. This spot can be identified as Unincorporated Colma, because there are no sidewalks. The Stoneson Company built sidewalks in Broadmoor. (Courtesy Roy Christopherson.)

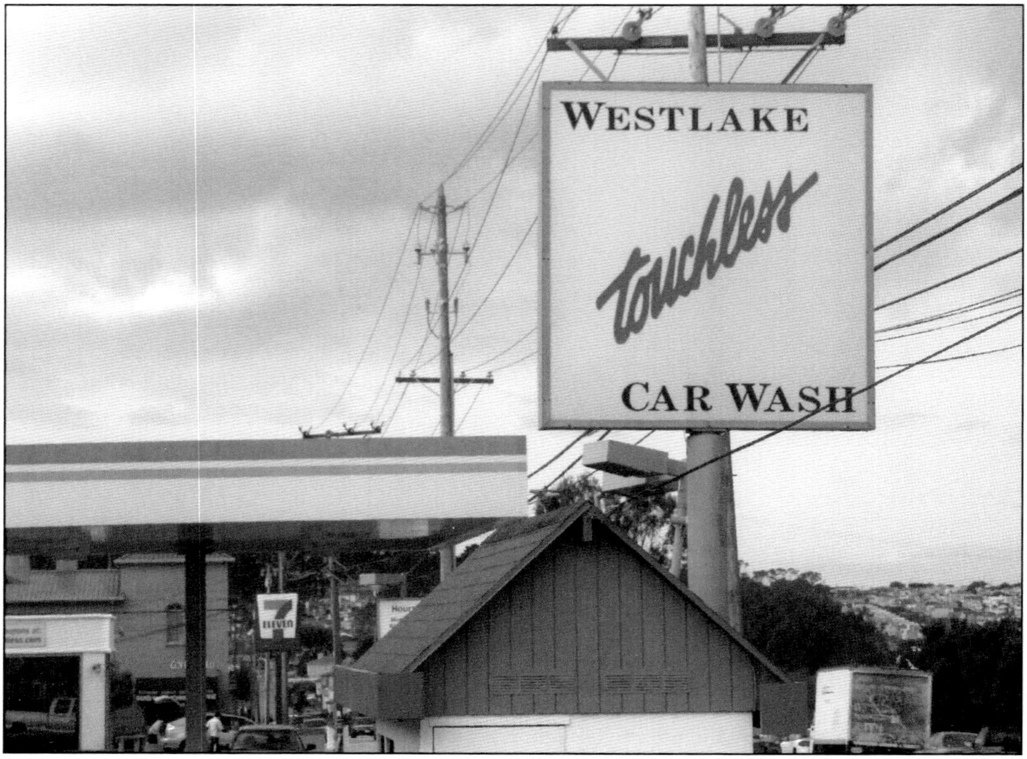

The same intersection of Sullivan Avenue and Eighty-seventh Street just a few feet to the west in 2010 is the Westlake Car Wash. This is part of the contiguous landmass including Broadmoor Village, Garden Village, and parts of Eighty-seventh Street. In an effort to simplify the situation, San Mateo County now considers all of these lands as Broadmoor. Thus, the Westlake Car Wash is not in Westlake; it is in Broadmoor.

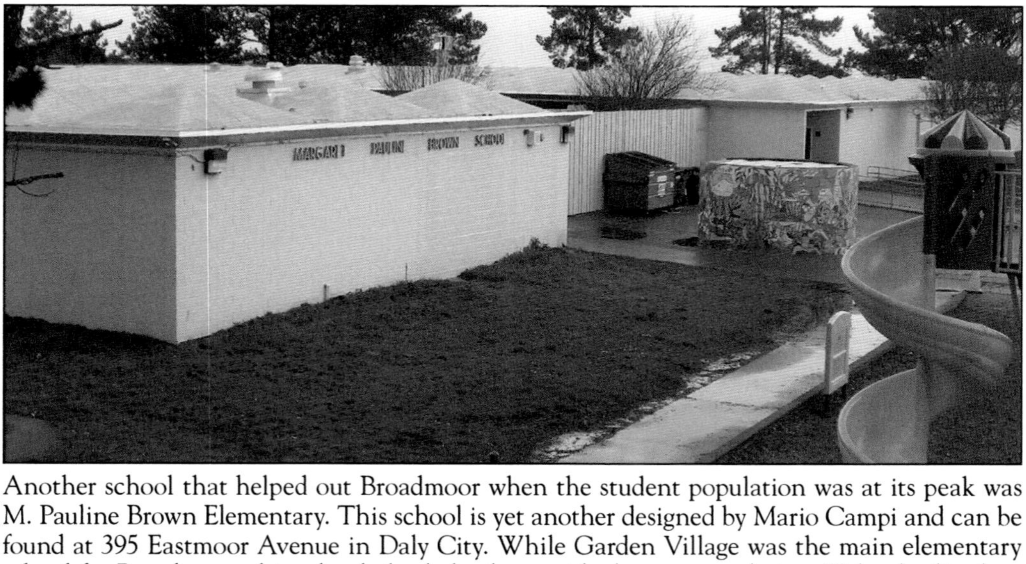

Another school that helped out Broadmoor when the student population was at its peak was M. Pauline Brown Elementary. This school is yet another designed by Mario Campi and can be found at 395 Eastmoor Avenue in Daly City. While Garden Village was the main elementary school for Broadmoor, this school also helped out with the overpopulation. Kids who lived on the east side (Sweetwood, Heather, etc.) went here.

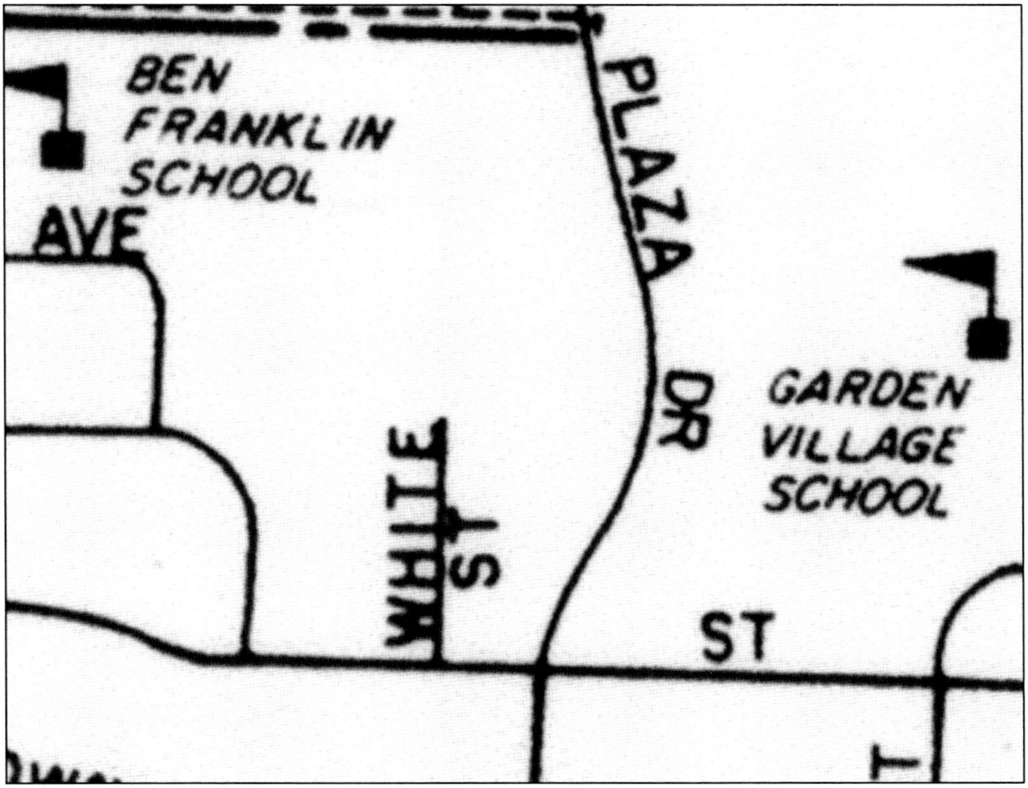

This is taken from a map dated 1971 highlighting White Street in Broadmoor. This illustrates how the street actually looks today. It is a dead-end street that is about a half block long and is located in between Garden Village Elementary School and Ben Franklin Junior High School. (Courtesy San Mateo County Public Works Department.)

Here is a map of the very same street from 1949. There is a huge difference in what exists today. In this map, White Street crosses Eighty-seventh Street and heads south. It also heads much farther north and has a left turn that takes it in a west direction. It is marked as East White Street. So the obvious question is, "What happened to the rest of White Street?"

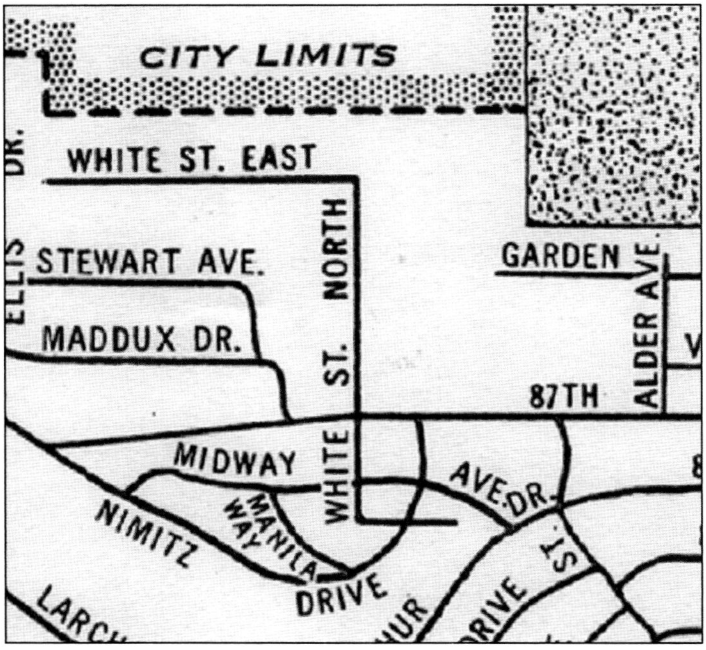

5/14/1959

The BPOA Digest

PUBLISHED BY THE BROADMOOR PROPERTY OWNERS ASSOCIATION
COLMA, CALIFORNIA

White Street Extension! - - Pro and Con

The Broadmoor Property Owners Association Board of Directors has had the subject of the extension of White Street brought before it many times.

We of the Board cannot take an official stand on this matter without knowing the wishes of the majority of the residents of Broadmoor. We, therefore, are presenting to you two views on the subject for your consideration.

ARGUMENT FOR WHITE STREET EXTENSION

Can you imagine living on a residential street that carries from 5,000 to 6,000 cars past your home every day?

That's what is happening along Maddux Drive as increasing numbers of people use this narrow, winding street to go to and from our neighboring communities. Nearly 100 families along Maddux Drive are exposed to this traffic hazard every day of the year. With the continued build-up around us, the problem can only become more critical.

Maddux Drive was never intended to be a connecting arterial between growing communities.

Not only is the problem become intolerable for the residents along Maddux Drive,

Continued on the inside

ARGUMENT AGAINST WHITE STREET EXTENSION

After two attempts and two subsequent failures the small and highly articulate group who are interested in trying to link Broadmoor Village and Westlake by means of a road through the Benjamin Franklin Garden Village School are at it again!

The perseverance of this group is to be admired, but certainly not their selfish motives.

Basically the pressure for this move continues to come from those persons with commercial interests in Westlake. A convenient road would increase the traffic into the Westlake area. Leases and rentals are based on traffic count. The advantage to COMMERCIAL Westlake is easily seen.

Continued on Pg. 4

THE BPOA DIGEST

PUBLISHED QUARTERLY BY THE BROADMOOR PROPERTY OWNERS ASSN., INC.
714 WHITE ST., COLMA, CALIFORNIA

BULK RATE
U. S. POSTAGE
PAID
Daly City, Calif.
Permit No. 19

KEN & BUNNY GILLESPIE
437 Lakeshire Drive
DALY CITY, CA 94015

OCCUPANT
767 Maddux Dr.
COLMA, CALIFORNIA

What happened, or rather what did not happen to White Street can be found in this copy of the Broadmoor Property Owners Digest dated May 14, 1959. The free information newsletter from the Broadmoor Property Owners Association was sent to all the residents of Broadmoor. (Courtesy Daly City History Guild.)

"FOR" cont'd from Pg. 1

but the thousands of people who daily shuttle back and forth between Westlake and Broadmoor for business and pleasure, deserve a more suitable and convenient route.

The map reproduced here shows such a route.

IT IS A ROAD THAT WAS PLANNED EVEN BEFORE YOUR HOMES WERE BUILT IN BROADMOOR.

The property for this proposed route has been deeded to San Mateo County expressly for the purpose of providing a critically needed connecting road between Westlake and Broadmoor. It is a county project and would not cost Broadmoor property owners a cent.

Since Broadmoor was developed right after World War II, the county has provided no major street improvements for the area. Such a project is long overdue.

Your property values would be enhanced by a good, straight road serving the area. The argument that the proposed road would constitute a hazard to the school children is not valid. There would be fewer children crossing the new street than are now crossing Maddux and 87th Street. Benjamin Franklin Upper Grade School and Garden Village Elementary School are separate school operations. Strong and attractive fencing along the route would completely eliminate any hazard to the children. Similar situations, where streets separate schools are common in this area and throughout California.

It was the Jefferson Elementary School District that deeded property for the proposed route to the county in 1950. This was in exchange for the White Street property which had originally been dedicated as the connecting route and was used for the construction of Benjamin Franklin School.

Even with the proposed new connecting road, Maddux will continue to serve Broadmoor as a route to Westlake and beyond. The people along Maddux realize this, but

Continued on Pg. 4

Because of the need for schools, the land that White Street was supposed to be on as a through street was given instead to the Jefferson Elementary School District to provide a home for what would become Ben Franklin Junior High School. Thus, the majority of White Street became what public works calls a "paper street." It was meant to be built but never was. (Courtesy Daly City History Guild.)

When Westlake Shopping Center was completed, there was a sharp increase in traffic on Maddux Drive, as it was the only road that went through to that area. Maddux Drive was not built to handle this increase in traffic that White Street was originally meant to take on. This solution was referred to as the White Street Extension, actually an extension of Park Plaza Drive. (Courtesy Daly City History Guild.)

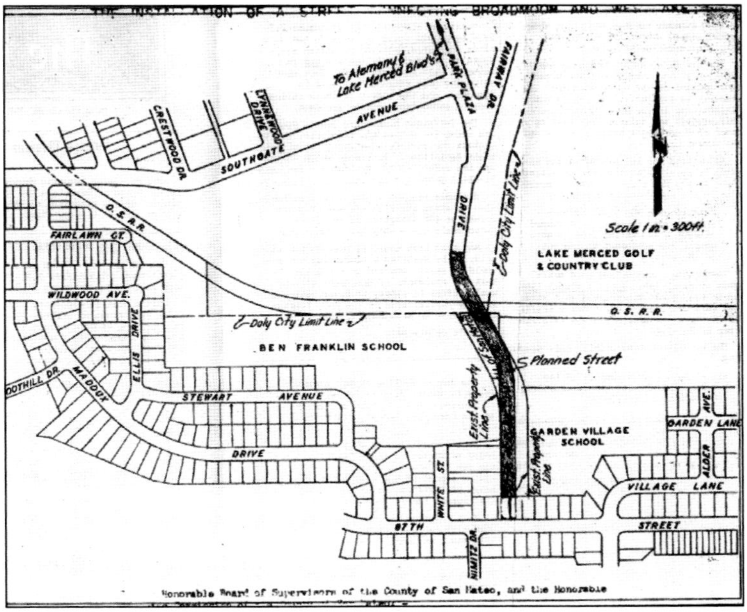

"FOR" cont'd from inside.

we have already reached the point where Maddux simply cannot stand the heavy traffic, plus anticipated increase.

The San Mateo county engineer and the county planning commission have urged the construction of the proposed road. The property is available. It can be built without cost to you from county road funds. This project was delayed last year by your Board of Supervisors because it was not in the budget.

Aside from the inconvenience and hazard which is involved in the present situation there is another point of utmost importance to the residents of Broadmoor:

Fire, police and Civil Defense services are severely handicapped without a connecting road to move people and equipment in and out of the area.

The proposed connecting road makes sense in every way. It is a direct link, and on both sides it connects with streets that were designed to carry heavy traffic --87th Street in Broadmoor, and Park Plaza Drive in Westlake.

The area is choking without this needed road.

All we need is the support of the people and this project can be achieved, for the benefit of Broadmoor.

Will you please indicate your opinion by a vote on this subject...just check one of the squares below and mail it to:

BROADMOOR PROPERTY OWNERS ASSOC.
714 White Street
Colma, California

☐ I am in favor of the White Street extension.

☐ I am against the White Street extension.

"AGAINST" cont'd from Pg. 1

Petitions circulated in Broadmoor Village by unpaid residents have on two occasions indicated that the unselfish residents of Broadmoor Village are not in favor of this proposed road. That they value the only recreational area in Broadmoor and the safety of their children above a convenient road is apparent.

The Jefferson Elementary School Board has among its duties the responsibility to protect the districts existing schools and their facilities. This road which threatens the safety of the Broadmoor - Benjamin Franklin Schools falls into this category.

A simple request to the County authorities to close the right-of-way of White Street or its alternate by the School Board would close this issue completely.

Any gain that would be made by individuals, or by Westlake's commercial interest would be small compared to the great loss that the residents of Broadmoor Village would suffer in safety to their children and the partial loss of the only recreational area in Broadmoor Village.

Don't be misled!!

The Annual Meeting of the Broadmoor Property Owners Association will be held on Thursday, May 14, 1959 at 8:00 P.M., at the Community Center, 714 White Street, Colma.

At this meeting you will elect the Board of Directors and Officers to serve you for the ensuing year. You will also hear a report of the activities of the Board of Directors and a complete financial report (where your $6.00 goes).

Your interest in the affairs of YOUR COMMUNITY can only be expressed by YOUR ATTENDANCE and PARTICIPATION.

We will be looking for you.

Refreshments will be served following the meeting.

A solution had to be found for the safety of the children that lived and played on Maddux Drive. The pros and cons of the White Street Extension are discussed in this informational handout for the Broadmoor Property Owners, who had to vote on whether to allow it or not. (Courtesy Daly City History Guild.)

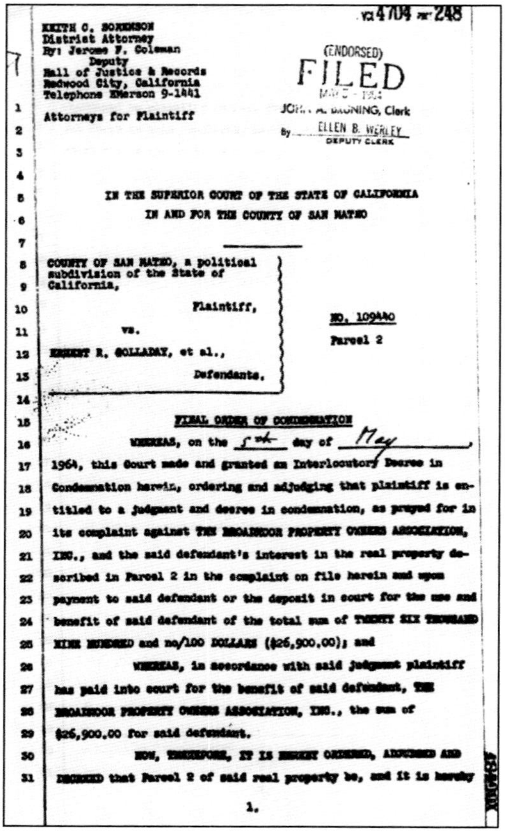

VOL 4704 PAGE 248

KEITH C. SORENSON
District Attorney
By: Jerome F. Coleman
Deputy
Hall of Justice & Records
Redwood City, California
Telephone EMerson 9-1441

Attorneys for Plaintiff

(ENDORSED)
FILED
MAY 5 - 1964
JOHN A. BRUNING, Clerk
By ELLEN B. WERLEY
DEPUTY CLERK

IN THE SUPERIOR COURT OF THE STATE OF CALIFORNIA
IN AND FOR THE COUNTY OF SAN MATEO

COUNTY OF SAN MATEO, a political subdivision of the State of California,
Plaintiff,
vs.
ERNEST R. GOLLADAY, et al.,
Defendants.

NO. 109440
Parcel 2

FINAL ORDER OF CONDEMNATION

WHEREAS, on the 5th day of May, 1964, this Court made and granted an Interlocutory Decree in Condemnation herein, ordering and adjudging that plaintiff is entitled to a judgment and decree in condemnation, as prayed for in its complaint against THE BROADMOOR PROPERTY OWNERS ASSOCIATION, INC., and the said defendant's interest in the real property described in Parcel 2 in the complaint on file herein and upon payment to said defendant or the deposit in court for the use and benefit of said defendant of the total sum of TWENTY SIX THOUSAND NINE HUNDRED and no/100 DOLLARS ($26,900.00); and

WHEREAS, in accordance with said judgment plaintiff has paid into court for the benefit of said defendant, THE BROADMOOR PROPERTY OWNERS ASSOCIATION, INC., the sum of $26,900.00 for said defendant.

NOW, THEREFORE, IT IS HEREBY ORDERED, ADJUDGED AND DECREED that Parcel 2 of said real property be, and it is hereby

1.

Here are court documents from May 1964 showing that the County of San Mateo paid the Broadmoor Property Owners Association the sum of $26,900. This is part of the White Street Extension solution. This was probably more of a formality than an actual lawsuit. (Courtesy San Mateo County Assessors Office.)

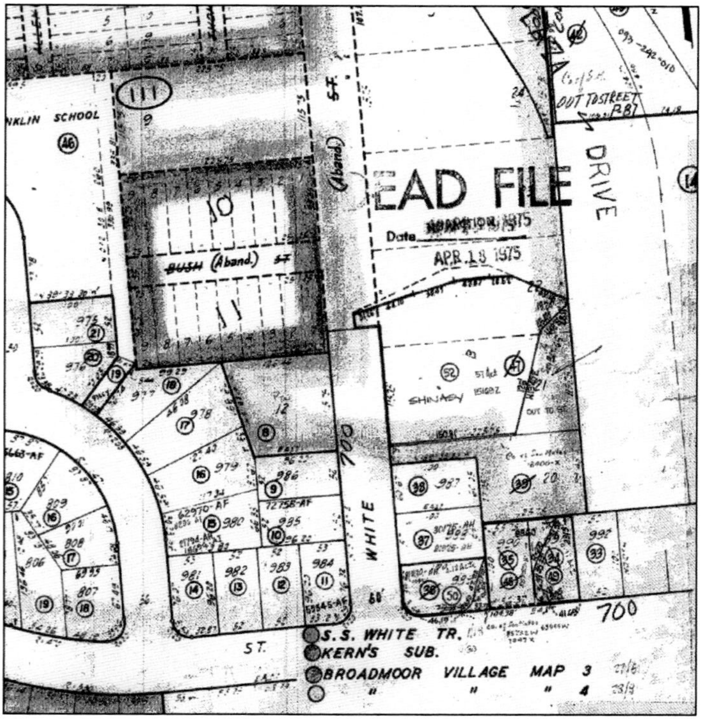

In this dead-file map was the proposed Park Plaza Drive connection to Eighty-seventh Street. In the lower right portion of this map is a parcel of land that looks like the state of Oklahoma on reverse. This is 714 White Street, the original Broadmoor Community Center built by the Stoneson Company. (Courtesy San Mateo County Mapping Department.)

The original plans called for the destruction of two homes on Eighty-seventh Street. The end result was the elimination of the original Broadmoor Community Center on 714 White Street and also the Hersbergs house at 540 Eighty-seventh Street. Also on this map, Bush Street, Thomas Street, and Allen Street are marked "aband" or "abandoned"—planned but never built, i.e. paper streets. (Courtesy San Mateo County Mapping Department.)

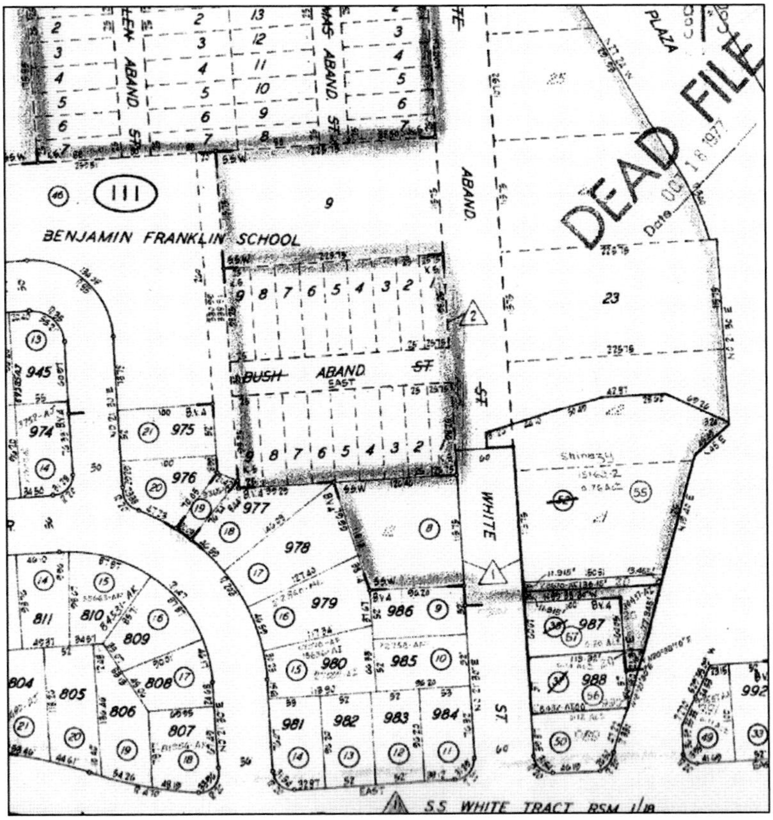

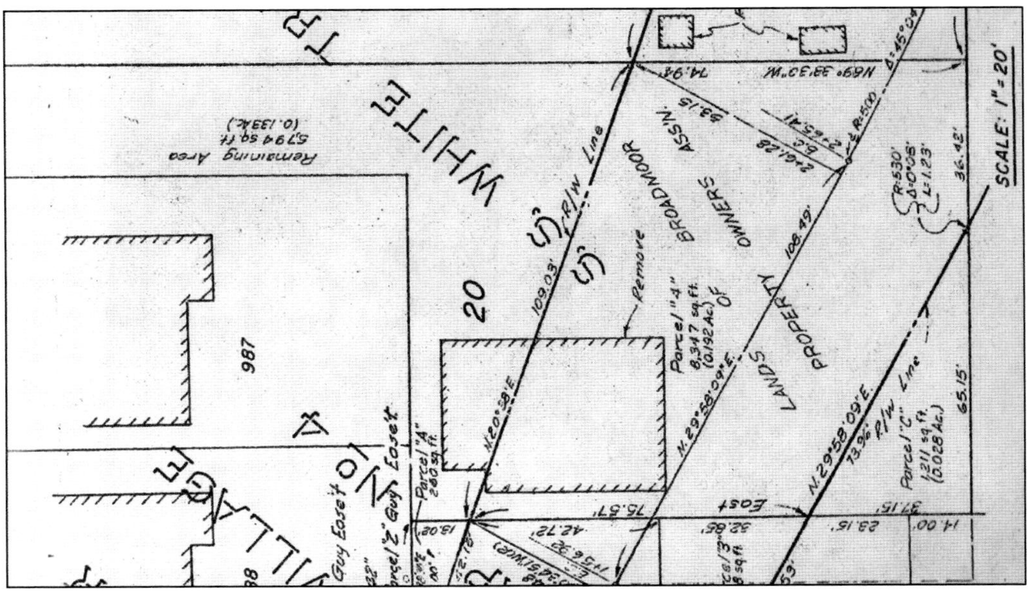

Here is a closer look at the parcel of land resembling a backwards Oklahoma. This parcel is also designated as "Lands Of Broadmoor Property Owners Association." The building to be removed is the original Broadmoor Community Center, and its address was 714 White Street. The construction on the Park Plaza Extension was completed in July 1964. (Courtesy San Mateo County Public Works Department.)

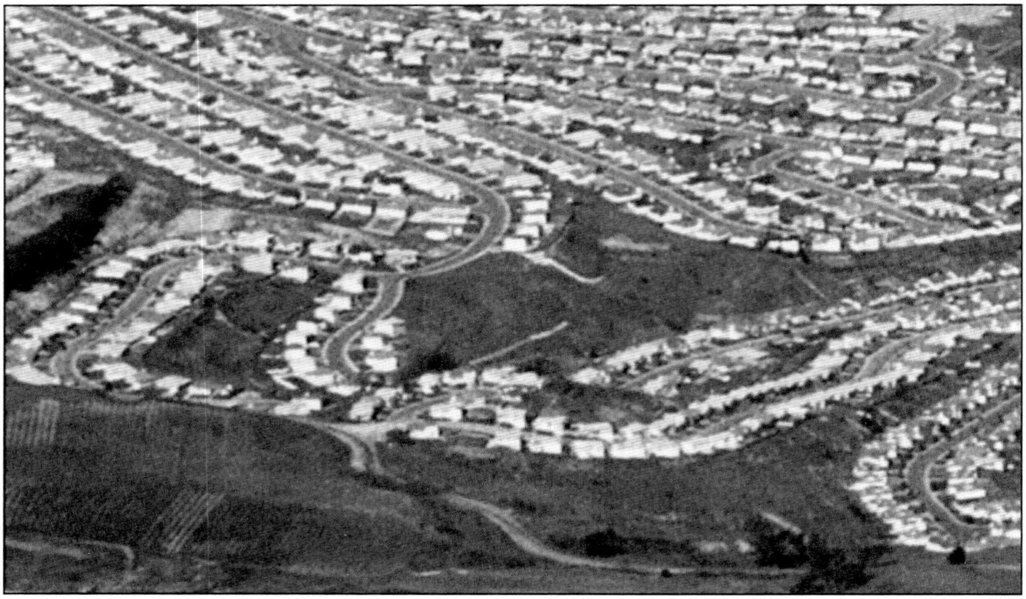

Here is an aerial photograph taken of the area in 1955. Below, Larchmont Drive intersects with MacArthur Drive. On the right (east) side of both Larchmont Drive and MacArthur Drive is a vacant area with no houses. There is no evidence of paper roads in this area of Broadmoor, so it is another mystery. (Courtesy HJW Geospatial Inc. and Pacific Aerial Surveys. Oakland, California.)

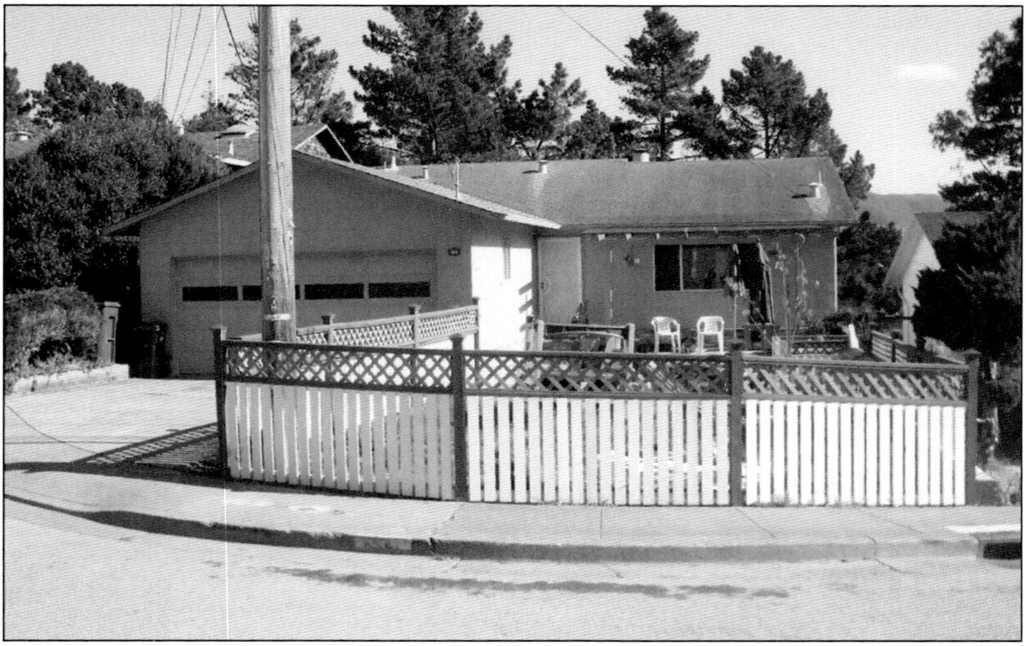

In 1968, seven houses were finally built in the lots left vacant for some 20 years. Here is one of the non-Stoneson houses. In all there are seven addresses, three on Larchmont Drive (654, 656, and 660) and four on MacArthur Drive (688, 684, 680, and 676). These houses have closed the access children had to play on Grasshopper Hill.

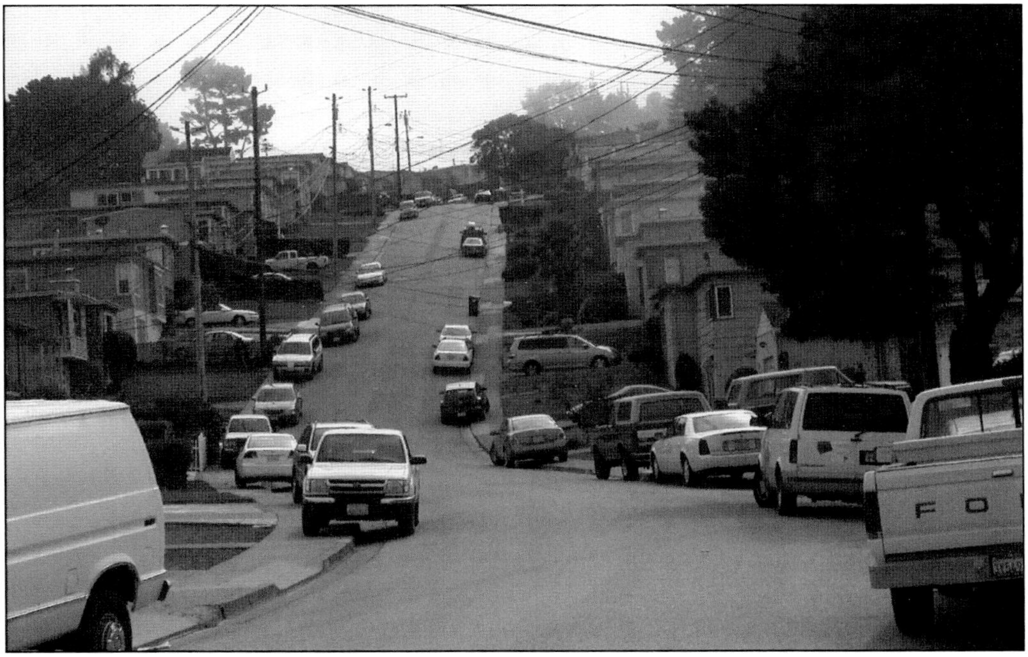

Pictured here is the bottom of Gilman Drive; it is very easy to see why a barrier had to be constructed at the top of the hill. There were many accidents involving cars going through the front of houses or totaling legally parked cars. One day in the mid-1970s, there was a fatality involving children playing in a yard. It was then the county heard the complaints and put in the barrier.

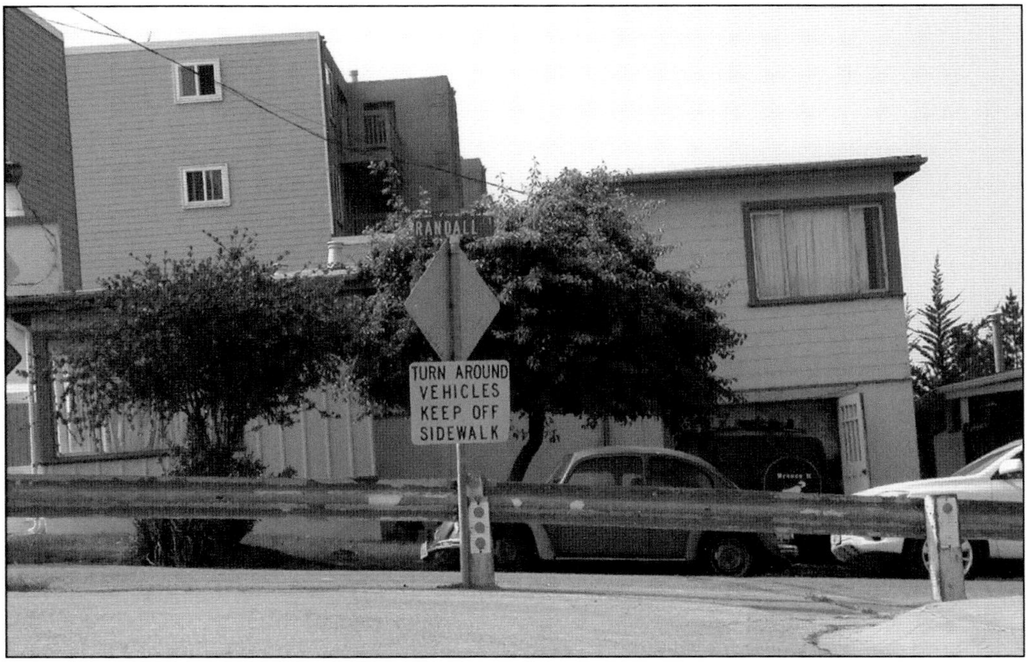

Here is the barrier that San Mateo County put in during the mid-1970s. One can drive down Randall Court, entering from Eastmoor Avenue, but can no longer drive down the hill on Gillman Drive. In the direct background (west) behind the barrier is a Stoneson built house on Randall Court (Broadmoor). Built in 1950, Randall Court is the youngest street in Broadmoor.

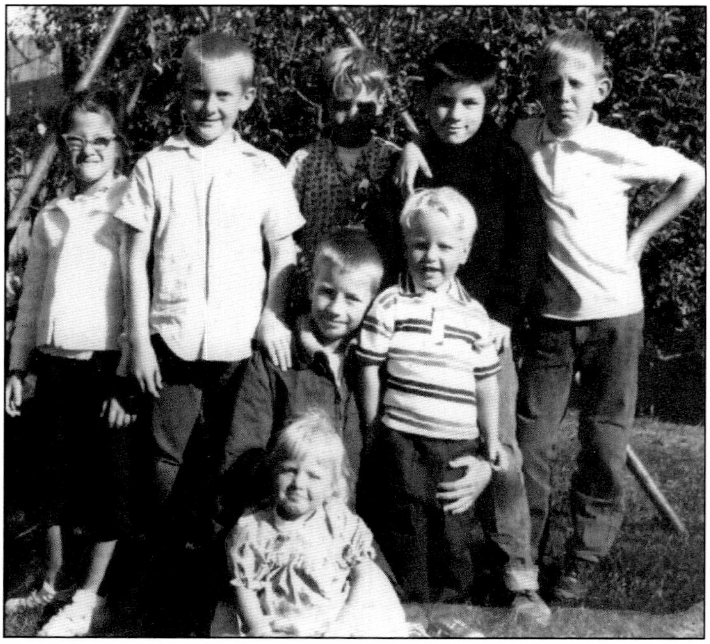

This is a photograph of the Louvaine Drive gang. Pictured from left to right are (first row) Julie Wright; (second row) Renny and Richard Wright; (third row) Jeannie Gerhardt, Greg Johnson, Roland Wright, John Gerhardt, and Bobby Wright. The Wrights lived on Washington Street and the Gerhardts on Louvaine Drive. John and Jeannie's dad, Jack, was a police officer for both Broadmoor and the San Mateo County Sheriff's Departments. (Courtesy Renny Wright.)

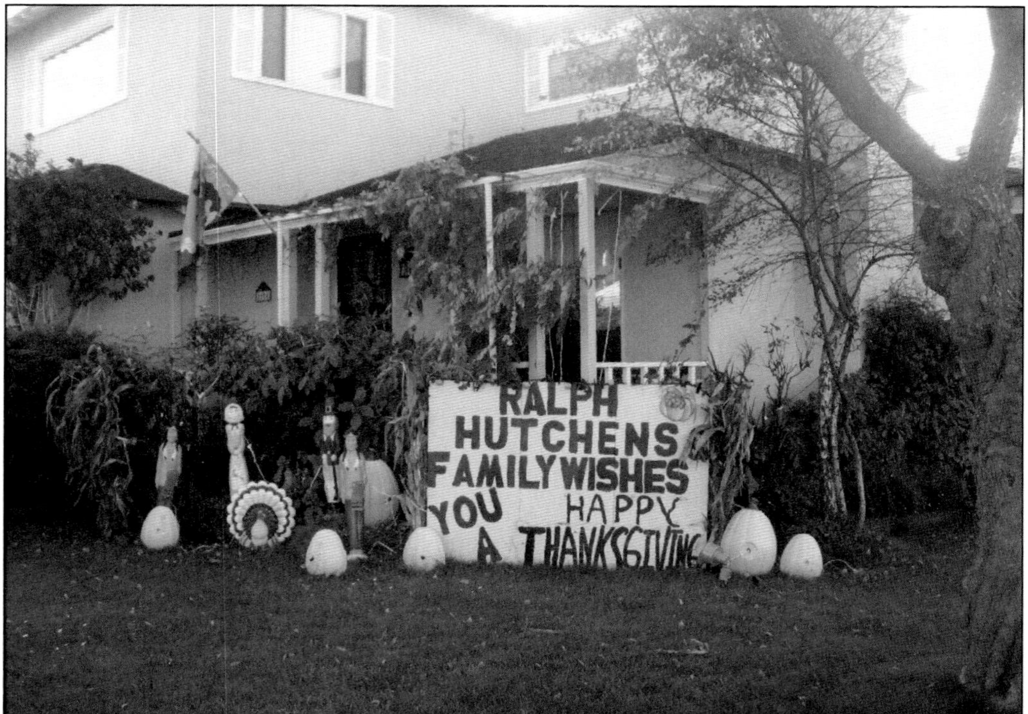

The spirited owner of this house is Ralph Hutchens. He and his wife, Cathy, live on the corner of Washington Street and Sweetwood Drive. There is always a reason to decorate the yard and celebrate even when no one else does. Here is their yard at Thanksgiving, and their decorations at Christmas get even more elaborate. Ralph is a realtor who specializes in Broadmoor, and Cathy is actually a former Miss Broadmoor.

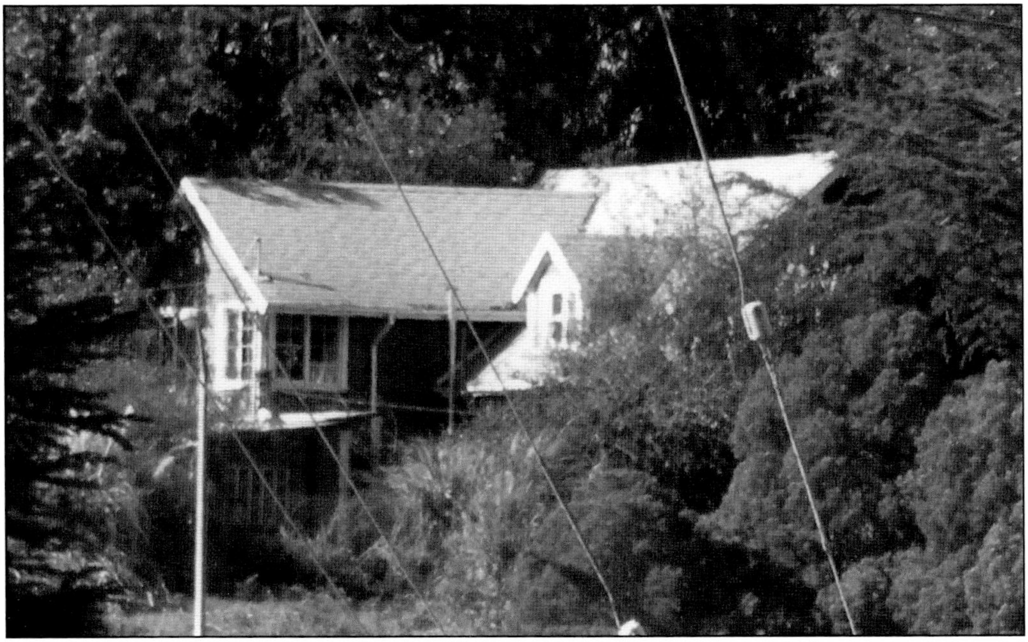

Hidden within the trees right in the middle of Broadmoor Village is the old house that belonged to the Shinazy family. According to San Mateo County records, this house was built in 1907, making it the oldest house in Broadmoor. It was built even before Daly City incorporated and is located at 716 White Street. George Shinazy, third generation, was an officer for the Broadmoor Police Department.

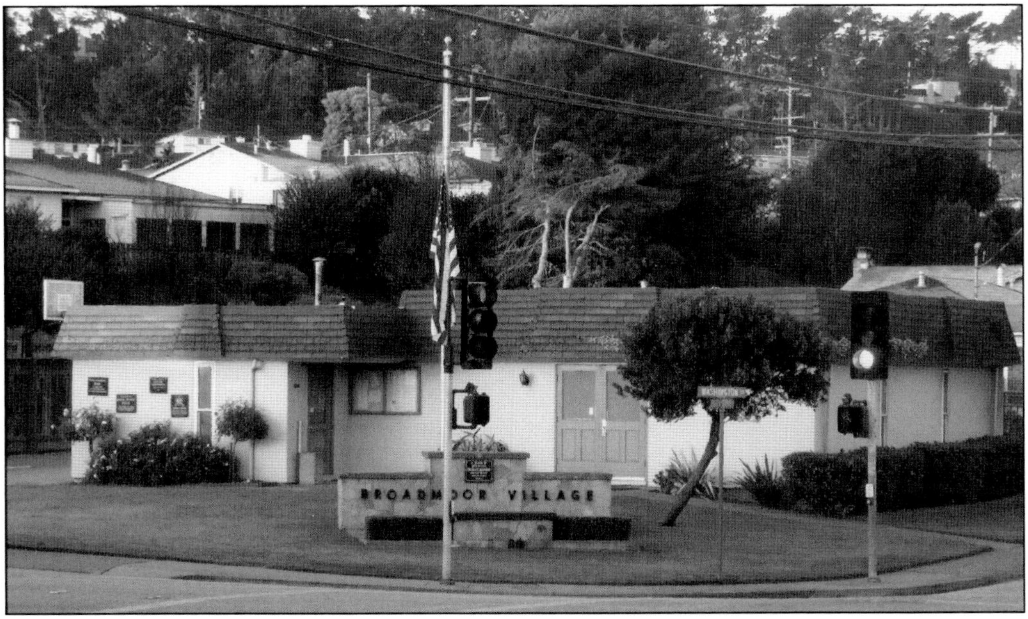

This is the Broadmoor Community Center at 501 Eighty-seventh Street on the corner of Washington Street. Built in 1967, it welcomes all who come to Broadmoor Village. It stands as a testimonial to all that this community has lasted some 65 years in the face of annexations, budget cuts, and all. This community, though unincorporated, shall last as it values the very ideal this country was made from—independence.

www.arcadiapublishing.com

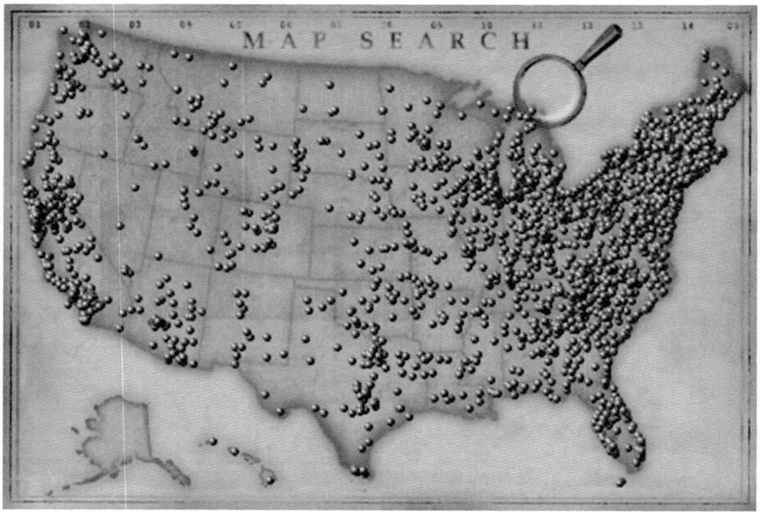

Discover books about the town where you grew up, the cities where your friends and families live, the town where your parents met, or even that retirement spot you've been dreaming about. Our Web site provides history lovers with exclusive deals, advanced notification about new titles, e-mail alerts of author events, and much more.

MADE IN THE USA

Arcadia Publishing, the leading local history publisher in the United States, is committed to making history accessible and meaningful through publishing books that celebrate and preserve the heritage of America's people and places. Consistent with our mission to preserve history on a local level, this book was printed in South Carolina on American-made paper and manufactured entirely in the United States.

This book carries the accredited Forest Stewardship Council (FSC) label and is printed on 100 percent FSC-certified paper. Products carrying the FSC label are independently certified to assure consumers that they come from forests that are managed to meet the social, economic, and ecological needs of present and future generations.

Find Your Place in History.